THE EUROPEAN UNION SERIES

General Editors: Neill Nugent, William E. Paterson, Vincent Wright

The European Union series is designed to provide an authoritative library on the European Union, ranging from general introductory texts to definitive assessments of key institutions and actors, policies and policy processes, and the role of member states.

Books in the series are written by leading scholars in their fields and reflect the most up-to-date research and debate. Particular attention is paid to accessibility and clear presentation for a wide audience of students, practitioners and interested general readers.

The series consists of four major strands:

- general textbooks
- the major institutions and actors
- the main areas of policy
- the member states and the Union

Published titles

Justin Greenwood
Representing Interests in the European Union

Fiona Hayes-Renshaw and Helen Wallace
The Council of Ministers

Simon Hix and Christopher Lord
Political Parties in the European Union

Brigid Laffan
The Finances of the European Union

Janne Haaland Matláry
Energy Policy in the European Union

Title of Series
Series Standing Order
ISBN 0–333–69352–3

If you would like to receive future titles in this series as they are published, you can make use of our standing order facility. To place a standing order please contact your bookseller or, in case of difficulty write to us at the address below with your name and address, the title of the series and the ISBN quoted above. (If you live outside the United Kingdom we may not have the rights for your country, in which case we will forward your order to the publisher concerned.)

Customer Services Department, Macmillan Distribution Ltd
Houndmills, Basingstoke, Hampshire RG21 6XS, England

Forthcoming

Simon Bulmer and Drew Scott
European Union: Economics, Policy and Politics

David Millar, Neill Nugent and William E. Paterson (eds)
The European Union Source Book

John Peterson and Elizabeth Bomberg
Decision-making in the European Union

Ben Rosamond
Theories of European Integration

Richard Sinnott
Understanding European Integration

•   •   •   •

Simon Bulmer and Wolfgang Wessels
The European Council (Second Edition)

Renaud Dehousse
The Court of Justice: A Brief Introduction

David Earnshaw and David Judge
The European Parliament

Neill Nugent
The European Commission

Hjalte Rasmussen
The Court of Justice

Anne Stevens
The Administration of the European Union

•   •   •   •

David Allen and Geoffrey Edwards
The External Economic Relations of the European Union

Michelle Cini and Lee McGowan
Competition Policy in the European Union

Martin Holland
The European Union and the Third World

Anand Menon
Defence Policy and the European Union

James Mitchell and Paul McAleavey
Regionalism and Regional Policy in the European Union

John Redmond, René Schwok and Lee Miles
Enlarging the European Union

Margaret Sharp and John Peterson
Technology Policy in the European Union

Hazel Smith
The Foreign Policy of the European Union

Mark Thatcher
The Politics of European High Technology

Rüdiger Wurzel
Environmental Policy in the European Union

•   •   •   •

Simon Bulmer and William E. Paterson
Germany and the European Union

Phil Daniels and Ella Ritchie
Britain and the European Union

Alain Guyomarch, Howard Machin and Ella Ritchie
France in the European Union

Other titles planned include

European Union: A Brief Introduction
The History of the European Union
The European Union Reader
The Political Economy of the European Union

•   •   •   •

Social Policy
Monetary Union
Political Union
The USA and the European Union

•   •   •   •

The European Union and its Member States
Reshaping the States of the Union
Italy and the European Union
Spain and the European Union

Political Parties in the European Union

Simon Hix

and

Christopher Lord

St. Martin's Press
New York

St. Martin's Press, Scholarly and Reference Division,
175 Fifth Avenue, New York, N.Y. 10010

First published in the United States of America in 1997

This book is printed on paper suitable for recycling and
made from fully managed and sustained forest sources.

Printed in Great Britain

ISBN 0–312–17291–5 (cloth)
ISBN 0–312–17292–3 (paperback)

Library of Congress Cataloging-in-Publication Data
Hix, Simon.
Political parties in the European Union / Simon Hix and
Christopher Lord.
p.   cm. — (The European Union series)
Includes bibliographical references and index.
ISBN 0–312–17291–5. — ISBN 0–312–17292–3 (pbk.)
1. Political parties—European Union countries.   I. Lord,
Christopher.   II. Title.   III. Series.

Contents

v

List of Tables and Figures

Tables

Figures

Preface

At the start of the European integration process in the early 1950s, several scholars predicted a central role for party politics in the construction of a European Community. For example, Ernst Haas devoted two chapters of his seminal work on *The Uniting of Europe* to predictions of how party competition at the domestic and European levels could promote integration (Haas, 1958). However, it was not until the decision in the early 1970s to hold direct elections to the European Parliament that a wider community of scholars began to focus on the role of political parties in European Community politics. Many of these new scholars argued that the first elections to the EP would facilitate the emergence of pan-European parties. For example, David Marquand optimistically expected a *'Europe des partis'* (Europe of parties) (Marquand, 1978). Nevertheless, a seminal work from this period – Geoffrey and Pippa Pridham's *Transnational Parties in the European Community* – constituted the first attempt at a comprehensive framework for analysing the organisational and behavioural links between the three key elements of the EC party system: the EP party groups, the European party federations, and the domestic parties in the EC member states (Pridham and Pridham, 1981).

However, the first European elections failed to produce a transnational mobilisation of political forces in Europe or coherent European-level party organisations. A deep disillusionment consequently set in among the Euro-party advocates. Few could now envisage political parties ever being able to challenge the national governments as the main articulators of citizens' interests and the main actors in European-level decision-making. As a result, political parties all but disappeared from the research agenda of scholars of European integration.

By the early 1990s, nonetheless, political parties have again emerged as (in Haas's words) 'crucial carriers of integration'. First, with the increased powers granted to the EP under the Single

European Act and the Maastricht Treaty, the behaviour of the EP party groups has a more direct impact on EU policy-making. Second, beginning with the drafting of the Maastricht Treaty in the 1990–91 Intergovernmental Conferences, the Socialist, Christian Democrat and Liberal party federations have held 'party leaders' summits' before each meeting of the European Council. As a direct result of these party leaders' summits, a 'Party Article' (138A) was inserted in the Maastricht Treaty: the first reference to the role of political parties in any EC Treaty or legislation. Finally, European integration has itself emerged as a major new 'cleavage' and source of intra- and interparty competition in the domestic arena. This was evident in the ratification of the Maastricht Treaty; in the 1994 EP elections; and in the arguments about the application of 'convergence criteria' for economic and monetary union. Many mainstream parties now have deep internal divisions on the question of Europe, and old and new parties and movements present anti-European platforms at the fringes of most domestic party systems.

Consequently, in the mid-1990s it is impossible to ignore the fundamental significance of political party organisation, behaviour and competition at the national and European levels in the continued development towards political, economic and monetary union in Europe. However, this book is the first attempt since Pridham and Pridham (1981) to present an integrated framework for understanding how party organisation and behaviour are linked throughout the complex and fragmented system of the EU – in the European Parliament, at national level, and within and between the other EU institutions. As part of a wider series of books on EU politics, this book fills a gap in the existing empirical research on EU politics and policy. The book includes a large quantity of new material based on several years of primary research (through interviews, direct observation and content analysis) in the European Parliament, at several party leaders' summits, and in a number of national capitals. However, this book is more than simply an empirical addition or summary. By placing party loyalties, actions, organisations and policies at the centre of our analysis, we present a fundamentally different theoretical and methodological perspective of how European integration and politics is best understood.

Numerous people have contributed to this book, either through interviews or through less formal comments and observations. We must thank in particular David Bell, Elmar Brok MEP, Peter Brown-Pappamikail, Ken Collins MEP, Richard Corbett, Pat Cox MEP,

Giorgos Dimitrakopoulos MEP, Brendan Donnelly MEP, Glyn Ford MEP, Fernand Herman MEP, Thomas Jansen, Karl Magnus Johansson, Francisco Lucas Pires MEP, Michael McGowan MEP, Giandomenico Majone, Graham Mather MEP, Neil Nugent, Manuel Porto MEP, Tapio Raunio, Barry Seal MEP, Michael Shackleton, Tony Teasdale, Thomas Tindemans, John Tomlinson MEP, Martin Westlake and Philip Whitehead MEP.

CHRISTOPHER LORD
SIMON HIX

List of Abbreviations

AGALEV	Ecology Party (Belgium: Flanders)
AN	National Alliance (Italy)
CC	Canaries Coalition Party (Spain)
CD	Christian Democrats (Italy)
CDA	Christian Democrat Party (Netherlands)
CDC	Catalan Democratic Convergence Party (Spain)
CDS	Christian Democrat Party (France)
CDS-PP	Centre Democrat Party (Portugal)
CDU	Christian Democratic Union (Germany)
CG	Greens (Ireland)
Con	Conservative Party (UK)
CSP	Confederation of Socialist Parties
CSP-EVP	European People's Party (Belgium: German minority)
CSU	Christian Social Union (Bavarian sister party of CDU)
CVP	Christian Democrat Party (Belgium: Flanders)
D'66	Radical Liberal Party (Netherlands)
DP	Democratic Party (Luxembourg)
DUP	Democratic Unionist Party (UK: N. Ireland)
EC	European Community
ECGP	European Co-ordination of Green Parties
Ecofin	Council of Economic and Finance Ministers
Ecolo	Ecology Party (Belgium:Wallonia)
ECOSY	EC Organisation of Socialist Youth
ECSC	European Coal and Steel Community
EDF	European Democratic Federation
EDG	European Democratic Group (EP group 1973–92)
EDU	European Democratic Union
EFA	European Free Alliance (Regionalists)
EFGP	European Federation of Green Parties
ELDR	European Liberal and Democratic Reform (federation and group in EP)

EMU	economic and monetary union
EN	Europe of the Nations (group in EP)
EP	European Parliament
EPP	European People's Party (federation and group in EP)
ERA	European Radical Alliance (group in EP)
ERM	exchange rate mechanism
EU	European Union
EUCD	European Union of Christian Democrats
FB	Anti-European Party (Denmark)
FDP	Free Democrats (Germany)
FE	Forza Europa (EP group 1994–5)
FF	Fianna Fáil (Ireland)
FG	Fine Gael (Ireland)
FI	Forza Italia (Italy)
FN	Front National (France)
FN (B)	Front National (Belgium: Wallonia)
FPÖ	Freedom Party (Austria)
FV	Greens (Italy)
G	Greens (group in EP)
GA/G	Greens (Luxembourg)
GAL	Greens (Austria)
GL	Greens (Netherlands)
Gr	Greens (Germany)
IAC	Institutional Affairs Committee (of European Parliament)
IGC	Intergovernmental Conference
IR	International Relations
IU	United Left (Spain)
IU-IVP	United Left (Spain: Catalanya)
JB	June Movement (Denmark)
KDS	Christian Democrat Party (Sweden)
KESK	Centre Party (Finland)
KF	Conservative Party (Denmark)
KKE	Communist Party (Greece)
KOK	National Coalition Party (Finland)
Lab	Labour Party (UK)
LF	Liberal Forum (Austria)
LI	Liberal International
Lib	Liberal Party (UK)
LN	Lega Norda (Italy)
LP	Labour Party (Ireland)

MAE	Majorité pour l'Autre Europe
MEP	Member of the European Parliament
MPG	Greens (Sweden)
MRG	Left Radicals (France)
MRP	Former French Christian Democratic Party
MS	Moderate Coalition (Sweden)
ND	New Democracy (Greece)
NEC	National Executive Council of Labour Party (UK)
NI	Non-inscrits MEPs without a party group
OUP	Official Unionist Party (UK: N. Ireland)
ÖVP	People's Party (Austria)
PASOK	Socialist Party (Greece)
PCF	Parti Communiste (France)
PCP	Communist Party (Portugal)
PCS	Christian Democrat Party (Luxembourg)
PDS	Party of the Democratic Left (Italy)
PES	Party of European Socialists (federation and group in EP)
PNV	Basque Nationalist Party
POLAN	Political Spring (Greece)
POSL	Labour Party (Luxembourg)
PP	People's Party (Spain)
PPI	People's Party (Italy)
PR	Republican Party (France)
PRI	Republican Party (Italy)
PRL	Liberal Party (Belgium: Wallonia)
PS	Parti Socialiste (France)
PS (B)	Parti Socialiste (Belgium: Wallonia)
PSC	Christian Democrat Party (Belgium: Wallonia)
PSD	Social Democrat Party (France)
PSD (P)	Social Democrat Party (Portugal)
PSDI	Social Democratic Party (Italy)
PSI	Socialist Party (Italy)
PSP	Socialist Party (Portugal)
PSOE	Socialist Party (Spain)
PvdA	Labour Party (Netherlands)
RC	Reformed Communist Party (Italy)
RDE	Rassemblement Démocratique Européen (former EP group)
REFA	Regionalist European Free Alliance
RPR	Gaullist Party (France)

RV	Radical Liberal Party (Denmark)
SAP	Social Democratic Labour Party (Sweden)
SD	Social Democrat Party (Denmark)
SDLP	Social Democratic and Labour Party (UK: N. Ireland)
SDP	Social Democrat Party (Finland)
SEA	Single European Act
SF	Socialist People's Party (Denmark)
SFP	Swedish People's Party (Finland)
SGP/GPV /RPF	Protestant Confessional Party (Netherlands)
SI	Socialist International
SNP	Scottish Nationalist Party (UK: Scotland)
SP	Socialist Party (Belgium: Flanders)
SPD	Social Democratic Party (Germany)
SPÖ	Socialist Party (Austria)
SVP	South Tyrol Party (Italy)
SYN	Synaspismo tis Aristeras (Greece)
UDC	Catalan Democratic Union (Spain)
UDF	Union Démocratique Française
UEL	Union of the European Left (group in EP)
UPE	Union for Europe (group in EP)
V	Liberal Party (Denmark)
V (S)	Left Party (Sweden)
VAS	Vasemmistoliitto (Finland)
VB	Vlaams Blok (Belgium: Flanders)
VIHR	Greens (Finland)
VLD	Flemish Liberal Party (Belgium: Flanders)
VU	Volksunie (Belgium: Wallonia)
VVD	Liberal Party (Netherlands)

1

Introduction

Why study political parties in the European Union?

The European Union (EU) is run by party politicians. All three branches of its political leadership – the Commission, the Council of Ministers and the European Council – are predominantly recruited from political parties. Most Commissioners, whose task it is to propose new initiatives, are selected from senior members of the leading political parties of the member states. It has also become customary for the presidency of the Commission, whose potential for political entrepreneurship was greatly extended by Jacques Delors, to alternate between the Union's main party political families of the centre left and centre right. The Council of Ministers, which makes decisions and laws based on the Commission's recommendations, involves government ministers from right across the range of specialist portfolios (foreign affairs, finance, industry, agriculture and so on). This means that *all* political parties that are members of a national governing coalition are automatically sucked into the management of the Union. The European Council, which does a great deal to set the overall direction of the Union and to link its sometimes diffuse processes, is made up of the heads of government, who are usually leaders of political parties, and often of the largest single party in each member state.

The Union's political leadership is, in turn, accountable to the European Parliament (EP) and to national parliaments. At the beginning of the 1994–9 Parliament, 101 of the political parties of the 15 member states of the Union are represented in the EP. For reasons that will be explored below, the EP tends to overrepresent national parties of opposition and fringe parties, thus increasing the number of political parties that have some access to an EU institution

1

and providing a limited counterbalance to the monopoly hold of parties of government on the Council of Ministers. Even more political parties are involved in the work of national parliaments and, although these are not Union institutions, membership compels political parties to debate and take up positions on a series of EU issues, as well as to review the performance of their own government on the Council of Ministers. A further challenge to political parties is presented by the need to organise for five-yearly elections to the EP, and to anticipate the possibility that EU issues will feature in national elections. This has, in turn, required various changes to be made to the organisational structures of national political parties. Many now have sections and bureaux specifically concerned with EU affairs and most include some senior EU-level politicians (such as MEPs) on their governing councils, to ensure that the party has sufficient understanding of the EU to function effectively in both the European and national arenas.

To improve their capacity to adapt to the new institutional environment presented by the Union, political parties have, however, also found it useful to develop transnational processes. These are of two kinds, the party groups in the EP and the extra-parliamentary party federations. The party groups in the EP bring together political parties from several EU member states into transnational parliamentary parties. The party federations, on the other hand, provide an element of extra parliamentary coordination of the electoral platforms of national parties in European elections and of the input of party leaders to meetings of the European Council. There are currently four pan-European party federations: the Party of European Socialists (PES), the European People's Party (EPP), the European Liberal Democratic and Reform Party (ELDR), and the European Federation of Green Parties (EFGP). To these must be added various near-federations, such as the Regionalist European Free Alliance (EFA) and the remains of the European Democratic Union (EDU), which used to be the coordinating mechanism for Conservative parties before most of these joined the Christian Democrats in the EPP to form just one federation of the centre right. In the EP, there are at the time of writing eight transnational party groups, four of which correspond to the party federations – the PES, the EPP, the ELDR and the Greens (G). Four others – the Union for Political Europe (UPE), the United European Left (UEL), Europe of the Nations (EN) and the European Radical Alliance (ERA) – are more ephemeral and free-floating in the sense that they have not existed across several parliaments. Nor do they have any continuing under-pinning in the shape of an extra-parliamentary federation, members of which are committed to form their MEPs into a transnational parliamentary group whenever they have the numbers to do so.

So, whether we are talking about the Commission, Council or Parliament, actors drawn from domestic party politics penetrate deep into the EU's institutions. The so-called domestic politics school of European integration has highlighted the extent to which each member state – and its internal party politics – needs to be regarded as a political sub-system of the EU's own decision- making bodies (Bulmer, 1983). This explains why it is that when a new country applies to join the EU, a long hard look is taken at its political parties and at its capacity to sustain a stable but competitive party system. Existing members know that they will be condemned to work with the party politicians of new member states: to sit with them in the Council and Parliament and to allow them to take part in the formation of majorities binding on everyone else. One reason why enlargement to Eastern Europe is such an unprecedented political challenge to the Union is that the countries in question have only nascent party systems of uncertain stability. Indeed, at a level of party politics, eastern enlargement would be a marriage of more doubtful compatibility than any of the Union's previous new relation-ships. With each earlier enlargement, the EU has taken on a country whose political families are recognisably the same as those in the existing member states. By contrast, not all East European countries show signs of developing party systems that centre around Christian and Social Democrats, Conservatives and Liberals as the dominant political forces.

Even amongst existing members the changing fortunes of domestic political parties may be viewed with some nervousness, especially where this signals a relative decline of national parties that have been supportive of European integration and the rise of those that show varying degrees of hostility to the Union's political system. In 1974, for example, the Community's programme of work was substantially disrupted when a new Labour government in the UK insisted on renegotiating the terms of EC membership arranged by its Conser-vative predecessor. In 1995, the election of a Gaullist to the French presidency for the first time since 1974 complicated the implementa-tion of the Schengen agreement for a frontier-free core of European states. It also created a two-way link between prospects for monetary union and the alternative ways in which President Chirac could construct his government and power base within and amongst the parties of the French right.

Some of the bargaining dynamics in the Union can also be traced to a sense that deals are forged as much between political parties, or even particular party leaderships, as between states and governments. In an effort to reduce the exposure of the Union's policies and achievements – its *'acquis communautaire'* – to the changing rhythms of domestic party politics, key players may rush to form agreements while there is a favourable conjuncture in the domestic politics of member states. They may also seek to neutralise future uncertainties in national party politics by locking successor governments into EU-level agreements. For example, when the French insisted at Maastricht that members should forego the right to think again about monetary union, should they meet the criteria in 1997 or 1999, it was for fear that future German coalitions might not be as favourable as Chancellor Kohl's to a single currency.

The need to give the Union a broad and durable political base in the domestic party politics of its member states means that there is a tendency for its political compromises to be struck at the centre of the left–right spectrum. It could be dangerous for the prospects of European integration were it to be seen as structurally biased towards the agenda of the centre right or the centre left, or as making it systematically more difficult for one of these to gain power and develop programmes of its choice. The EU can, arguably, no more afford to offend the core values of one of its mainstream party political families of Western Europe than the key interests of a member state. The need to maintain a left–right balance in European integration accounts, for example, for the drive to develop a social policy in parallel with the single market programme. However, another powerful reason for the centripetal bias in EU decision-making has to do with the peculiar way in which party politicians are recruited into its political leadership. Qualification for membership of the Commission, Council of Ministers or European Council is linked to the success of parties in the national and not the European political arena. This has two related consequences. First, the bodies that run the Union will always include a wide spread of the mainstream parties of West European politics. Since 1958, there has been no moment when they have not included representatives of all four dominant political families: Christian Democrats, Conservatives, Liberals and Social Democrats. By contrast, even those countries that are accustomed to coalitions will usually only include two or three of these in government at any one time, leaving at least one to play the role of principal opposition party. Second, the party politicians that participate in the Commission, Council of Ministers or European Council are thrown together by circumstance, rather than choice. This means that they have no collective electoral mandate to develop a particular party perspective at the European level. Nor do they amount to a deliberately constructed coalition, based on careful forethought as to how party political priorities are to be balanced and blended. All of these factors combine with decision-making rules that stress consensus and the need for oversized majorities to prevent the Union ever becoming the property of just one – or even just two or three – party political perspectives.

By identifying those who are most likely to win and lose from the above patterns of European-level decision-making, we can also make some predictions as to which parties are most likely to support or oppose integration. Mainstream parties – and those nearest the centre of the political spectrum – are far more likely to get what they want from the EU. By contrast, the further out a strand of opinion to the left or the right, the more those associated with it are likely to feel alienated by the consensual ways of the Union. Yet, in a sense, this analysis also captures the strategic weakness of Euro-scepticism. While political alliances in support of integration are facilitated by contiguity on a left–right scale, its opponents are holed up in the outlying positions on the left and right, and often prevented from making common cause by their fundamental incompatibility on all questions other than integration itself. The only political arena in which this does not hold is, significantly, the UK, where other factors, the practices of single-party government and adversarial politics, mean that it is the supporters of integration who are separated by institutional factors, and prevented from making common cause, while either party of government will, inevitably, have some Euro-sceptics in its ranks.

If national party politics change the policy outputs of the Union, the converse is also true. The EU confronts domestic political parties with a new structure of threats and opportunities. They have to adapt to the EU and organise themselves for participation in its institutions and rule-making, if they are to maintain their influence over all the political processes that shape the distribution of values in their own national societies. This may be a source of stress for both parties and party systems at the national level, for European integration may suggest patterns of cooperation and conflict that cut across long-standing political alignments in the domestic arena. The split in the Labour Party in the 1980s, the attempted creation of a Social Democratic Party in the UK and the easy ascendancy that the Conservatives consequently enjoyed throughout that decade before they too split over dilemmas presented by European integration provide one illustration of how the exposure of previously self-contained national party systems to the politics of the Union can unleash complicated political dynamics, the full effects of which can take several years to ramify through the party politics of a member state.

Indeed, the choices presented by the EU provide a new source of political competition in West European politics. By taking up different positions on EU issues, parties – or factions within them – can compete for different niches in public and elite opinion. They can also split their opponents, or wrong-foot them tactically. It is worth considering a few examples from French and German politics, which, incidentally, cast doubt on the (often Anglocentric) argument that a strong sense of pro-European consensus only exists in those countries because of an elite understanding to keep EU issues out of party political debate and competition. At the end of the 1970s, Europe seemed to provide an ideal issue for Jacques Chirac to challenge the sitting President, Valéry Giscard d'Estaing, for the leadership of the French right. Giscard was widely identified with pro- integration attitudes, and too heavily committed to his personal diplomacy with German Chancellor Helmut Schmidt to be able to do everything possible to cover his flank from a 'Euro-sceptic' onslaught. By contrast, Chirac expected to consolidate his leadership of the most cohesive section of the French right and underscore his claims to be de Gaulle's political heir by remobilising the Gaullists around the General's notion of a Europe of states (Shields in Gaffney, 1996). Fifteen years later, both the content of the Maastricht Treaty and the decision to put it to a referendum in France were heavily influenced by Mitterrand's attempts to split the French right (Dinan, 1994, p. 186; Moravcsik, 1993b). Meanwhile, in Germany, elements of the Bavarian Christian Democrats, the CSU, attempted to capitalise on the post-Maastricht malaise of 1992–4. Although by no means completely successful in capturing the party's policy platform, they hoped to use a more critical position on Europe to reinforce *Land* rights for Bavaria, while edging the CSU towards the role of a pan-German conservative party (Paterson in Gaffney, 1996). Likewise in the *Land* elections in 1996, the German Social Democrats (SPD) adopted a cautious approach to monetary union. Faced with a progressive haemorrhaging of their support to the Christian Democrats to their right and the Greens to their left, German anxiety about monetary union seemed to offer the ideal opportunity for the SPD to revive their flagging fortunes.

In spite of the foregoing examples, it is unusual for the European Union to be analysed in terms of party politics. Even those who accept that the EU is peopled by party politicians deny that it is a field of party politics. They further suggest that the political science of party politics and the study of the European integration are incapable of contributing very much to one another. Before taking up this debate, we need, however, to do two more things in this introduction: first, to give a peremptory summary of what parties do and how they develop and, second, to provide a historical analysis of how the EU has arrived at its present mix of national and transnational party politics.

Political parties and party systems

Western European political systems are liberal democracies, but it is the representatives of the people who rule and not the people themselves. One of the main functions of parties is to link the represented with their representatives. They are often described as intermediators between society and government. This is not immediately obvious to those who complain about the elitist character of representative politics in Western Europe. But parties do more than select individuals for public office and political leadership. They also have to compete for votes and this puts them under continuous pressure to adjust their policies to the needs and values of publics and societies. The only exception to this is where they succeed in 'cartelising' a certain political issue: in reaching a stable agreement between themselves to keep an issue out of political debate and competition. Otherwise, parties are said to act as 'aggregators', adding together social demands, channelling them into the political system and reaching crucial decisions as to how they are to be traded off in a context of limited resources. As this will often require significant political innovation and a degree of uncertainty as to which solutions will be easiest to sell to the public, there is also a sense in which parties are the 'political entrepreneurs' of effective liberal democratic systems.

In performing their various roles, parties usually settle into a division of labour between themselves. It is common for some to function as parties of government and others as parties of opposition. In the former case, parties also provide a mechanism for coordination across the arms of government, executive and legislative, as well as across the levels, local and central. Their work in organising and maintaining parliamentary majorities, as well as in simplifying the negotiation of coalitions, arguably adds to the stability and predictability of government. The institutional disciplines they bring to these tasks are, in turn, justified by the way in which party politics structure electoral choice. By giving all individuals in a political system the opportunity to vote for entire teams and packages of policies, they provide each voter with a simple and understandable mechanism for making choices about the overall approach to government over an extended period. And because the political parties that present themselves at future elections are usually the same as those who fought previous ones, the opportunity to punish parties for poor performance is a key mechanism by which liberal democratic systems bring politicians to account, weed out failure, and renew themselves. One issue which is of central importance to the EU is whether the effective performance of the various roles mentioned in this paragraph require a political system to develop a single set of political parties, each with some kind of presence throughout the territory covered by the political system. An obvious advantage of such an arrangement is that it allows parties to function as a mechanism for the coordination of voter preferences from right across the political unit. In the case of the EU, changes in patterns of support would be more clearly attributable to trends in public opinion on European questions, and harder to dismiss as the chance accumulation of a series of localised political debates that have little to do with the Union itself. On the other hand, existing national parties may represent a kind of sunk investment in the construction of a political infrastructure in Western Europe and any erosion of their role could involve serious costs in terms of political socialisation and well-established mechanisms for mediating contacts between society and political institutions, the EU included.

Analysis of how political parties develop has often focused on the deep divisions, or cleavages, that are to be found in West European societies. S. M. Lipset and S. Rokkan found that most parties represent some definable segment of their home society and that they develop – or import – an ideology that is well-adapted to the interests of that core political base (Lipset and Rokkan, 1967). As we will see, parties often follow the dividing lines of class, religion, region and ethnicity. Because Western European countries have many similarities in their internal social divisions, they have mostly developed political parties that profess like attitudes to government. Indeed, many have similar names. Parties that are to be found in many different countries – Conservatives, Christian Democrats, Socialists, Liberals, Far Left, Far Right and Regionalists – are often known as the political families of Western Europe.

Political parties have, historically, had a role in shaping political systems around them, or even in completing the formation of societies and nations themselves. Yet there are also important instances of the opposite effect: of parties having to adapt to preexisting constitutions or rules for obtaining and exercising political power. One result of this is that parties may group together people who see themselves as representing a diversity of interests and ideologies. We need to beware of treating parties as unitary actors, and remember that they may have a complex inner party politics of different tendencies and factions. Attitudes towards European integration may be as much the product of conflict within parties as across them. Needless to say, parties also differ markedly in how they distribute power internally between the various components of ordinary member, elected representative and overall political leadership. Determination of official policy on EU questions and appointment of individuals to positions within the Union's institutional processes may, therefore, be hierarchically and centrally decided in some parties, while others may have various mechanisms of inner party democracy that allow even the ordinary member to have some influence.

It is also important to note that there are different kinds of party system as well as various sorts of political party. Party systems are commonly distinguished according to the number and relative size of their political parties, their stability, and the extent to which individual parties consider the rules of the political system to be fair and acceptable. These are, of course, related questions, for 'anti-system' parties will only render a system dysfunctional to the extent that 'pro-system parties' are unable to manage it or provide it with sufficient competition on their own. Amongst specific variables, there is a clear difference between a bipolar system dominated by two major parties and a multipolar one. The former will often produce alternating one-party government, while the latter will usually depend on multi-party coalitions. However, this is not to suggest that there is any simple relationship between the number of parties in a system and its stability or consensual/conflictual character. The structure of electoral preferences and the rules for winning power may still encourage centripetal, as opposed to centrifugal, patterns of party competition. Likewise, there may be other factors apart from a multiplicity of parties that compel a consensual approach to party politics. Where, for example, a political system is multinational, acceptability of decisions and consent will often require the involvement of party politicians representing a wide cross-section of nationalities and not just simple majorities of the whole. Such approaches to party politics are said to be 'consociational'. The problems of anti-system parties and multinational politics probably constitute the two clearest structural differences between party politics at the EU and national levels. There is scarcely any national political arena in Western Europe in which the principal political parties still disagree about the basic shape of the political system itself. This can scarcely be said of the EU, even though the more 'sceptical' national parties claim to take issue only with certain methods of European integration, and not with the need for some kind of Union.

From what we have said so far, it is clear that the roles of political parties are complex and multifaceted, as well as open to being played in different ways by different political parties: parties shape the public's political preferences and they help construct its understanding of the political system, but they also respond to what the public wants; they govern, but they also exist to oppose, criticise and even protest. Yet underlying all of this is one defining feature that sets them off from all other organisations: they exist to influence the *overall* formation of policy in the *public* sphere. Were they only interested in particular policies, they would be no different from interest groups. Were their core goals concerned with following, rather than shaping, the general framework of rules and laws by which other, more particular, economic and social activities are governed, they would be no different from private organisations like companies. It is for this reason that parties are often characterised by some overall set of attitudes, or ideology, about the manner in which societies *ought* to be governed: about the proper purpose of government, the extent of its intervention in economy and society and its relationship with the nation and the international scene. In contemporary circumstances, these questions are unanswerable without raising issues of European integration.

A history of party politics in the EU

The early European Community was heavily influenced by postwar patterns of party politics. Many of the attitudes towards the postwar integration of Western Europe were formed within the political parties that emerged least discredited from the Second World War. Those that had been closest to resistance movements were often the most keen, though the far left cooled to integration as the formation of a European Community came to be associated with the Western side in the Cold War. Meanwhile Christian Democrats took up much of the running, as the cause of West European reconciliation came naturally to those who believed that the conflicts and divisions of the age of nationalism had disguised a deeper past, based on a single European civilisation of shared religious and social values. Robert Schuman of the French MRP, Konrad Adenauer of the German Christian Democrats and Alcide De Gasperi of the Italian Christian Democrats formed a bond of mutual understanding that provided an early suggestion that horizontal cross-national feelings of ideological affinity really could break through the vertical divisions of the nation state. The early record of the Social Democrats was more ambiguous. The leadership of the German SPD initially opposed the European Community on the grounds that it would complicate relationships with the East and thus prejudice the cause of national reunification. Although the French Socialists were largely supportive of integration in the 1950s, they were less relaxed than the MRP about a small Community of Six that excluded Britain and gave priority to Franco-German reconciliation. From the start, there was also a clear split on the centre left between those who believed that European integration would be essential to manage markets and complete the formation of national welfare states and those who thought that it would only interfere with this objective. Prominent in the latter camp was the British Labour Cabinet which made the fateful decision that Britain should not be a founder member of the European Community in 1950. Across the original Six, Liberals and Radicals were largely favourable, with economic liberals looking forward to trade liberalisation and radical liberals finding inspiration in an arrangement that could curb the power of the state to make war or dominate its own citizens. By contrast, West European Conservative parties were almost universally opposed to the formation of the European Community. It is no coincidence that the six countries that accepted a supranational approach to European integration in the 1950s were all those where Christian Democrats, rather than Conservatives, formed the main party of government on the centre right and as soon as this situation was reversed in one key country – de Gaulle's Fifth French Republic – the Community found itself being pulled in a more intergovernmental direction. Even Churchill's enthusiastic support for European integration turned out on closer inspection to preclude the supranational option, at least for Britain itself.

Whether hostile or opposed, similarity of attitude towards European integration was in itself a justification for the party families of Western Europe to meet, exchange views and coordinate action. However, the formation of a definite set of transnational institutions with a potential to make important decisions about matters that the parties cared about added urgency to these practices. Several of the political families had long experimented with federations or internationals of various kinds, so a basis for collaboration was already there. From 1948, the early meetings of the Council of Europe also required national parliamentary parties to send six-monthly delegations to Strasbourg and there were some moves to make this into a democratic forum, or even Constituent Assembly, for the continent as a whole. It was not, however, until the formation of the European Coal and Steel Community (ECSC) and the first meeting of its Assembly in 1953 that any attempt was made to experiment with transnational parliamentary groups. With the formation of the EPP, the PES and the ELDR, the High Authority of the ECSC became the first international body accountable to an Assembly whose deputies sat in transnational blocs.

With these faint stirrings of transnational party activity, early theorists, like Ernst Haas and Leon Lindberg, invested much hope in political parties as potential 'carriers' of European integration. Working with a pluralist model of politics in which institutions and parties are always under pressure to adapt to the needs and demands of the different groups and sections of their societies, and predicting that the European Community would be able to deliver political benefits that were beyond the reach of the nation state, Haas and Lindberg argued that parties which failed to redirect some of their efforts to influencing the institutions of the EC on behalf of their voters would lose out in the competition for political support. What was interesting about this theory was that it suggested political parties would come under competitive pressure to adapt to the European political arena, regardless of whether they were hostile or enthusiastic about integration (Haas, 1958; Lindberg and Scheingold, 1971). At first, it was predicted, attempts to influence the new Community might take the form of *ad hoc* alliances between various agglomerations of interests and parties from different countries. However, political socialisation – positive experience of consensus-building in EC institutions-would eventually blend with the search for competitive advantage to impel parties towards more permanent and integrated formations at the European level. Even in the short term, it was hoped that party politicians could provide a supplementary source of new initiatives and political entrepreneurship to a largely technocratic European Commission. Over a longer period it was anticipated that they might be capable of agreeing comprehensive programmes at the European level, and of offering alternative leaderships to people all of the Community's institutions. Such hopes were critical to the EC's political development, for, as we have seen, the classic route to democratisation and the widening of electoral choice in Western Europe was to rely on parties to present the voter with competing policies and teams for government.

Contrary to these early predictions, the development of party activities at the European level was, however, at best sluggish, at least until the end of the 1970s.The federations and the party groups appeared to be mired in a lowest common denominator character of decision-making, suggesting not only that they had little ability to make national parties do what they would not have done anyway, but, more damagingly, that they were not even very important as sites for learning and socialisation. In most national parties, liaison with the transnational federation was usually left to relatively marginal officials, or treated as an excuse for occasional political tourism. Meanwhile, the EP remained unelected before 1979, with the consequence that its party groups consisted of those who primarily saw themselves as national members of parliament, thrown together for just one week a month in Strasbourg. There was, therefore, little sense of the groups emerging as politicians specifically selected to specialise in EC affairs. The only developments that did occur in the groups were, arguably, retrograde. The Gaullists, who had originally been in the ELDR, left in 1965 to form a group all on their own. Although they were by instinct prickly defenders of national independence, this move showed a remarkably low tolerance of constraints on national freedom of action, given the powerlessness of the Assembly as it then was. It also suggested that early experiments in transnational party formation might relapse into the practice common to other international assemblies of representatives sitting in national party blocs. Nor did the first widening of the EC in 1973 hold out much hope that the party groups could be commensurately enlarged without experiencing problems of their own. The British and Danish Conservatives confirmed the trend set by the Gaullists towards greater fragmentation and lower levels of transnational party organisation, by forming a fifth group of their own, the European Democratic Group (EDG). Although the Labour Party did eventually enter the PES, it did not even take up its seats in the Assembly in the first two years of British membership, and, even then, it remained for years to come a powerful source of internal division in the wider group.

Ideological diversity and conflicts of national and partisan interest seem plausible explanations for this unimpressive record of transnational party development before 1979 (Pridham and Pridham, 1981). However, differences in the ideological roots and sociological bases of national parties are constant factors and they cannot readily explain why, after such a disappointing start between the 1950s and 1970s, both the federations and the groups should have become more active and integrated during the 1980s and 1990s. As will be shown in following chapters, the federations ceased to be confined to the faintly futile task of drafting European manifestos for elections that were largely fought on national lines. They increasingly developed an additional role as sites for consensus-building by means of party leaders' summits held immediately prior to meetings of heads of government in the European Council, which, arguably, constitute the most authoritative forum for settling the Union's agenda and wider issues of European integration (Hix, 1995a). Meanwhile, studies of the groups in the EP noted their growing cohesiveness, even though successive enlargements of the Union meant that there were more national parties that needed to be accommodated in group agreements, and increased parliamentary powers meant the groups had to make more contentious choices about the distribution resources and allocation of political values (Attina, 1990).

The development of transnational party activities was probably stimulated more by reforms to the institutions of the Union during the 1980s and 1990s than by changes in the character of political parties. The problem with early optimism about the prospects for transnational party development was that it had assumed institutional contexts that simply did not exist during the first thirty years of the EU. Conversely, a combination of a directly elected parliament (1979), its empowerment by the Single European Act (1986) and

Maastricht Treaties (1992), and the curtailment of the national veto on the Council has meant that parties that are good at organising themselves transnationally will receive certain pay-offs that may be denied to others. Yet, institutional change has so far been lopsided in the kind of transnational party activity that it has catalysed. The experience of 1979 to 1996 would seem to suggest that there is a threshold between elite and mass politics that parties are unable – or unwilling – to cross in the transnationalisation of their activities. From the public's point of view, the federations and the groups are invisible elements in the Union's political infrastructure. Even in the most recent European election in 1994, it was the familiar national parties that appeared on ballot sheets; there was negligible awareness or discussion of the transnational parliamentary groupings to which candidates would adhere if elected; and, although some of the manifesto commitments agreed in the federations did percolate into the debate, public understanding of both their provenance and significance was hazy.

Indeed, even the intensification of transnational party activity in the EU in the 1980s and 1990s did little to remove the national foundations of party politics. In many ways, it is national, rather than transnational, parties that function as the 'carriers of European integration'. The continued ability of national parties to monopolise the mass political arena while reserving European-level activities for elite contacts between senior party figures and MEPs can be seen as evidence of their remarkable capacity to ensure that the transnationalisation of party activity does little to diminish their own role. Likewise, it is hard to avoid the impression that national political parties are key influences in shaping the political culture of each country's membership of the EU. There are two reasons for this. First, public attitudes towards European integration seem to be less rigidly formed than on domestic issues and they are, consequently, more open to political leadership by domestic parties, who often dominate national debates and media. Second, it is political parties who recruit elites and shape their basic political assumptions. The prejudices for or against European integration that they transmit from one generation of political leaders to another may help explain the significant continuities of approach towards the politics of the EU that are to be found in certain member states.

Amongst changes at the level of national party politics in the 1980s and 1990s that have, arguably, affected the practice of transnational party collaboration are the following: first, the problems that globalisation and the 'crisis of the welfare state' have presented for left-of-centre parties in particular, and the attendant search for 'solutions' at the European level (Delwit and De Waele, 1993); second, the presence of new cleavage structures and a consequent need to accommodate new arrivals on the political scene, such as the Greens; and, third, the degree of *Parteiverdrossenheit* or public disillusionment with political parties and party democracy. The latter compels political parties to consider whether European integration is a 'problem' or a 'solution' in terms of their own political credibility, and supporters of the EU to ponder the implications of building the Union around party politicians who are not as authoritative as they once were in the domestic arena.

Argument and organisation of the book

Before presenting our particular view of the significance of political parties in the EU, it is helpful to set out systematically the main views of those who are more sceptical about the relevance of party politics to the study of the EU. These might be summarised as follows:

- EU politics are about contending 'national interests' rather than party ideologies. Although each member state is riven by internal conflict about the positions that should be adopted at EU level, there are authoritative domestic institutions for determining the 'national line' (Moravcsik, 1993a). Such majoritarian procedures that exist in the EU are only artifices to facilitate *interstate* bargaining (for example, by speeding decision-making). Few claim that they produce or 'sanctify' party political majorities at the European level.
- In so far as the EU is a political system that has to respond to social forces and not just interstate bargaining, it is argued that it is not political parties but economic interests that are most influential with the Commission and the Council (Gaffney, 1996, p. 21). According to this point of view, economic interests have little difficulty in organising themselves for international political influence. Transnational settings may even make it easier for them to escape controls, play off competing authorities and dominate the weak and diffuse decision-making processes typical of multi-state political systems (Holland, 1980). Policy networking

approaches further emphasise the extent to which EU agencies –
at a practical level of policy formulation and implementation –
become highly dependent on the expertise and cooperation of the
very private interests that they are supposed to regulate (Mazey
and Richardson, 1993). By contrast, it is suggested that parties,
like democracy itself, are essentially nation-bound institutions.
They are inherently constrained in their ability to organise,
aggregate and communicate across political frontiers.

- The Union has only had very modest success in stimulating the
  development of its own political parties. The EU does not have
  pan-European parties that directly engage the electorate in a
  competition around alternative approaches to European integration or in the aggregation of votes; and although transnational
  party activities touch on many individual aspects of the EU's
  governance, these do not amount to a classic model of party
  government, for it would be a heroic leap to describe the
  federations and party groups as having *overall responsibility* for
  government and opposition in the Union, or as the main linking
  mechanisms between all branches and levels of government. In so
  far as the EU has a party politics, it borrows heavily from the
  efforts of national political parties. Even the federations and party
  groups – which come nearest to endowing the EU with a party
  system of its own – are more *trans*national than *supra*national.
  That is to say, they are not composed of individuals and local
  branches, but of preexisting national parties, many of which were
  fully developed before the foundation of the Union itself. This,
  inevitably, leads to a very different balance of power between the
  whole and the parts than anything to be found in a single-state
  political party, with neither the federations nor the groups being
  able to command the same levels of loyalty and authority over
  national parties as the latter, in turn, enjoy over their own
  membership. In addition, the cultural segmentation of the Union
  along national and linguistic lines carries over into even the most
  assiduously 'European' of the federations and party groups.
- Most sceptically of all, it can even be argued that the only impact
  of European integration on party politics has been negative and
  that it has greatly contributed to a general decline in their
  importance in Western Europe. To a degree this argument
  overlaps with the foregoing observations that the EU has changed
  the locus of decision-making from the natural habitats of political
  parties – national parliaments and elections – to interstate

bargaining in the Council of Ministers and to transnational technocracies (Gaffney, 1996). However, a further problem is that the emphasis of the Union on consensual decision-making and oversized majorities has meant that decisions are often agreed by all or most of the main political families of Western Europe – the Conservatives, Christian Democrats, Liberals and Socialists. In other words, there is a tendency for the EU to suspend party political competition, rather than provoke it. There is an absence of political contestation – of sharp delineations between parties of government and opposition – that is so important for political parties to differentiate themselves and become relevant in the eyes of the public. Brigid Laffan, for example, writes of a 'blurring of the left–right divide' and of EU 'governance structures' that serve to dilute political preferences because an all-party Commission faces an all-party Council and Parliament (Laffan, 1996, p. 93).

The argument of this book is that 'naive' and 'sceptical' assessments are equally unsatisfactory, for neither can resolve the central paradox of party politics in the EU. The evidence of subsequent chapters leaves us in the uncomfortable position of confirming two propositions that, at first sight, cannot both be true. It suggests *both* that the Union is a system of very weak party organisation by West European standards *and* that its decision-making is systematically affected by the activities of political parties. Part of the difficulty is that academic commentators have expected successful Euro-parties to resemble their equivalents in domestic politics, and treated any continued role for national parties in EU institutions as a sign of failure. The problem with this is that it precludes appreciation of how far the trio of national parties, transnational federations and parliamentary groups, *cumulatively*, perform many of the roles expected of any system of party politics. These three elements have, in other words, adapted to one another, and formed a rational and defensible division of labour for this stage in the Union's political development. We will see that they come together to form a party system of a kind, even if no one component of the system amounts to a full political party in relation to EU politics: transnational parties because they make no direct contact between society and EU governance and national parties because they are too small to organise themselves individually to influence the outputs of EU institutions.

The danger of dismissing the role of parties at the European level, so long as Euro-parties do not come up to standards of integration we would expect in some imaginary Union constructed in the image of a single-state political system, is thus one of underestimating the suitability even of present arrangements to the messy part-national and part-European political system that we have in fact got. Various images such as 'two-level games' and 'joint-decision traps' have been used in recent years to underline the extent to which the EU and its member states have come to be linked political arenas in Western Europe (Scharpf, 1988; Dyson, 1994). Parties are important yet neglected elements in that linking, even if their activities have only been explicitly Europeanised at the cross-over point between the two arenas, and contacts with mass society are largely left to national parties.

To develop this argument, Chapters 2 and 3 will attempt a more detailed analysis of how national parties, the federations and party groups in the EP fit together into a single system of party politics. They will begin by returning to the domestic micro-foundations of West European politics and examining the positions of national parties on the key issues of left–right politics and European integration. They will then show how national parties have been pulled together at the EU level and demonstrate that the four main political families of Western Europe have made a like organisational response to the political growth of the EU. This can, in turn, be summed up in a single 'organigram' of what a transnational party at the European level looks like, indicating that there are certain uniformities both in the pressure on parties to organise themselves for EU politics, and in the responses they have made. Chapters 4 to 6 will turn to a detailed analysis of the EU's experiment with transnational parliamentary parties. The extent to which the EP groups are the joint product of national and European-level party politics will be revealed through a detailed examination of the recruitment of MEPs, the election of the EP and the formation of national party delegations into parliamentary coalitions. Attention will then turn to the inner workings of the groups, the way in which decisions are taken and consensus is reached. Finally, an assessment will be made of the kind of party politics that is required by the powers and functions of the EP, and of the success of the groups in delivering it in terms of their individual unity and overall coherence as a system of parliamentary parties.

Chapter 7 will show how, in constructing party activities outside the EP, parties at the European level began by imitating the classic function of extra-parliamentary parties, that of coordinating electoral programmes, only to find that the EU's distinctive institutional environment made it sensible for the transnational party federations to concentrate on a task that has no parallel in national politics: that of coordinating the positions of party leaders prior to meetings of the EU's main agenda-setting body, the European Council.

2

Shape of the EU Party System

The aim of this and the following chapter is to provide an analytical framework for the understanding of party behaviour in the European Union system – on European issues at the national level, in the European Parliament, and in the other arenas at the European level (such as the European Council). This chapter focuses on the motivations behind party behaviour (their goals) and the shape of the EU party system (the strategic environment): the dimensions of party competition, and the positions and strengths of the party families within the system. Chapter 3 turns to the organisation of parties in the EU (the institutional environment): the links between the various party structures in the EU system. These two chapters together constitute a 'tool-kit' of concepts and methods to help understand and explain party activity at all levels of the EU system.

Parties and their environment

If political parties are central actors in EU politics, we need to understand how they behave. In other words: what are the basic goals of political parties, and how do they pursue these goals in the EU system? The main goal of a political party in any system is political office: parliamentary seats, cabinet portfolios, and prime ministerial or presidential office (Downs, 1957; Riker, 1962). Political office gives party leaders control of the organs of the state, and usually increases their personal prestige and financial security. In other words, political office gives politicians the rare possibility of obtaining power, fame and fortune at the same time. In the EU system, political

21

offices are national ministerial positions, European Commission posts, and seats in the national and European parliaments.

However, in democratic systems, parties can only obtain political office by winning elections. To win an election parties promise voters that if they obtain office they will implement policies to make their voters better off. Consequently, a secondary party goal in democratic systems is public policy: the outputs of political decision-making (Strom, 1990). In concrete terms, party policies are the positions taken in party programmes, electoral manifestos, and party leaders' statements. In the EU system, policy goals are secured through the outputs of the domestic and European decision-making processes. Sometimes, ideal policy and office goals can be obtained simultaneously. More often than not, however, there is a trade-off between office and policy goals.

The trade-off between office and policy goals results from an interaction between the basic party objectives and the constraints of the environment in which parties operate. This environment has two elements. First, the *strategic environment* is the structure of competition (the divisions and alliances) between the parties in the political system – the shape of the party system. The strategic environment in EU politics is thus the political and representational strengths, the policy positions, and the divisions and alliances between the various European party families. Second, the *institutional environment* is the set of formal and informal rules of the game: the organisational structure within political parties, and the decision-making structure of the political system. In EU politics, these constraints are the relations between the different party organs in the national and European arenas and the vertical and horizontal decision-making structures of the EU system.

However, parties are not purely dependent on their environment. Parties possess significant political and financial resources, which also gives them a degree of autonomy. Under certain circumstances, parties can use these resources to modify the environmental constraints and make the obtainment of their goals easier. In the EU system, parties are not the dominant political organisations, and are rivalled by governments, interest groups and businesses. Parties are thus less able to alter the constraints on their behaviour at the European level than at the domestic level. Nevertheless, under certain conditions parties can make 'environmental choices' at the European level. For example, they can alter the strategic environment by choosing not to compete on certain issues (such as the question of European integration), or can alter the institutional environment by changing the structure of EU decision-making (such as by giving more powers to the EP).

In this chapter the basic elements of the strategic environment in which parties operate in the EU are introduced: the historical and political context of the EU party system. The organisational constraints on parties in EU politics and the implications of this environment on party behaviour in the EU are subsequently covered in Chapter 3. This chapter first looks at the historical determination of the dimensions of party competition in the EU, and subsequently analyses the positions and strengths of the individual party families within this space.

Dimensions of party competition

As Table 2.1 illustrates, each 'critical juncture' in modern European history produced a particular societal and political cleavage; and successive junctures have created a complex matrix of cross-cutting cleavages in European politics (Lipset and Rokkan, 1967). First, the Reformation and Counter-Reformation in the sixteenth and seventeenth centuries produced a division between the interests of the State and the Church, and between the secular and religious groups associated with these institutions. Second, the formation of the European nation states between the seventeenth and nineteenth centuries produced a cleavage between the centre and periphery interests. Third, the birth of modern democracy in the wake of the French Revolution (in 1789) produced a conflict between the authoritarian interests of the *ancien régime* and the emerging middle classes. Fourth and fifth, the agricultural and industrial revolutions produced the first real cleavages between groups based on socio-economic rather than political interests: between urban and landed interests, and between owners and workers.

When the precursors of modern political parties began to emerge in the last half of the nineteenth century they mobilised around these cleavages. In states that had been allied to Rome after the Reformation, nascent Christian parties defended the interests of the state; whereas in states with national churches this role was fulfilled by Conservatives. Liberals emerged to challenge these forces and demand political representation for the middle classes; Agrarian movements began to articulate the interests of rural elites; and Socialists

TABLE 2.1

Critical junctures, cleavages and party families in EU politics

Critical juncture	Cleavage	Party family	Salient issues in EU politics
Reformation	Church v. state	Christian Democrats v. Conservatives	Abortion, bioethics, social policy, free market, crime, military
National integration	Centre v. periphery	v. Regionalists	Regional policy, language rights, EMU, political union
Democratic revolution	Authority v. liberty	v. Liberals	Free trade, competition policy, internal market, civil linerties
Agricultural revolution	Urban v. rural	v. Agrarians	Common Agricultural Policy
Industrial revolution	Owners v. workers	v. Socialists	Social policy, industrial policy, civil liberties, corporatism
UNIVERSAL SUFFRAGE			
Russian revolution	Democratic v. Revolutionary Left	v. Communists/ Radical Left	Workers' rights, trade protection, women's rights, anti-military
Fascist dictatorship	Democratic v. Revolutionary Right	v. Fascists/Extreme Right	Immigration, drug-trafficking, anti-fraud, street-crime, abortion
Post-industrial society	Materialists v. Post-materialists	v. Greens	Environmental policy, bioethics, women's rights, anti-nuclear
European integration	Euro. integration v. national sovreignty	v. Anti-Europeans	Institutional reform, EMU, political union, EU citizenship

emerged to represent the working classes against the 'capitalist bosses'. With the introduction of universal suffrage around the turn of the century, mass political parties solidified the links between these various political movements and the sections of society they sought to represent.

Successive junctures since the advent of universal suffrage have also produced new cleavages. The Russian Revolution (in 1917) divided the Socialist movement between groups attached to the democratic institutions and groups committed to their overthrow. Similarly, the period of Fascist dictatorship in Europe created a new anti-democratic ideology on the extreme right. The onset of post-industrial society in the 1960s and 1970s led to new movements which demanded political resolutions on 'post-material' issues such as women's rights, anti-nuclear weapons, and protection of the environment. This also coincided with the rebirth of the regionalist and substate nationalist movements, which sought to articulate the interests of the peripheries that had been marginalised in the process of state-formation. Finally, the growth of European integration in the 1980s and 1990s led to the formation of new anti-European movements.

However, the movements based on these post-universal suffrage cleavages have been unable to challenge the dominance of the classic *familles spirituelles*. This is only partially because value-divisions between traditional social groups have remained even after some of the basic societal conflicts have declined (Franklin *et al.*, 1992). Above all, the classic party families have persisted because the traditional party organisations have proved remarkably adaptable to changes in the structure of electoral and political competition. The only original party family that has almost disappeared is the Agrarians, who have been subsumed in one or other of the families of the right: the Liberals, Christian Democrats, or Conservatives.

The European *familles spirituelles* consequently seek to compete on the political issues that defined their ideological identities and the interests of the social groups they emerged to represent. The issues in EU politics that are of particular concern to each party family are shown in the last column of Table 2.1. However, as a result of nearly a century of party competition in democratic elections, the party families have used the concepts of 'left' and 'right' to simplify the multiplicity of cleavages and issues in a single dimension of political conflict. This does not mean, however, that there is a single universal left–right conception; simply that on almost all issues in European politics, parties take up positions on one or the other side of a left–right dichotomy. For example, sometimes the left–right dimension is based on economic issues, such as taxation and employment: where the Socialists and Christian Democrats are on the left; and Liberals and Conservatives are on the right. At other times, the left–right refers to sociopolitical divisions, such as abortion rights: where Socialists and Liberals are on the left; and Christian Democrats and Conservatives are on the right.

When new cleavages emerge and new issues are brought up, new parties often try not to compete on this left–right continuum. For example, in the late 1970s and early 1980s Green parties attempted to define a 'new politics' that was not related to either the left or the right (Offe, 1985). However, the main parties invariably demand that new movements also compete on the traditional political issues; which forces new issues to be amalgamated into the original left and right concepts, and new parties to be aligned on the left–right dimension. By the late 1980s, the majority of Green parties had thus taken up positions on the left on most political issues. This flexibility of the meanings of left and right has enabled them to persist as the dominant concepts in strategic behaviour between political parties.

However, there is one cleavage in EU politics that cannot be squeezed into the single left–right dimension: the division between interests that support European integration, and interests that are adamantly opposed. One reason for this unsqueezability is that this is a new dimension and the traditional party families have not (yet!) been able to take up stable positions on either side of the issue. However, a more fundamental reason for the stubbornness of the 'integration–sovereignty' cleavage is that it inherently undermines the cohesion of the main party families. The traditional parties distinguish between themselves in the domestic arena over the role of state authority in the making of social and economic policies, and not on the question of the institutional design of the emerging supranational political system in Europe. In other words, after a century of relatively stable democratic state structures in Europe, the main *familles spirituelles* represent ideologies about who gets what under a particular institutional structure. However, political interests about the question of European integration are more determined by national and cultural factors than by party affiliation. Consequently, whereas parties in different European states from the same party family tend to have similar views about the role of the state (the left–right question), they are likely to have different views as regards European integration.

The Christian Democrats and Conservatives are a partial exception to this rule. From the rebirth of Christian Democratic parties after the Second World War, they have been unanimously committed to the process of European integration. This is rooted in Catholic social doctrine, and the reluctance of the Church to treat the nation state as the 'natural' political structure. In contrast, most Conservative parties are more eager to protect the traditional state structures. Contemporary Conservatism contains a definite streak of 'national liberalism', which defends the right of each European nation to its own self-determination. This division is thus a throwback to the earliest political juncture in the formation of the domestic European states: where Christians Democrats had an allegiance to a supranational institution; and Conservatives were wedded to state structures that were defined independently of Rome.

Similarly, two of the smaller party families directly contradict this rule: both of which are more coherent on the integration–sovereignty cleavage than on the left–right dimension. First, Regionalist parties inherently question the structure of the state in Europe since its establishment between the seventeenth and nineteenth centuries, and advocate European integration to facilitate the destruction of this organisation. Regionalist parties are thus unanimously pro-European, but come from many different positions on the left–right political spectrum. Second, a small number of movements have begun to emerge that directly derive from the European integration cleavage. In most cases these movements have not been formally established as political parties, and only come together as a single political force to fight in European elections. In domestic electoral competition, when politics returns to the classic Left-Right issues, these movements consequently disappear as the members rejoin the mainstream political families from whence they came. Like the Regionalists, these anti-European movements are thus coherently aligned on the integration–sovereignty dimension but are fragmented on left–right issues.

Overall, therefore, the strategic environment of party politics in the EU system has two fundamentally irreconcilable dimensions. First, the left–right dimension is an abstract summary of socioeconomic and political cleavages. Second, the integration–sovereignty dimension is a conflict about more or less European integration derived from deep social, cultural, national and territorial traditions. Party politics in the EU is conducted within this two-dimensional space. However, the main party families prefer to compete on the left–right dimension, to minimise internal conflicts between different member parties of the same party family.

Position and strength of the party families

The coherence of the European *familles spirituelles* in the EU political space is shown by the positions of the member parties of the party families on the two dimensions. On the first (left–right) dimension, the parties can be located from empirical data compiled from judgements by 'party systems experts' in each of the European states. In these judgements, each party is positioned on a scale from 1 (at the left end of the spectrum) to 10 (at the right end). The predominance of a single left–right dimension is confirmed in empirical research, regardless of whether expert judgements, voter orientations or content analysis is used (Castles and Mair, 1984; Budge, Robertson and Hearl, 1987, Laver and Hunt, 1992; Huber and Inglehart, 1995). The data on the positions of the parties on the left—right dimension that are used here are taken from Huber and Inglehart (1995), except for Greece, which is taken from Mavgordatos (1984). However, no survey has been conducted by experts on the positions of parties on the second (European integration) dimension. Nevertheless, a reasonable indicator of the position of parties on the integration–sovereignty dimension of EU politics are the views of individuals who 'identify' with that party. Few works have exclusively addressed the question of party attitudes towards European integration. The exceptions are Morgan and Silvresti (1982); European Parliament (1988); Featherstone (1989); Haahr (1993); and Gaffney (1996). In the tables below, the figures for the positions of the parties on the second dimension hence refer to the number of people who identify with a particular party who think the EU is a 'good thing' minus the number of people who identify with the same party who think the EU is a 'bad thing'. On these two dimensions, the standard deviation of the parties (the average deviation from the mean position of each party family) and the range (the difference between the lowest and highest party positions in each party family) are indicators of the level of coherence of the party families on each of the dimensions.

Apart from the location of the party families in EU politics, the other main aspect of the EU party system is the relative strengths of the party families. In the tables below, the strength of each individual party is the average percentage of the electorate that voted for it in national elections between 1990 and 1994 and in the 1994 European election. The mean strength of a party family is the total number of European citizens that voted for the parties in that family in this period. This is calculated by weighting the individual party scores according to the size of the EU member state; for example, the German electorate comprises 22.1 per cent of the EU citizenry, the Luxembourg electorate is only 0.1 per cent; and the British electorate is 15.7 per cent.

Christian Democrats and Conservatives

Starting with the first cleavage in modern European politics, in the EU states that were traditionally aligned with the Church of Rome during the Reformation and Counter-Reformation period (as in Germany and the Benelux states), Christian Democracy is the main political family on the right (see Irving, 1979; Hanley, 1994). In contrast, in the states with national Churches that were independent of Rome (as in Britain, Scandinavia and France), Conservatism is the dominant political force on the right (Layton-Henry, 1982; Girvin, 1988). The only exceptions to this rule are Spain, Portugal and Italy, where deep Christian Democratic traditions have declined since the 1970s, and where the contemporary forces on the right have taken more 'national' and/or 'secular' positions, which are similar to the Conservative or Liberal families.

On sociopolitical issues, such as divorce and abortion, Christian Democrats are usually to the right of the Conservatives. On economic issues, however, they are usually to the left of the Conservatives. Consequently, as economic issues are generally more salient than sociopolitical issues, the average position of the Christian Democrats is to the left (6.7) of the Conservatives (7.7), as Tables 2.2 and 2.3 show. The only real exceptions to this rule are the minor Scandinavian Christian Democratic parties. However, this is because Scandinavian Christian Democracy is inherently 'Christian fundamentalist', against the liberalism of the Scandinavian states, whereas the 'social Catholicism' of the continental Christian Democrats facilitates compromise with Liberal and Social Democratic parties. Nevertheless, on the left–right dimension, the Christian Democratic and Conservative families are both fairly coherent: with a low deviation from the mean (standard deviations of 0.8 and 0.4 respectively) and a small difference between the most centrist and most extreme parties (ranges of 2.7 and 1.1 respectively).

On the integration–sovereignty dimension, the 'supranational' origins of Christian Democracy, as opposed to the 'national' origins of Conservatism, are reflected in the opinions of the Christian Democrat and Conservative voters. The average difference between Christian Democrat voters in favour of EU integration and those opposed to EU integration is almost +75 per cent, whereas for the Conservatives it is only +54 per cent. On this dimension, however, the Conservatives are more internally divided than the Christian

TABLE 2.2

The Christian Democrats

Member state	Party name		Date established	Left/Right	Pro-/Anti-EU	% 90–94
AUSTRIA	Österreichsche Volkspartei	ÖVP*	1945 (1889)	6.3	–	39.8
BEL. Flem.	Christelijke Volkspartij	CVP*	1968 (1884)	5.7	74	16.9
Francoph.	Parti social-chrétien	PSC*	1968 (1884)	6.0	64	7.5
DENMARK	Kristeligt Folkeparti	KRF	1970	6.2	–	1.7
FINLAND	Suomen Kristillinen Liitto	SKL	1958	8.5	–	3.1
FRANCE	Centre des démocrates-Sociaux	CDS*	1976 (1945)	5.8	–	≈5.0
GERMANY	Christlich Demokratische Union	CDU*	1950 (1870)	6.4	60	33.9
	Christlich Soziale Union	CSU*	1946 (1870)	7.0	–	6.4
IRELAND	Fine Gael	FG*	1933 (1922)	7.0	68	24.4
ITALY	Partito popolare italiano	PPI*	1994 (1919)	6.3	75	16.5
	Centro Cristiano Democratico	CCD*	1994 (1919)	–	–	2.3
LUXEMB.	Parti chrétien social	PCS*	1914	7.1	95	31.5
NETHERL.	Christen Democratisch Appèl	CDA*	1980 (1879)	6.3	88	26.5
PORTUGAL	Partido do Centro Democrático e Social	CDS*	1974	8.4	66	8.5
SWEDEN	Kristdemokratiska Samhällspartiet	KDS*	1964	7.0	–	7.1
		Mean:		6.71	73.8	15.9
		Standard Deviation:		0.83	11.4	
		Range:		2.79	35	

Notes: The dates in the fourth column refer to the establishment of the current organisation bearing the name of the party. The dates in parentheses refer to the establishment of the earliest incarnation of the current organisation.

All the parties in the table are members of the European Union of Christian Democrats (EUCD).

The parties marked with an asterisk are also members of the European People's Party (EPP) party federation. Most CCD MEPs sit in the Group of the EPP in the EP. The ÖVP, CDU, CSU, PPI and PCS are also members of the 'Conservative' European Democratic Union (EDU).

The data used here on the positions of the parties on the integration-sovereignty dimension are taken from *Eurobarometer*, No. 37e (1992).

The data on party strengths are taken from the election reports in various editions of the *Journal of Electoral Studies*.

TABLE 2.3

The Conservatives

Member state	Party name		Date established	Left/Right	Pro-/Anti-EU	% 90–94
DENMARK	Det Konservative Folkeparti	KF*	1916 (1850)	7.6	70	16.9
FINLAND	Kansallinen Kokoomus	KOK*	1918 (1894)	7.4	–	19.3
FRANCE	Rassemblement pour la République	RPR	1976 (1947)	7.9	54	≈18.0
	Parti républicain	PR**	1977 (1965)	7.2	–	≈10.0
GREECE	Nea Dimokratia	ND*	1974 (1902)	8.3	57	39.6
	Polotiki Anixi	PA	1994 (1902)	–	–	2.9
ITALY	Forza Italia	FI	1994	–	–	19.2
SPAIN	Partido Popular	PP*	1989 (1910)	7.5	56	37.7
SWEDEN	Moderata Samlingspartiet	MS*	1968 (1902)	8.3	–	21.9
UK	Conservative Party	CP**	1867 (1830)	7.7	34	34.4
	Mean:			7.7	54.2	18.9
	Standard Deviation:			0.4	11.6	
	Range:			1.1	36	

Note: All the parties in the table, except FI are members of the European Democratic Union (EDU). The parties marked with a single asterisk are also members of the European People's Party (EPP) party federation and sit in the Group of the EPP in the EP, and the parties marked with a double asterisk are not members of the EPP but sit in the EPP Group nonetheless. The RPR, FI, and PA sit in the 'Union for Europe' Group in the EP.

Democrats. The supporters of the Christian Democrats are strongly pro-EU integration in all EU states: where the German CDU voters are the least pro-European Christian Democrats. In contrast, the difference between British Conservative voters in favour of the EU and those opposed is only +34 per cent, whereas for the Danish Conservatives (and probably for the other Scandinavian Conservatives) this figure is +70 per cent. This difference was hence revealed in the ratification of the Maastricht Treaty, where all Christian Democratic parties were unanimously in favour of the treaty, and there were deep divisions in many of the Conservative parties (particularly in the British CP and the French RPR). Consequently, although the religious cleavage that traditionally divided Conservatives and Christians in Europe may have almost disappeared since the 1960s, the difference between a fundamental allegiance to a European-wide entity and an allegiance to the nation state may prevent the two main political families of the Right from organising together at the European level.

Liberals

The ideology of Liberalism relates to personal social and political freedom as well as economic freedom (see Kirchner, 1988). On the issue of social and political freedom Liberal parties are hence usually to the left of Christian Democrats; whereas on the issue of economic freedom they are often to the right of Christian Democrats. Moreover, this duality of Liberal ideology has produced two main streams within the contemporary Liberal family: *Radical Liberals* emphasise social and political freedoms, whereas *Economic Liberals* emphasise economic freedom. Consequently, as Table 2.4 shows, the mean position of the Liberal family on the left–right dimension is 6.4, which is only slightly to the left of the Christian Democrats, and there is a high level of internal cohesion (with a standard deviation of 1.0 and a range of 3.5, from 4.8 to 8.3). However, the average left–right position of the twelve Liberal parties where the Radical stream is dominant is 5.5 (which is clearly to the left of the Christian Democrats) – marked with an 'R' in Table 2.4. This is thus in contrast to the average position of 7.1 for the eleven parties where the Economic stream predominates (which is between the Christian Democrats and the Conservatives) – marked with an 'E' in Table 2.4.

On the question of European integration, however, Liberal supporters are even more integrationist than the Christian Democrats:

with an average difference between 'support for' and 'opposition to' the EU of +75 per cent. On European issues, moreover, there is only a minor difference between the supporters of Radical Liberals (+71 per cent), and Economic Liberals (+78 per cent). Radical Liberals argue that greater social and political freedom is gained through the development of a larger sociopolitical unit in Europe. Economic Liberals, on the other hand, see European integration as the only way to deregulate the restricted national economies in Europe. However, as with the Christian Democrats and Conservatives, these pro-European views are not consistently held within the Liberal streams. Among the Radical Liberals, the Greek, Spanish and British parties are less Euro-enthusiast than Italian and German parties; and among the Economic Liberals, the Belgian Flemish party is not as pro-European as the Dutch and Danish parties. Nevertheless, all the Liberal parties supported the ratification of the Maastricht Treaty.

Finally, a further complication in the position of the Liberal family in EU politics is the underlying 'agrarian' background of some of the parties who now claim to be Liberal. These parties are shown in Table 2.4 with an 'A'. As previously discussed, the Agrarians were a coherent party family based on a deep urban–rural cleavage in European politics. For a number of reasons, however, these parties have increasingly occupied the centre ground in the party systems where they are present: in Denmark, Finland, Ireland, and Sweden. The mean left–right position of these *Agrarian Liberal* parties is 6.8, which is very close to the Christian Democrats. However, the significance of these parties for the behaviour of the Liberal family in EU politics is that they have a very specific attitude towards European integration: related directly to the status of the Common Agricultural Policy (CAP) – which constitutes more than one-third of the EU budget. Agrarian parties are staunch defenders of the CAP, and are thus strongly in favour of the EU as it stands at present. However, if the CAP is radically reformed, through an opening up of the European agricultural market as a result of rulings by the World Trade Organisation (WTO) or EU enlargement to Central and Eastern Europe, the Agrarian Liberals may begin to oppose the EU. In stark contrast, the rest of the Liberal family (and particularly the Economic Liberals) advocates the introduction of more free market measures into the CAP. This would thus undermine the coherence of the Liberals on the second dimension in EU politics.

TABLE 2.4
The Liberals

Member state	Party name		Date established	Left/Right	Pro-/Anti-EU	% 90–94
AUSTRIA	Liberales Forum[R]	LF	1993	6.3	–	3.0
BEL. Flem.	Vlaamse Liberalen en Democraten[E]	VLD	1993 (1846)	7.3	59	11.7
Francoph.	Parti réformateur libéral[E]	PRL	1979 (1846)	7.4	80	5.3
DENMARK	Venstre: Danmarks Liberale Parti[A]	V*	1870	8.1	78	17.4
	Det Radikale Venstre[R]	RV	1905 (1870)	5.7	80	6.0
	Centrum-Democraterne[E]	CD	1973	6.0	87	3.0
FINLAND	Suomen Keskusta[A]	KESK	1906	7.0	–	24.8
	Suomen Maaseudun Puolue[A]	SMP*	1959	7.0	–	4.8
	Liberaalinen Kansanpoulue[E]	LKP	1965 (1894)	6.3	–	1.2
FRANCE	Parti radical[E]	RAD	1901	6.7	–	≈2.0
	Mouvement des Radicaux de Gauche[R]	MRG	1972 (1901)	4.8	–	≈6.0
GERMANY	Freie Demokratische Partei[R]	FDP	1948 (1861)	5.6	83	7.1
GREECE	Hellenic Liberal Party[R]	HLP	1982 (1910)	5.3	68	2.8
IRELAND	Fianna Fáil[A]	FF*	1926 (1905)	6.8	74	37.1
	Progressive Democrats[E]	PD	1985 (1905)	8.3	–	5.6
ITALY	Partito repubblicano italiano[R]	PRI	1895	5.6	79	2.0
	Radicale[R]	Rad.	1962 (1955)	–	70	1.4
	Federazione dei liberali italiani[E]	FLI	1994 (1848)	7.3	77	1.2

LUXEMB.	Demokratesch Partei[E]	DP	1945	8.3	78	18.8
NETHERL.	Volkspartij voor Vrijheid en Democratie[E]	VVD	1948 (1885)	7.2	88	18.9
	Democraten '66[R]	D'66	1966	4.8	88	13.6
PORTUGAL	Partido Social Democrata[E]	PSD	1974	6.4	79	42.2
SPAIN	Centro Democrático y Social[R]	CDS	1982 (1977)	5.4	46	.8
	FORO[E]		1993	–	–	.2
SWEDEN	Folkpartiet Liberalerna[R]	FPL	1934 (1900)	5.9	–	9.1
	Centerpartiet[A]	CP*	1921 (1913)	5.9	–	8.5
UK GB	Social and Liberal Democrats[R]	SLD	1988 (1839)	5.2	63	17.0
N. Ireland	Alliance Party of Northern Ireland[R]	APNI	1970	5.8	–	.1
		Mean:		6.4	75.1	11.0
		Standard Deviation:		1.0	11.1	
		Range:		3.5	42	

Note: All the parties in the table, except the CD, MRG, Rad. and FF, are members of the European Liberal, Democratic and Reform Party (ELDR) and sit in the Group of the ELDR in the EP. MRG and Rad. sit in the 'European Radical Alliance' Group in the EP and FF sits in the 'Union for Europe' Groups in the EP.

Socialists

Like the Liberals, the Socialist party family exists in all the member states of the EU (Paterson and Thomas, 1986; Padgett and Paterson, 1991). Furthermore, like the three main party families of the centre right, the Socialist party family is fairly coherent on the left–right dimension. As Table 2.5 shows, the left–right mean position of the 19 EU Socialist parties is 4.3. There are some ideological differences within the Socialist family. For example, SAP is more 'pacifist' than the British LP, the PDS is more interventionist than PSOE, and the SPD prefers a coalition with a Liberal party whereas the PvdA, the SPÖ and the SP prefer coalitions with Christian Democrats. Nevertheless, all the parties in the Socialist family are moderately in favour of state intervention to correct 'market failures', and universally advocate a reduction of state interference in individual social and political relations (such as abortion rights, freedom of consciousness, and freedom of sexuality). Consequently, the Socialist family is highly cohesive on the left–right dimension: with a standard deviation of only 0.5 and a range of only 1.8 (3.5 to 5.3).

However, compared to the level of cohesion on the left–right dimension, on the question of European integration the Socialist family is historically divided. In the 1950s, the Socialist parties in the original six member states were less reluctant than the other main party families to approve the Paris and Rome Treaties. In the 1960s and most of the 1970s, the Socialist parties in Britain, Ireland, Denmark and Norway were officially opposed to their countries becoming members of the European Economic Community. Although all the European Socialists supported the Maastricht Treaty, the Socialist parties in Britain, Denmark, France and Greece suffered deep internal divisions when it came to ratifying the Treaty in the national parliaments. Finally, these internal divisions were repeated in Austria, Finland, Sweden and Norway in the 1994 referendums on joining the EU and in the September 1995 Swedish elections to the EP. Overall, however, Socialist parties are generally in favour of European integration, but in some member states they are careful not to antagonise their supporters. As Table 2.5 shows, there is a vast difference between the high levels of support for the EU among Socialist voters in Ireland, Portugal and the Netherlands, and the low levels of support in Denmark, Britain, Greece, and even among the francophone Belgians.

TABLE 2.5

The Socialists

Member state	Party name		Date established	Left/Right	Pro-/Anti-EU	% 90–94
AUSTRIA	Sozialistische Partei Österreichs	SPÖ	1889	4.8	–	31.4
BEL. Flem.	Socialistische Partij	SP	1978 (1889)	4.0	72	11.5
Francoph.	Parti Socialiste	PS	1978 (1889)	4.2	61	12.5
DENMARK	Socialdemokratiet	SD	1871	4.2	21	26.6
FINLAND	Sosiaalidemokraattinen Puolue	SDP	1899	4.4	–	22.1
FRANCE	Parti Socialiste	PS	1969 (1905)	4.1	63	17.4
GERMANY	Sozialdemokratische Partei Deutschlands	SPD	1891 (1863)	3.8	64	33.2
GREECE	Panhellinio Socialistiko Kinema	Pasok	1974 (1935)	4.6	57	41.0
IRELAND	Labour Party	LP	1912	4.1	77	15.2
ITALY	Partito Democratico della Sinistra	PDS	1991 (1921)	3.5	67	19.8
	Partito Socialista Italiano	PSI	1892	5.0	74	5.6
	Partito Socialista Democratico Italiano	PSDI	1947 (1892)	5.3	–	1.4
LUXEMB.	Parti Ouvrier Socialiste Luxembourgeois	POSL	1903	4.0	74	24.8
NETHERL.	Partij van de Arbeid	PvdA	1946 (1894)	4.2	81	23.5
PORTUGAL	Partido Socialista	PS	1973 (1875)	4.9	75	32.0
SPAIN	Partido Socialista Obrero Español	PSOE	1879	4.0	72	34.9
SWEDEN	Socialdemokratistiska Arbetarparti	SAP	1889	4.1	–	37.6
U.K. GB	Labour Party	LP	1900	4.4	42	38.3
N. Ireland	Social Democrat and Labour Party	SDLP	1970 (1949)	3.7	–	1.0
		Mean:		4.3	64.3	30.1
		Standard Deviation:		0.5	15.4	
		Range:		1.875	60	

Note: All the parties in the table, except the PSDI, are members of the Party of European Socialists (PES) and sit in the Group of the PES in the EP. The Italian PSDI was expelled from the PES in 1994 for its support of the Berlusconi government, but it still considers itself part of the Socialist family.

Greens

The Greens are the only other party family that exists in all the EU
member states (see Müller-Rommel, 1989). The first formal political
party in this tradition was the British Ecology Party, which was
established in 1973. However, the German Die Grünen are usually
treated as the 'mother of the Greens' because they were the first to
achieve electoral success and have dominated the ideological debates
in the Green movement. Green ideology mixes the original commitments to environmental protection and pacifism with a radical
agenda for reforming the European economic and political system.
Rather than justifying these positions in terms of economic interests,
as most of the Radical Left parties do, the Greens are fundamentally
'post-materialist': arguing that society should move beyond the
narrow aims of economic and political security. However, there is
an ongoing debate as to whether the Greens should wholly reject the
present system of representational politics (as advocated by the
fundamentalists ('fundis')) or should compromise with the traditional
parties to achieve incremental change (the position of the pragmatists
('realos')). In the 1990s, most Green parties have only been able to
secure electoral success when adopting this later position. To be able
to participate in the electoral process, however, the Greens have been
forced to define their positions on the main issues dividing the other
main party families (i.e., questions of economic policy) and thus to
take up a position on the left–right spectrum. As Table 2.6 shows, in
so doing the Greens have positioned themselves between the Socialist
and Radical Left families (with an average of 3.2).

By defining their identity in left–right terms, however, the Greens
are as incoherent as the other main party families when it comes to
the question of European integration. In ideological terms, the
Greens are torn between supporting European-level initiatives for
environmental protection that cannot be implemented at the national
level, and a deep scepticism of the 'democratic deficit' in EU decision-
making. In 1992, however, all the Green parties either voted against
or abstained in the ratification of the Maastricht Treaty in the
national parliaments; and the Green parties in Austria, Sweden
and Finland opposed EU membership in the 1994 referendums. As
Table 2.6 shows, the Green voters are also unevenly distributed
between pro- and anti-EU positions. Nevertheless, on average the
difference between Green voters 'in favour' and those 'opposed' is

TABLE 2.6

The Greens

Member state	Party name		Date established	Left/Right	Pro-/Anti-EU	% 90–94
AUSTRIA	Die Grüne Alternativen	GAL	1986 (1982)	2.9	–	4.8
BEL. Flem.	Anders Gaan Leven (AGALEV)	AGA	1981	3.4	66	5.8
Francoph.	Écolo	ECO	1978	3.5	62	5.0
DENMARK	De Grønne	DG	1983	2.0	–	0.4
FINLAND	Vihreä-De Gröna	VIHR	1982	4.0	–	6.8
FRANCE	Les Verts	V	1984 (1978)	4.4	65	5.2
	Génération Écologie	GE	1991 (1978)	4.4	–	1.4
GERMANY	Die Grünen	G	1979	2.9	55	7.9
GREECE	Ecologistes Alternatives	EA	1989	–	40	0.5
IRELAND	Camhaontás Glas	CG	1981	–	–	4.7
ITALY	Federazione dei Verdi	FV	1986	2.6	–	3.1
LUXEMB.	Déi Greng Alternative/Glei	GA/G	1993 (1983)	2.3	70	9.8
NETHERL.	Groen Links	GL	1989	1.8	63	4.8
	De Groenen	DG	1986	–	–	0.1
PORTUGAL	Os Verdes	OV	1982	–	–	≈1.0
SPAIN	Los Verdes	LV	1986	–	73	0.8
SWEDEN	Miljöpartiet de Gröna	MPG	1981	4.3	–	3.3
U.K.	Green Party	GP	1985 (1973)	–	77	2.4
	Mean:			3.2	63.4	4.6
	Standard Deviation:			0.9	10.3	
	Range:			2.5	15	

Note: All the parties in the table, except GE, are members of the European Federation of Green Parties (EFGP) and sir in the Green Group in the EP (if they have any MEPs).

over 65 per cent, which suggests that they are more pro-European than the 'materialist' supporters of the Socialist or Radical Socialist parties. This could mean that the anti-European positions of the Green party leaderships are unsustainable in the long term.

Radical Left

Turning to the first of the smaller party families that arose after the extension of the franchise in Europe, there is a group of parties in many EU member states to the left of the Socialists (Baumgarten, 1982). These parties, which are shown in Table 2.7, derive from two separate political traditions: the Communist parties that emerged around the time of the Russian Revolution; and the Independent Socialist parties that emerged in the late 1950s and 1960s against the so-called 'sell out' of the governing Socialist and Social Democratic parties. After the fall of the Berlin Wall in 1989, however, most European Communist parties dropped their commitment to a complete overthrow of capitalist and liberal democratic institutions (and many dropped the word Communist in their name). This consequently pushed the two traditions together, in a 'united front' to campaign for a democratisation of European political and economic institutions (see Bell in Gaffney, 1996). In contemporary EU politics, therefore, these parties are effectively a coherent *famille spirituelle*: with an average position on the left–right of 2.3, and a standard deviation of only 0.8.

This treatment of the Radical Left as a single party family in EU politics is further justified by the coherence of their positions towards European integration (see Fiesci, Shields and Woods in Gaffney, 1996). Almost all the parties in Table 2.7 are officially opposed to further European integration, and all except the Spanish IU voted against or abstained in the ratification of the Maastricht Treaty in 1992. However, there are some radical differences in the opinions of the EU among the voters for these parties. As Table 2.7 shows, the average difference between Radical Left voters 'in favour of' or 'opposed to' the EU is +34 per cent. Nevertheless, this figure masks striking differences. At one extreme, about 60 per cent more voters for the Greek SYN and Irish DL are in favour of the EU than are opposed; whereas, at the other extreme, 32 per cent more voters for the Danish SF are opposed to the EU than are in favour (hence a figure of −32).

TABLE 2.7
The Radical Left

Member state	Party name		Date established	Left/Right	Pro-/Anti-EU	% 90–94
AUSTRIA	Kommunistische Partei Österreichs	KPÖ	1918	–	–	0.2
DENMARK	Socialistisk Folkeparti	SF*	1958	2.9	–32	8.5
	Venstresocialisterne	VS	1967	–	–	0.5
FINLAND	Vasemmistöliitto	VAS*	1990 (1918)	3.5	–	10.1
FRANCE	Parti Communiste Française	PCF*	1920	2.3	19	7.1
	Lutte Ouvrière	LO	1968	1.0	–	0.8
GERMANY	Partei Demokratisch-Sozialistische	PDS	1990 (1918)	1.5	–	3.8
GREECE	Synaspismos tis Aristeras	SYN*	1977 (1918)	2.4	68	6.8
	Kommounistiko Korima Hellados	KKE*	1918	1.8	33	5.3
IRELAND	Democratic Left	DL	1991 (1907)	2.7	54	3.2
ITALY	Rifondazione Communista	RC*	1991 (1921)	1.0	48	6.0
LUXEMB.	Nouvelle Gauche	NG	1990 (1921)	–	–	2.6
NETHERL.	Socialistische Partij	SP	1957	–	–	1.2
PORTUGAL	Partido Communista Portugues	PCP*	1921	3.6	31	≈9.0
SPAIN	Izquierda Unida	IU*	1986 (1920)	2.4	54	11.6
SWEDEN	Vänsterpartiet	V*	1990 (1917)	2.6	–	4.5
UK N. Ireland	Workers' Party	WP	1970 (1921)	2.8	–	0.1
			Mean:	2.3	34.4	5.2
			Standard Deviation:	0.8	29.0	
			Range:	2.6	100	

Note: The nine parties in the table that have MEPs that are marked with an asterisk sit in the Confederal Group of the United European Left in the EP.

Extreme Right

At the other end of the left–right dimension are the various parties that make up the Extreme Right in European politics (Georg-Betz, 1994). There are three main streams to this grouping. First, there are the *neo-fascist* organisations that advocate the economic and social policies of the Nazi and Fascist movements of the 1930s and 1940s (and often use the same symbols) – these are indicated with an 'F' in Table 2.8. Second, there are several overtly nationalist and *xenophobic* parties that either derive from monarchist traditions (such as AN or EPEN) or emerged as protest movements against immigration in the 1970s and 1980s, but actively deny any links to Fascism or Nazism – marked with an 'X' in the table. Third, in the 1980s several new Extreme Right parties emerged that combined nationalist ideology with a strong *anti-tax protest* against the modern welfare state – marked with an 'A' in the table. The Austrian FPÖ, which derives from a 'national liberal' tradition from the middle of the nineteenth century, does not easily fit this typology. However, it can be considered part of the Extreme Right family because in its present incarnation it combines nationalist/xenophobic and nationalist/anti-tax ideologies.

These parties can be treated as a single party family in EU politics for a number of reasons. First, they have a strongly coherent position on the left–right dimension: with an average of 9.3, and a standard deviation of only 0.4. On economic issues some Extreme Right parties are more free market than others. However, they have common policies on many sociopolitical issues: for example, they are all anti-immigration, anti-abortion, anti-homosexual rights, and anti-parliamentarian (preferring 'strong presidentialism'). Second, moreover, despite some voters for these parties being relatively pro-European (such as the supporters of the VB), the parties of the Extreme Right are strongly opposed to European integration. All the parties of the Extreme Right opposed the ratification of the Maastricht Treaty in 1992; and the FPÖ and NYD campaigned against Austrian and Swedish membership of the EU in the 1994 referendums. There is a tension in Far Right ideology as regards European integration: between a preservation of national identities, and an emphasis on a deeper cultural commonalty between 'White Europeans'. However, the groups that advocate this second position (the neo-Fascists) are electorally and organisationally small. Consequently, the

TABLE 2.8

The Extreme Right

Member state	Party name		Date established	Left/Right	Pro-/Anti-EU	% 90–94
AUSTRIA	Freiheitliche Partei[X/A]	FPÖ*	1955 (1885)	8.6	–	16.6
	Nationaldemokratische Partei[F]	NDP	–	–	–	.1
BEL. Flem.	Vlaams Blok[X]	VB*	1978	9.8	43	7.2
Francoph.	Front National[X]	FN*	1985	–	–	2.1
DENMARK	Fremskradtspartiet[A]	FRP	1972	9.1	31	4.7
FRANCE	Front National[X]	FN*	1972	10.0	0	10.7
GERMANY	Republikaner[X]	Rep.	1983	9.3	–43	3.1
	Nationaldemokratische Partei Deutschlands[F]	NPD	1964 (1920)	–	–	.2
	Deutsche Volksunion[F]	DVU	1987	–	–	.1
GREECE	Ethniki Politiki Enosis[X]	EPEN	1977 (1946)	9.4	–	.7
ITALY	Alianza Nazionale[X]	AN*	1994 (1946)	9.3	57	10.4
LUXEMB.	D'National Bewegong[X]	NB	1988	–	–	.3
NETHERL.	Centrum Democraten[X]	CD	1980	9.5	–	1.1
PORTUGAL	Movimento Acçao Nacional[X]	MAN	–	–	–	.4
SPAIN	Fuerza Nueva[X]	FN	1976 (1934)	–	–	.1
SWEDEN	Ny Demokrati[A]	NYD	1990	9.1	–	6.7
U.K. GB	British National Party[F]	BNP	1982 (1967)	–	–	.1
	National Front[F]	NF	1967	–	–	.1
	Mean:			9.3	17.6	5.3
	Standard Deviation:			.38	35.7	
	Range:			1.4	100	

Note: The five parties in the table that have MEPs that are marked with an asterisk sit together as 'non-attached members' in the EP. See text for an explanation of X, A and F.

contemporary Extreme Right family is predominantly 'nationalist' in orientation and hence vehemently anti-European integration.

Regionalists

The first of the two political families that are less coherent on the left–right dimension than on the question of European integration are the Regionalists (Rokkan and Urwin, 1982; Rudolph and Thompson, 1989). The label 'Regionalists' encompasses a diverse mix of ethnic, linguistic, substate nationalist, autonomist, separatist, and irredentist groups. The single common strand between these groups, nonetheless, is that they advocate a reform of the territorial structure of the state in which they operate, which encompasses anything from decentralisation or devolution, to complete independence or accession to a different state. Most of these parties also support an eventual goal of a 'Europe of Regions', where the existing nation states are wholly replaced by a European-wide political system based on a mosaic of small territorial units. As Table 2.9 shows, therefore, the supporters of Regionalist parties are generally more pro-European integration than the supporters of any other party family.

By defining itself in terms of 'territorial politics' rather than on socioeconomic issues, however, the Regionalists are deeply divided on the left–right dimension (with a standard deviation of 2.2). Some parties, like the Spanish HB, the Irish SF or the Welsh PC, are at the extreme left of the spectrum (advocating public ownership of the industries in their region), whereas others are at the far Right of the spectrum (supporting anti-foreigner positions). The majority of Regionalist parties, however, contain left and right wings within a single party, and consequently adopt a centrist position in the party system (hence a mean of 5.4). This central position has allowed many of the larger Regionalist parties to coalesce in the national and European arenas with the mainstream party families. For example: Lega Nord has formed alliances with the PDS or Forza Italia in Italy, and with the Liberal group in the EP; the UDC, CDC and PNV have been aligned with PSOE in Spain, and with either the Christian Democrats or the Liberals in the EP; and the SNP and VU have coalesced with some of the parties in the Radical stream of the Liberals in the EP to form the Group of the European Radical Alliance. In general, therefore, if the main European party families all adopt pro-European positions, the Regionalist party family may find it difficult to define a common identity.

Anti-Europeans

Finally, the only other group of parties that define themselves more on the European integration dimension than on left–right issues are the Anti-Europeans. These groups do not strictly constitute a party family, as few of them have ongoing party organisations. However, they can be compared to the traditional party families because the electoral and organisational strength of all four parties in Table 2.10 is directly dependent on the salience of the new integration–sovereignty cleavage in EU politics.

Three of the Anti-European movements, the Danish FB and JB and the French MAE, only compete as political organisations during European elections. The Danish FB was the earliest anti-European party to be formed, in the 1972 Danish referendum on membership of the European Community. It was originally composed of many leading individuals from the Danish Progress Party (FRP), but was also allied with the Socialist People's Party (SF). During the 1992 and 1993 referendums on the Maastricht Treaty, however, the 'No' campaign split into two factions: a right-wing group based on the original FB, with many of the supporters of the FRP (and won 10.3 per cent in the 1994 European elections); and a left-wing group, the JB, with the supporters of the SF that refused to back the 'Danish compromise' of the December 1992 Edinburgh European Council (and won 15.2 per cent in the 1994 European elections).

The French MAE was also a side-product of the 'No' campaign in the 1992 French referendum on the Maastricht Treaty. The leaders of MAE – such as Philippe de Villiers, James Goldsmith and Charles de Gaulle (the grandson of the former French President) – were prominent figures in the French Gaullists (RPR). It was thus formed out of the right of French politics. MAE has only fought one election campaign, the 1994 European elections, and may not survive as a coherent movement. However, the level of support for the movement, 12.5 per cent, and the organisational resources of leading the Europe of Nations Group in the EP, suggest that it will at least live to fight the 1999 European elections. Moreover, the relative success of the 'No' campaigns (against the united opposition of the main political parties) in the 1994 referendums in Austria, Finland and Sweden suggests that similar parties to these Danish and French groups may emerge in future European elections in the new EU member states. This would further enhance the identity and strength of an Anti-European political family.

TABLE 2.9

The Regionalists

Member state		Party name		Date established	Left/Right	Pro-/Anti-EU	% 90–94
BELGIUM	Flem.	Volksunie	VU*+	1954 (1919)	6.5	70	5.2
	Francoph.	Front Démocratique des Francophones	FDF	1964	7.0	100	.7
	German-speaking	Partei der Deutschsprachigen Belgier	PDB+	1971	–	–	.1
FINLAND		Svenska Folkpartiet	SFP**	1906 (1894)	6.6	–	5.5
FRANCE	Alsace	Elzaessiche Union/Union pour l'Alsace	EU+	–	–	–	.0
	Basque	Eusko Alkartasuna-Iparraide	EA-I+	1986	–	–	.0
	Brittany	Union Démocratique Bretonne	UDB+	1963	–	–	.1
	Corsica	Unione di u Populu Corsu	UPC+	1977	–	–	.2
	Flanders	Vlaams Federalistische Partij	VFP+	–	–	–	.0
	Occitania	Partito Occitan	PO+	–	–	–	.0
	Perpignon	Unitat Catalana	UC+	–	–	–	.0
	Savoy	Mouvement Région Savoie	MRS+	–	–	–	.0
	Fruili	Union Furlana	UF+	–	–	–	.0
ITALY	N. Italy	Lega Nord	LN**	1992 (1986)	7.5	–	7.2
	Piedmont	Movimento Autonomista Occitano	MAO	–	–	–	.0
	Sardinia	Partito Sardo d'Azione	PSA+	1921	–	–	.3
	Slovene-Fruili	Slovenska Skupnost	SS+	–	–	–	.0
	South Tyrol	Südtiroler Volkspartei	SVP***	1945	–	–	.6
		Union für Süd-Tirol	UST+	1972	–	–	.0
	Trentino	Unione Autonomista Trentino-Tirolese	UAT T	–	–	–	.1
	Val d'Aosta	Union Valdôtaine	UV+	1945	–	–	.1
	Venice	Union del Populo Veneto	UPV+	1982	–	–	.1

NETH. Freisland	Fryske Nasjonale Partij	FNP+	–	–	–	.0
SPAIN Andalucia	Partido Andalucista	PA+	1977	6.1	–	.9
Basque	Partido Nacionalista Vasco	PNV***	1895	4.7	–	2.9
	Eusko Alkartasuna	EA+	1986	1.0	–	1.1
	Herri Batasuna	HB	1978	–	–	.9
Canary Islands	Coalición Canaria	CC*	–	–	–	.6
Catalonia	Unió Democràtica de Catalunya	UDC***	1931 (1906)	6.2	72	2.4
	Convergència Democràtica de Catalunya	CDC**	1974 (1906)	6.2	–	2.2
	Esquerra Republicana di Catalunya	ERC+	1931	4.1	–	.1
U.K. Cornwall	Mebyon Kernow	MK+	1951	–	–	.0
N. Ireland	Democratic Unionist Party	DUP****	1971 (1905)	8.0	–	1.0
	Official Unionist Party	OUP***	1974 (1905)	8.1	–	.8
	Sinn Féin		1921	1.8	–	.3
Scotland	Scottish National Party	SNP*+	1934 (1928)	4.4	60	3.2
Wales	Plaid Cymru	PC+	1925	3.40	–	1.1
		Mean:		5.4	75.5	3.8
		Standard Deviation:		2.2	14.9	
		Range:		7.1	40	

Note: The eleven parties with MEPs are marked with the asterisks. The parties with one asterisk sit in the 'European Radical Alliance Group' in the EP, the parties with two sit in the ELDR Group, the parties with three sit in the SPP, and the party with four sits with the 'non-attached' members. The parties marked with a cross are members of the European Free Alliance (EFA) party federation.

48   *Political Parties in the European Union*

TABLE 2.10

The Anti-Europeans

Member state	Party name		Date established	% 89–94
DENMARK	Folkebevaegelsen Med EF	FB	1972	14.6
	Junibevaegelsen	JB	1993	7.6
FRANCE	Majorité pour l'Autre Europe	MAE	1992	6.2
NETHERL.	Staatkundig Gereformeerde Partij/	SGP/	1984 (1918)	
	Gereformeerd Politiek Verband	GPV/		7.2
	Reformatorisch Politieke Federatie	RPF		
			Mean:	1.6

Note: The % votes for each party are the average results in the 1989 and 1994 European elections, not the averages for all elections between 1990 and 1994 (as in the other tables). All the parties in the table sit in the 'Europe of Nations' Group in the EP.

The other party included in Table 2.10 is fundamentally different to the movements that were directly spawned by the integration–sovereignty cleavage. The SGP, GPV and RPF are Protestant fundamentalist parties in the Netherlands, that originally date from 1918. However, since the 1984 European elections, they have deliberately campaigned against European integration; with European election manifestos entitled *For National Independence in the European Cooperation* and *Unity in Diversity*. Moreover, whereas in national elections (and in the 1979 European election) the two parties usually poll under 2 per cent, in the 1984, 1989 and 1994 European elections they have averaged 7 per cent. Finally, after the 1994 European elections, the SGP/GPV/RPF joined the Danish and French parties in a new Europe of Nations Group in the EP. The electoral support for these parties in European elections (which they fight as a 'united front'), and their legislative behaviour at the European level, is therefore based more on mobilisation around the integration–sovereignty cleavage in EU politics than their original position on the left–right dimension.

Consequently, the Anti-Europeans are fairly coherent on the integration–sovereignty dimension of the EU party system. Also in direct contrast to the traditional party families, and like the Regionalists, the Anti-Europeans are deeply divided on left–right issues. All these anti-European movements were initially led by politicians who broke away from right-wing parties (as in the FB and MAE), or were right-wing parties that increasingly took an anti-European position (as with the SGP/GPV/RPF). However, when left-wing parties which were formally Euro-sceptic (as in the case of the Greens and Radical Left) turn to support European integration, many left-wing activists and voters may move to the anti-European movements. Strategic movements on the left towards pro-European positions may thus increase the support base of the Anti-European parties. However, this will inevitably undermine their internal cohesion. This was dramatically exposed in the Danish Anti-European movement. The leadership of the Danish Socialist People's Party changed its position between the two referenduns on the Maastricht Treaty (from the 'No' to the 'Yes' campaign). Many party activists and voters consequently defected from the party in the second referendum and joined the FB. However, this influx of Left-oriented voters in the FB produced a new division in the Danish Anti-European movement, which eventually led to the establishment of a separate left/Anti-European party: the JB.

Shape of the EU party system

By way of a summary and conclusion, therefore, the shape of the EU party system is the strengths and positions of the party families in the two-dimensional space. The positions of the party families are summarised in Figure 2.1: the mean positions are shown by an 'X', and the ranges are shown by the ellipses. As the ellipses reveal, only two of the party families are more coherent on the integration–sovereignty dimension than on the left–right dimension: the Regionalists and the Anti-Europeans. These are thus the only families that can openly compete on European issues. The 'core' families of all the domestic European party systems, in contrast, are fairly coherent on the left–right dimension, but have wide ranges on the integration–sovereignty dimension. This consequently means that these families risk internal divisions if they are unable to couch EU issues in terms of the traditional Left–right continuum.

However, the mean positions of the Socialists, Liberals, Christian Democrats and Conservatives in the early 1990s (shown by 'X' in Figure 2.1) suggest that this is exactly the strategy that these party families have attempted to pursue. In the 1990s, the mean positions of the core families are close together on the integration–sovereignty

FIGURE 2.1   Positions of the party families

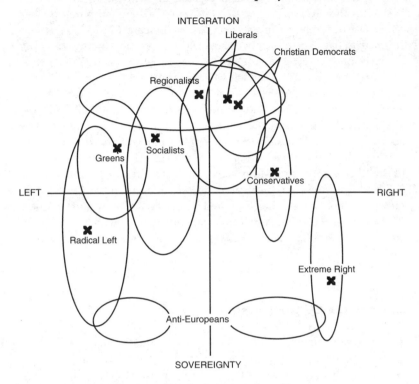

Note: The mean position of each party family is shown by an X.
         The ellipses represent the ranges of the member parties of each party family.

dimension, in moderately pro-European positions, and are far apart on the left–right. This implies that they do not compete on EU issues. For example, whereas in the 1970s the majority of the Socialist parties were anti-European integration, in the 1990s they are universally moderately pro-European. This has thus narrowed the gap between the Socialists and the three right-wing families on European issues, which has enabled them to compete purely in left–right terms and to reduce the risk of internal divisions within their family.

Ironically, this convergence on pro-integration positions among the main party families, and subsequent concentration on left–right issues, is likely to undermine the two families that are primarily aligned on the integration–sovereignty dimension. First, the larger Regionalist parties will be inclined to join one or other of the main blocs as the Regionalist family fragments on the left–right dimension. Second, as the Socialists, Greens and Radical Left become more pro-European, this will leave a space for the Anti-European family to expand. The price of this expansion, however, is likely to be the eventual division between left and right Anti-Europeans (as represented by the two ellipses in the figure).

The positions of the families in the policy space consequently suggest that there are three main political blocs in the EU party system: a left bloc and a centre-right bloc that are coherent on the left–right dimension; and a pro-Europe bloc that is coherent on the integration–sovereignty dimension and consequently cuts through the other two blocs. In addition, there are two openly anti-integration party families – the Extreme Right and the Anti-Europeans – and three party families that are ambivalent – the Radical Left, the Greens and the Conservatives. However, these families do not constitute a coherent 'bloc' against the pro-European families. The likely shape of party competition in the EU system is not only dependent upon the positions and existence of these blocs but also on their relative electoral strengths.

As Table 2.11 hence illustrates, between 1990 and 1994 the left and centre-right blocs were fairly evenly balanced (with between 40 and 46 per cent of the votes across the EU). However, whereas the Socialists were the largest party in the left bloc in every EU member state, the Liberals, Christian Democrats and Conservatives were each dominant in about a third of the national systems. Moreover, the four political families who are strongly in favour of European integration (the pro-Europe bloc) together constituted about 60 per cent of the vote. Nevertheless, half of this support came from the Socialist family, which easily splits into pro- and anti-European voters when the integration–sovereignty cleavage is manifest (as in European elections or referendums on the ratification of changes to the EU Treaty).

Overall, therefore, no single political bloc is dominant on either of the two main dimensions in the EU party system. This may mean that if a majority party-political coalition is constructed in the European arena it will reflect a balance of electoral opinion on both main issues in the EU. Another possibility, however, is that if both dimensions are salient in the EU party system, the political blocs (and some of the political families) may fragment into four distinct blocs: left–integration (Socialists and the left-wing Regionalists); left–sovereignty (Radical Left, Greens and the left-wing Anti-Europeans); right–integration (Liberals, Christian Democrats and the right-wing

TABLE 2.11

Strengths of political blocs and party families

	LEFT BLOC			PRO-EUROPE BLOC		CENTRE-RIGHT BLOC				
	Rad. LEFT	GREEN	SOCS	REGS	LIBS	CHR. DEMS	CONS	Extr. RIGHT	ANTI-EUROS	Total
AUSTRIA	.2	4.8	**31.4**		3.0	**39.8**		16.7		95.9
BELGIUM		10.8	**24.0**	6.0	17.0	**24.4**		9.3		91.5
DENMARK	9.0	.4	**26.6**	5.5	**26.4**	1.7	16.9	4.7	22.2	107.9[1]
FINLAND	10.1	6.8	**22.1**	.3	**30.8**	3.1	19.3			97.7
FRANCE	7.9	6.6	**17.4**		8.0	5.0	**28.0**	10.7	6.2	90.1
GERMANY	3.8	7.9	**33.2**		7.1	**40.3**		3.4		95.7
GREECE	12.1	.5	**41.0**		2.8		**42.5**	.7		99.6
IRELAN	3.2	4.7	**15.2**	8.4	**42.7**	24.4				90.2
ITALY	6.0	3.1	**26.8**		4.6	18.8	**19.2**	10.4		97.3
LUXEMB'G	2.6	9.8	**24.8**		18.8	**31.5**		.3		87.8
NETHERL'DS	1.2	4.9	**23.5**		**32.5**	26.5		1.1	7.2	96.9
PORTUGAL	9.0	1.0	**32.0**		**42.2**	8.5		.4		93.1
SPAIN	11.6	.8	**34.9**	11.1	1.0		**37.7**	.1		97.2
SWEDEN	4.5	3.3	**37.6**		17.6	7.1	21.9	6.7		98.7
UK	.1	2.4	**39.3**	6.4	17.1		**34.4**	.2		99.9
Avg. Strength	5.2	4.6	**30.1**	3.8	11.0	15.9	**18.9**	5.0	1.6	96.1
	39.9%			60.8%		45.8%				

Note: The total percentage for Denmark is over 100% because the average votes for the anti-EU parties are for the 1989 and 1994 European elections, whereas the average votes for the other parties are for all the national and European elections between 1990 and 1994. The numbers in bold are the strongest parties in the centre-right and centre-left blocs in each member state.

Regionalists); and right–sovereignty (Conservatives, Extreme Right and the right-wing Anti-Europeans). Only if the core party families of the centre left and centre right refuse to compete on the integration–sovereignty dimension could this fragmentation be avoided.

In conclusion, therefore, the significance of the shape of the EU party system is that this particular set of positions and alliances structures the way parties relate to each other when pursuing their political goals in EU politics. The historical and ideological nature of the *familles spirituelles* suggests that this shape is relatively stable over time. For example, although Christian Democrats and Conservatives may cooperate at present in the EP, we cannot assume that this in perpetuity (unless one or other of the families completely dissolves). Similarly, the above findings suggest that opposition to European integration is not simply a passing fad. The question of more or less integration into a new European system is a manifest dimension of political conflict that seriously undermines the coherence of the traditional party families. This is fundamentally because the institution of the political party is deeply rooted in the establishment of democratic institutions at the level of the nation state. Moreover, with this framework to understand political interaction *between* parties on issues in EU politics (the strategic environment) we can now turn in the next chapter to political interaction *within* the party family organisations.

3

Organisation of Parties in the EU

This chapter continues the outline of an analytical tool-kit for understanding party behaviour throughout the European Union system. Whereas in the previous chapter we concentrated on the motivations of parties and the relations between the political families in the EU party system, in this chapter we turn to the other major determinant of party behaviour in any political system: the structure of party organisation. This chapter begins by painting a generic picture (an organigram) of the organisation of a major party family in the institutional structure of the EU system. The subsequent sections, discuss, first, how far parties in the EU system are unitary entities or are comprised of several separate organisational forms and, second, how the different elements of the party organisation fit together in the making of party policy on European issues. As with the first chapter, therefore, this chapter aims to provide a set of instruments to help understand the overall structure and behaviour of political parties in and towards the EU, rather than to explain any specific party activity in a particular national or European-level situation. The final section of this chapter is hence an overview of the framework set out in Chapters 2 and 3. The general conclusion is that although the strategic and institutional environment of the EU system limits the linear development of a 'Europe of parties', the main party families have begun to adapt their organisational and policy strategies to accommodate these constraints.

Organigram of a party in the EU system

There are several advantages to using an organigram to analyse the organisation of parties in the EU. First, an organigram is a 'heuristic device' that is used to express large quantities of information about party structures in a single form (this is a summarising role) (see Katz and Mair, 1992). Second, by contrasting the individual party families with a 'generic type', the level of development of each family can be easily compared without delving into the minutiae of party rules and statutes (a static-comparison role). Finally, an organigram is a description of a particular stage in the development of party organisations in the EU system, with which previous and future stages can be compared, and towards which the less organised party families are evolving (a temporal-comparison role). The organigram of a political party in the EU system is hence shown in Figure 3.1.

In the organigram, the executive and legislative offices held by party actors at the national and European levels are shown in bold type. The party bodies that are legally recognised under the statutes, rules of procedure or constitutions of the national and European-level party organisations are shown in capitals (the official party organs). The relationships between these structures are shown by a series of arrows. An arrow with a thin line means that a group is 'unofficially represented' in a party organ (i.e., can attend but not vote); or that there is a loose connection between two sets of party actors holding political offices in the national and European arena. A medium-thickness arrow means that an individual or group is officially represented in a party organ (i.e., has the right to vote). Finally, a thick arrow shows that a party organ can make a recommendation (which may or may not be binding) to another party organ, or group of party actors holding political office.

As the organigram hence shows, the EU system has two levels of political institutions: in the national arena (the domestic parliaments, governments and other institutions); and in the European arena (the European Council, the Commission, the Council of Ministers, the EP, and other institutions). Party activity is primarily organised within these arenas (in the national and European parliaments). However, party activity is also linked between these two levels. First, party activity is linked between the national and European levels via direct channels of representation and organisation. Party actors holding national governmental office sit in the European Council and the Council of Ministers. Moreover, the MEPs are directly connected to the national party organisations through the process of selecting candidates for European elections; which is controlled by domestic (national and/or local) party structures.

However, the second way that activity is linked between the two levels, and the main way that party actors are connected across the European-level institutions, is through a relatively new set of EU

FIGURE 3.1   Organigram of a political party in the EU system

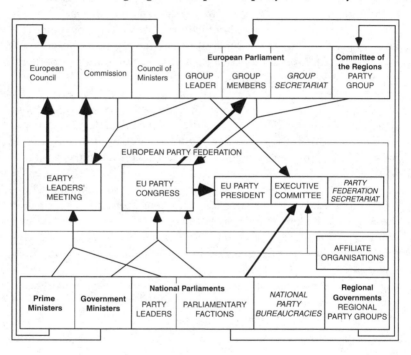

NATIONAL LEVEL

Key:

⟶	= Is unofficial represented in/informally connected to
⟶	= Is officially represented in
⟶	= Makes policy recommendations to
Bold	= Political offices at the European and national levels
CAPITALS	= Official party organs
Italics	= Party Secretariats

party organisational structures: the European party federations. Socialist, Christian Democrat and Liberal party federations were established in the mid-1970s and Green and Regionalist party federations began to take shape in the mid-1980s. However, the party federations were not really significant organisations until the late 1980s. (The development of the party federqations is discussed in more detail in Chapter 7.) Like the party organisations within the national and European parliaments, the party federations have their own set of legal rules and statutes governing their activities. These rules establish regular channels of communication between key national and European-level party actors. Moreover, through the involvement of the party actors in all the EU institutions in their activities, the party federations have established a new set of links between like-minded actors at the European level.

This organigram does not show the exact organisational structure of all the European party families. It is only an approximation of the organisation of the Christian Democrats (with some of the Conservatives), the Socialists, the Liberals, the Greens, and the Regionalists. The Radical Left, the Extreme Right, and the Anti-Europeans have only tenuous links between the party organisations in the national and European arenas. Nevertheless, the five party families that do organise at the national and European levels, and have formal structures to link these levels of organisation (through the establishment of party federations), have all the elements illustrated in the organigram. Moreover, the other three party families have some interlinking structures and are experimenting in establishing more formal intermediate organisations. Overall, the organigram serves as a general reference point as we go on to analyse how the various elements of party organisation in the EU system fit together.

One, three or fifteen organisations in each party?

The organigram can be conceptualised in a variety of ways. First, the main EU party families have some form of party organisation in each EU member state, which are the member parties of the family (as discussed in Chapter 2). Under this conceptualisation, there are at least fifteen separate party organisations within each party family, not considering that most families have several member parties from at least one member state. Second, if the national member parties are treated as a single level of party organisation, the groups in the EP and the Committee of the Regions as a second level, and the party federations as interlinking organisations, then there are three sets of party organisations within each main party family. This is also valid since each of these three types of organisation has its own independent administration and legal status: the national party bureaucracies and constitutions, the EP group secretariats and rules of procedure, and the party federation secretariats and statutes. There is, however, a further way of conceptualising party organisation in the EU: that each party family represents a single complex organisation. This is also legitimate since the statutes of the party federations refer to the national parties and the EP groups as separate sub-units. This unitary conception of the party families has particularly grown with the evolution of the Party Leaders' Meeting as the central organising institution in the Socialists, Christian Democrats and Liberals. However, while the internal organs of the party federations remain weak relative to the organs of the EP and national sub-units, the unitary conception of party organisation in the EU masks a more complex reality. To illustrate these points, the national party organisations, the party organisations in the European institutions, and the intermediate party federation organisations are analysed separately. Finally, a key element of the organisational coherence of each party family is the role and significance of the Party Leaders' Meeting.

The national party organisations

By far the most developed party organisational structures in the EU system are in the legislative and executive institutions at the national level. These are the membership and decision-making structures of the national parties, that began to be formed in the middle of the nineteenth century. The party structures in the domestic arena are the only true 'party membership organisations' in the EU system, where individual citizens pay fees to participate in the selection of party leaders and electoral candidates, and in the choice of party policies. The national party organisations are primarily financed out of individual and corporate membership dues, but most parties also receive subventions from the public accounts to fight election campaigns and to run their parliamentary activities. The party organs at the national level consequently command far more financial and political resources than either the groups in the EP or the party federations.

At the leadership level, party organisations in the national institutions are divided into three groups: party elites that hold government office; parliamentary elites that do not hold executive office; and elites that do not hold any national-level political office. However, the most senior figure in each national party organisation (and indeed in the whole of the EU party system) is the national party leader. The party leader is usually the leader of the party group in the national parliament. Moreover, when a party is in government the national party leader is usually the Prime Minister, or is a senior minister if the party is a junior coalition partner. On rare occasions the Prime Minister is not the party leader but is another member of the party leadership cadre. Even in such circumstances, however, the party leader of the Prime Minister's party is often more influential in deciding the direction of government policy than the Prime Minister (as was the case for years in the Italian system). Finally, the dominance of the national party organisations is further illustrated in the fact that, in contrast to the European-level organisations, no reference is made to either the groups in the EP or the party federations in the statutes and rules of almost all national parties (Katz and Mair, 1992). It is not surprising, therefore, that very few individual members of a national party are aware that they are also *de facto* members of a 'party at the European level'.

The dominance of the national party organisations in the system is demonstrated in the direction of the connections (the arrows in the organigram) between the domestic organisations and the actors in the European institutions. The first type of connection is the direct representation of national party actors in the EU institutions. Most importantly, the party elites holding executive office in the domestic institutions sit in the European Council and the Council of Ministers. Less significantly in the workings of EU politics, the main party officials holding political office in regional governments and assemblies (as in Germany, Spain or France) sit in the Committee of the Regions. In both these cases, however, the primary party political allegiance of these actors is to their national parties and not to any European-level party organisation. This is a function of the internal accountability mechanisms of the domestic party machines. If a party member holding ministerial office goes against the policy of the domestic party leadership when acting in the Council of Ministers, they will at least be severely cautioned and at most be demoted.

However, these direct links between party activity at the domestic and European levels do not exist for parties in opposition at the national or regional levels. There are, nevertheless, two further indirect connections to the European level for domestic parties in government and in opposition. First, the European Commissioners are formally nominated by the governments of the member states. In practice, however, the position of the Commissioners depends on the support of their national party leaderships. For example, while the British Labour Party was in opposition, it ensured that Neil Kinnock replaced Bruce Millan as the second UK Commissioner. Similarly, after the Danish government had changed from Conservative to Socialist in 1993, Commissioner Henning Christopherson (a Conservative) was duly replaced by Ritt Bjerregaard (a Socialist) when the new Commission was appointed in 1994. There are numerous other examples of this power of the national party to ensure the loyalty of their Commissioners.

Nevertheless, a more significant indirect connection is the relationship between the domestic parties and their MEPs. This relationship is a two-way channel: of MEPs playing a role in domestic party activity; and of national parties putting pressure on their MEPs. However, the second of these channels is stronger than the first. Most MEPs take part in domestic party congresses and vote in party leadership elections. Relative to national parliamentarians, however, the status of MEPs in the national party apparatus is weak. Moreover, and more importantly for the behaviour of MEPs, the structure of European elections ensures that MEPs are dependent upon internal mechanisms in the national (or subnational) party organisations for their reselection. In the June 1994 elections, for example, candidates were selected by national electoral committees in seven member states, by regional electoral committees in four member states, and by local party organs in one member state (Britain). Consequently, in none of the party families were the EP groups or the party federations able to influence who was put on the ballot papers. The ELDR required that the list of candidates of their member parties was 'communicated' to the executive committee of the party federation, but the committee was not allowed to protest any selection of the national parties. This selection procedure hence gives national parties the ultimate sanction over their MEPs; and ensures that where national party and EP party group allegiances conflict in the EP, the national party allegiance invariably wins out. This was dramatically revealed in the July 1994 EP vote on the candidacy of Jacques Santer for Commission President – where all national delegations whose party leaders were prime ministers (after the prime ministers had collectively supported Santer in the European Council) broke from the positions of their EP party groups if they were different to their domestic parties' positions (Hix and Lord, 1996). Overall, the national parties are by far the strongest party organisations in the EU system.

Party organisation in the European institutions

In the European institutions, formal party organisations only exist in the EP and the Committee of the Regions. Party groups were first established in the EP soon after its creation in the early 1950s. However, these groups have only commanded significant financial and secretarial resources since the first direct elections of the EP in 1979. Each party group now has: a hierarchical leadership structure, with a president (or chairperson) and several vice-presidents (usually one from each national party in the group); an executive bureau; a series of working groups; a detailed statute or rules of procedure, by which all the individual MEPs must abide or risk expulsion from the group; and a secretariat that is comparable to the size of the support staff of the party factions in the domestic parliaments. Party groups have also been set up in the Committee of the Regions. The Committee of the Regions was established by the Maastricht Treaty, and first met in 1993. Christian Democrat, Socialist, and Liberal groups were subsequently established in early 1994, with Statutes and leadership structures based on those of the groups in the EP. Following the Maastricht Treaty Party Article (138A), the statutes of the main groups in the EP were changed to establish the fact that the groups are the official organs of the party federations in the EP. This principle was also laid down when the groups in the Committee of the Regions were first formed. A cosmetic indication of this change was the change of the names of the three main EP groups to: the Group of the European People's Party; the Group of the Party of European Socialists; and the Group of the Liberal, Democratic and Reform Party.

However, a major difference between the EP groups and the groups in the Committee of the Regions is that the EP groups are funded out of the budget of the EP (which is a separate line in the overall EU budget). There are at present no such provisions to finance the work of the groups in the Committee of the Regions out of EU resources. Consequently, the groups in the Committee of the Regions usually use the secretarial and financial resources of the

EP groups. Moreover, a further significant difference is that the party organisations in the Committee of the Regions are primitive structures, and are less cohesive than the groups in the EP. Whereas the EP groups have established procedures to which the majority of the Group members adhere, the groups in the Committee of the Regions are not accepted as legitimate in the eyes of many of the Committee members. For example, when the Socialist Group in the Committee was established, several SPD members from the German *Länder* refused to join the group because they argued that their primary political allegiance was to their region and not to their party (Authors' interview with PES official). Although there is also a tension between national and party-group loyalties within the EP groups, it is extremely rare that an MEP voluntarily leaves a group because he feels that his national allegiance is compromised.

There are also party actors in the other institutions at the European level. As discussed, the parties holding the office of domestic governmental office sit in the European Council and the Council of Ministers. However, there are no formal European-level party organisational structures within either of these institutions. Similarly, most European Commissioners are senior figures from domestic and/or European party organisations. The personal cabinets of the Commissioners are also filled with policy advisers from the same national party background as the Commissioners they serve. Like the Council of Ministers, however, there are no formal party political links between the members of the Commission from the same party family. Nevertheless, an informal 'caucus' among the Socialist members of the Santer Commission was established in early 1995, and the Christian Democrat and Liberal Commissioners have been known to hold informal meetings.

There are legal limitations on the ability of external political organisations (such as political parties) to influence the European Commissioners: Article 157.2 of the EC Treaty states that Commissioners should be 'completely independent in the performance of their duties . . . [and] shall neither seek nor take instructions from . . . any other body'. However, this Article is specifically aimed at the governments of the member states, because it goes on to state that 'each member state undertakes to respect this principle and not to seek to influence the members of the Commission in the performance of their tasks'. Without any explicit reference to 'party' influences, there is thus no formal reason why party organisations cannot be established within the European Commission. At this stage, however, the links between the Socialist Commissioners are inconsequential in comparison to the level of party organisation in the executive branch of the domestic institutions (the national governments) or in the legislative branch of the European institutions (in the EP). Consequently, the party groups in the EP are the only genuine party organisations in the European institutions.

The European party federations

Finally, the third set of party organisations in the EU system are the party federations. Socialist, Liberal and Christian Democratic party federations were established between 1974 and 1976, in the build-up to the first direct elections to the EP. A Regionalist European Free Alliance was also established in the early 1980s, but is not as developed as the main party federations. Furthermore, the insertion of the Party Article in the Maastricht Treaty, the names of the Socialist and Liberal organisations were changed to include the word 'Party' instead of 'Confederation' or 'Federation' (in November 1992 and December 1993, respectively) and a new Green party federation was established (in June 1993). Consequently, the four current party federations are: the European People's Party – Christian Democrats (EPP), together with several Conservative parties; the Party of European Socialists (PES); the European Liberal, Democratic and Reform Party (ELDR); and the European Federation of Green Parties (EFGP). Like the national party organisations and the EP groups, the party federations have their own statutes, decision-making mechanisms, leadership structures, budgets, and secretariats that are legally separate from the EP groups and the national parties.

However, the organisations of the party federations are fundamentally different to both the national parties and the EP groups in two key respects. First, the party federations are not linked to an electoral process or a parliamentary arena. Second, the party federations draw their finances from other party organisations and not from individuals or public resources. The EP groups and the national member parties each pay for about half of the total running costs of the federations. The party federations are thus not real political parties if they are considered independently from the organisations in the national and European parliaments. However, this simple conclusion is false. The party federations are simple coordinating structures, like the central offices of any domestic party. Consequently, the party federations should be regarded as umbrella organisations that bring together the party organisations within the national and European institutions. This can be seen by looking at who participates in the work of the federations.

The party federations uphold a 'permanent presence' (this phrase comes from the statues of the European People's Party) at the European level through a series of offices and organs. First, each party federation has an Executive Committee (the Bureau of the PES, the Political Bureau of the EPP, and the Councils of the ELDR and the EFGP), which is comprised of delegates of the national parties (usually the International Secretaries) and the EP groups, and which meets about six times each year. Second, each party federation has a Party President, who is usually a national party leader, and a number of Vice-Presidents, who are senior party figures in the national institutions (such as party spokespersons on European policy or foreign ministers) and in the European institutions (such as the EP group Leader or European Commissioners). Third, the Christian Democrats and the Liberals have a special Leadership Committee (the Presidency of the EPP, and the Bureau of the ELDR) to manage the day-to-day running of the activities of the party federation. The members of this Committee are the President and Vice-Presidents of the party federation. Fourth, the President, the Executive Committee and the Leadership Committee are assisted in their tasks by the Party Federation Secretariat.

In addition to these ongoing organs, the official bodies for coordinating the work of the party federations are the Party Congresses. These Congresses are held every two years, with an additional Congress in the build-up to the EP elections to adopt a European Election Manifesto. The participants in the Congresses are the delegates from the national member parties of the party federation and the party groups of the federation in the EP and the Committee of the Regions. As the organigram also illustrates, representatives from affiliate organisations, such as trade unions or party political societies, are entitled to attend Party Congresses, but usually do not have the right to vote on resolutions. The role of the Party Congress is to elect the Party Federation President and to set the long-term policy goals of the party federation (which are usually contained in an Action Programme). As the organigram shows, the policy resolutions of the Congress are implemented by the executive bodies of the party federation and provide an agenda for the EP party group.

However, there are two important differences between the party federation Congresses and the congresses of the national party organisations. First, the participants in the party federation Congresses are national and European parliamentarians (the 'middle-level elites'), whereas the participants in national party congresses are rank-and-file party members. The activities of the party federations are hence only indirectly accountable; which puts them in a weak position in relation to the national party organisations. Second, the party federation Congresses do not constrain the behaviour of party actors holding executive office at the European level. The party officials in the Commission and the Council are not accountable to the party federation Congresses. In contrast, national party Congresses scrutinise the behaviour of party leaders holding ministerial office. However, these vital links between EU party organisations and the party actors in the EU institutions have begun to develop through the institutions of the Party Leaders' Meeting.

Party leaders' meetings: 'Central Committees' of the EU party system

Since their birth in the 1970s, the Christian Democrat, Socialist and Liberal party families have held unofficial meetings of the national party leaders. From the mid-1980s, however, Party Leaders' Meetings (which are sometimes referred to in the media as 'party leaders' summits') have grown in significance. First, in the early 1990s, the Party Leaders' Meeting was institutionalised in the PES, ELDR and EPP statutes as the supreme internal decision-making organ of the party federation. For example, the Action Programmes and Election Manifestos are always approved by a Party Leaders' Meeting before going to the party federation Congresses, and the executive organs of the party federations report directly to the Party Leaders' Meetings. Second, Party Leaders' Meetings have established a new role in monitoring the behaviour of party officials holding executive offices at the European level. By bringing prime ministers and European Commissioners together, the Party Leaders' Meetings are the only arenas where all the officials fulfilling executive functions at the European level from the same party family meet to discuss the medium- and long-term EU agenda. The direct impact on behaviour in the Commission and the European Council may still be limited, but this is the first time that these figures have been jointly attached to a European-level partisan institution. Third, the Party Leaders' Meetings have begun to play a new role in coordinating the development of party policy on issues in EU politics at national and European level (see the next section).

The participants at these meetings are the national party leaders of the member parties of the party federation, the prime ministers from the member parties of the federation (that are not party leaders), the presidents and vice-presidents of the party federation, the Leader of the EP group of the federation, and the members of the European Commission from the member parties of the federation. Party Leaders' Meetings are held at least twice a year, usually in the week immediately before a European Council. The Socialist party leaders also try to meet in the same venue as the European Council. The policy positions of the Party Leaders' Meetings are contained in Party Leaders' Declarations that are presented at press conferences at the conclusions of the meetings. The Party Leaders' Meetings (particularly of the EPP and the PES) have consequently established a place in the general media jamboree surrounding the six-monthly meetings of the European Council. With the growing attendance of party policy advisers, the EPP and PES Party Leaders' Meetings are attended by at least one hundred top officials. However, this growing number makes private discussions between party leaders increasingly difficult, and thus defeats the original object of the meetings. As a result, the PES has also begun to hold annual party leaders' conclaves that are away from the European Council meetings, are attended only by the party leaders themselves, and where no Declaration needs to be negotiated and presented to the press.

This new status of the Party Leaders' Meetings has arisen from demand-and-supply factors. The demand factors result from a search for new institutional frameworks by national party leaders. As discussed in the previous chapter, European issues (on the integration–sovereignty dimension) undermine the existing bases of party competition. The rise of these issues in domestic politics in the late 1980s and early 1990s consequently pushed national party leaders to seek ways to couch these issues in traditional left–right terms. A starting point in this aim is to discuss this problem with like-minded parties in other national systems and learn from the strategies of the EP party groups. This means establishing regularised contacts at the highest political level within each party family. In addition, the supply-side factors result from the inadequacy of existing transnational party institutions to meet this demand. Neither the Party Congresses nor the executive committees of the party federations possess the political authority to agree credible and/or binding commitments about party behaviour at national and European level. As pointed out in the discussion of domestic party organisation, the only persons in the EU system who are able to make these sorts of promises are the national party leaders. It was thus in the interests of both the domestic party leaders and the European party officials to institutionalise the informal leaders' gatherings as the main organ of European party cooperation and coordination.

Overall, therefore, a 'party in the EU' is made up of two separate organisations within the national and European parliaments, that are brought together under the umbrella organisation of a party federation. The key coordinating institution in this arrangement is the Party Leaders' Meeting. In a similar sense, the German SPD is made up of state-level membership organisations and the federal-level faction in the Bundestag, that are brought together in the central offices of the Party in Bonn and in the Annual Congress. Nevertheless, under different circumstances, the singular, triangular and fifteen-piece conceptualisations still hold. In day-to-day domestic legislative politics in the member states, each party family is separated into fifteen clearly independent sub-units. In day-to-day EU politics, moreover, the EP party groups operate independently of the national parties, and the party federations play hardly any role. Nevertheless, in the adoption of more medium and long-term EU policy goals (such as party attitudes towards economic and monetary union), each party family increasingly works as a coherent organisation, where policy is developed through an interaction between the national parties and the EP groups, and the party federations play a crucial coordinating role. How this interaction works is the subject of the next section.

The making of party policy on Europe

One of the main purposes of partisan organisation is for like-minded actors to agree on common goals. The establishment of common policy frameworks allows politicians to create a 'common identity' in the minds of the electorate. This identity significantly reduces the amount of work needed to develop policy ideas and to present them to the voters. In this sense, party organisation can be used to reduce the 'transactions costs' of policy development (see Cox and McCubbins, 1993). For example, in the European party systems, where individual politicians make prior commitments to an election manifesto, a single campaign can be run by each political party. In the

United States, in contrast, where the Democrats and Republicans do not adopt single electoral platforms, each candidate bears the costs of developing his own ideas and getting them across to the electorate. Without the structure of powerful party organisations, running for political office in the USA is much more expensive than anywhere in Europe.

For the same cost-reduction reasons, the national member parties and the EP party groups from the same party families have begun to use the framework of the party federations to develop common policy platforms on a number of European issues. There are two main reasons why advocating separate policies on these issues is costly for national parties in the same party family. First, if a party is saying something different to a like-minded party in another member state, competing parties can use this against them. For example, the British Conservatives have suffered from being 'out of step', while the Labour Party has gained credibility on European questions by reminding the voters and the media that its policies are the same as those of the rest of the Socialist family. Second, developing party policy on European issues is inherently more difficult than on more traditional questions in party politics. European issues – such as EU institutional reform, EU enlargement, economic and monetary union, and EU environ-mental and social policies – are not only new to (and cross-cut) party competition at the national level, but also require a detailed technical knowledge of EU institutions and policy-making. Conse-quently, by talking to other parties and their EP group, the member parties of a party federation can hope to improve the quality, consistency and coherence of party policies towards medium- and long-term issues in EU politics. In the Socialists, Christian Democrats and Liberals (and to some extent in the Greens), party policy on these issues is increasingly made through a series of connections between the three types of party organisation that were described in the previous section. How this policy network operates is summarised in Figure 3.2.

Developing and adopting policies

In the policy development stage, each national party, the EP party group, and the party federation establishes a working group. For example, during the Intergovernmental Conferences (IGCs) in 1990 and 1991 that led to the Maastricht Treaty, the British Labour, Liberal and Conservative parties discussed the development of the

FIGURE 3.2   The making of party policy on European issues

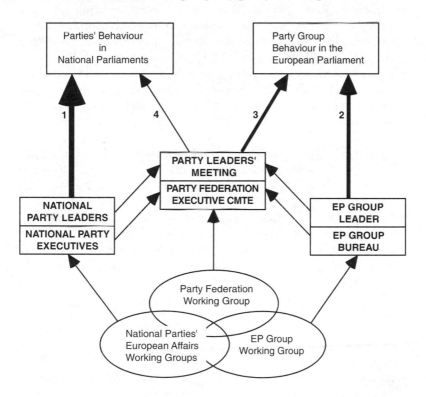

IGC agenda at regular meetings of their European Affairs working groups. These groups were chaired by a senior spokesperson in the case of Labour and the Liberals and by the Minister for European Affairs in the case of the Conservatives. Moreover, in the EP each party group set up separate working groups on economic and monetary union (EMU) and political union. In the party federations, the PES (which at that stage was still the Confederation of Socialist Parties in the EC), the EPP and the ELDR also divided the work into committees. Each of these groups met at regular intervals (usually every month) throughout the negotiation of the Maastricht Treaty, between December 1990 and December 1991.

By coincidence as much as by design, as the figure shows, there is usually a large overlap between the three levels of working groups. The national party European Affairs committees usually contain

MEPs from their own parties (who are also often in the EP working group on the same subject). And in some cases, the national groups even involve MEPs or national figures from other national parties (who are also usually members of the party federation working group). For example, during the IGCs, David Martin MEP (the chairman of the Socialist Group's working group on political union) was a member of the British Labour Party's working group; and there were regular contacts between the German and French Socialists' European Affairs committees. The party federation working group, on the other hand, involves the leading spokespersons from the national and EP working groups, and other specialists in the subject area (such as academics or policy advisers from the European Commission or the Council of Ministers). There are, however, no hard and fast rules for who participates in each level of working group, and how far these groups overlap. Indeed, in some policy areas there are no overlaps at all. Nevertheless, this description is a fairly accurate picture of how policy was developed in the main party families during the 1990–91 IGCs and in a number of other EU policy areas (such as environmental policy and the 1993–94 EU strategy on employment, growth and competitiveness).

As Figure 3.2 shows, when the working groups have finished their policy preparation, they each present a report to their prospective leaderships: the national party executives, the EP group bureau, and the party federation executive committees. In the national party organisations, the key figures in the transformation of the recommendations of the working groups and the executive committees into official party policy are national party leaders. A similar role is played by the group leader in the EP party group bureau. In the party federations, however, the national party leaders and the EP group leaders play a collective role in the adoption of official policy statements (which are contained in Declarations from the biannual Party Leaders' Meetings). However, what is significant for parties and their electorates is how these policies are turned into actions.

Connecting policy adoption to legislative behaviour

If the policy network operates successfully, the positions adopted by the national and European party leaders influence the behaviour of parties in the national and European parliaments. Party policy statements constrain the day-to-day behaviour of the parties' representatives: determining which legislative proposals a party can support, and with which other parties alliances can be built. Nevertheless, the degree of correspondence between policy adoption and legislative behaviour depends by whom the policy was finally adopted. This is illustrated in Figure 3.2 by the size of the arrows from the leadership organs to the actors in the legislative arenas. The strongest connections are the direct links between the national and EP group leaderships and the respective behaviour of their actors in the national and European parliaments. First, if a member of the national parliament breaks from the policy position adopted by the national party executive he or she is usually reprimanded and may even be expelled from the parliamentary group (this is shown by arrow 1 in the figure). Second, an MEP who breaks from the group policy position can be warned against further defections (arrow 2). However, unlike national parties, it is very difficult to expel an individual MEP from a group, particularly if he or she is backed by their national delegation. Consequently, the strongest connection from policy adoption to party action is between the national party leaders and their national parliamentary factions.

In addition to these direct connections, there are two indirect (and consequently weaker) links between the policies agreed by the Party Leaders' Meetings and the behaviour of the EP party groups and the national parliamentary factions (arrows 3 and 4). These connections are weaker because, unlike the national and EP leaderships, the Party Leaders' Meeting·has very few mechanisms for enforcing its policy statements on either national or European actors. The Socialists and Christian Democrats have experimented with ways of binding the member parties and the EP groups to the Leaders' Declarations, but no party has ever been expelled from a party federation for breaking the promises it made at a Leaders' Meeting. The only real power of the Leaders' Meeting is to provide a platform for national party leaders to scrutinise (and usually criticise) each other's behaviour and the behaviour of the EP group leader. This power of scrutiny is more effective on the actions of the EP group leader than on the national parties because the party leaders have the collective power (through the Party Leaders' Meeting) to force his or her resignation (arrow 3 is hence thicker than arrow 4 in the figure).

Case-study: the British Labour Party and EMU

The operation and significance of this policy network is clearly illustrated in the changing policies of the British Labour Party on the issue of economic and monetary union during the build-up to, and negotiation of, the IGCs between 1990 and 1991. Prior to the IGCs, British Labour Party policy towards Europe consisted simply of a 'socialist vision of the EC', which involved European-level environmental, social and regional policies, and a vague commitment of EC institutions to economic growth and job creation (Labour Party, 1990a, p. 79). Following the recommendations of the Labour working group on European Affairs, with the participation of several MEPs, in February 1990 the National Executive Committee (NEC) adopted a new position paper on EMU. The central policy of the paper was to support a 'hardening of the ERM' but to oppose a single currency (Labour Party, 1990b). This was almost identical to the position of the Conservative Government. In other words, because the Labour Party saw EMU as a question of 'more' or 'less' European integration (i.e., on the integration–sovereignty dimension discussed in Chapter 2), it was safer to minimise party competition on this issue by adopting the same policy as the Conservatives.

Nonetheless, at the Party Leaders' Meeting of the Confederation of Socialist Parties (CSP) in Madrid on 10 December 1990 – immediately prior to the launch of the IGCs at the European Council in Rome on 14–15 December – the Labour Party leader (Neil Kinnock) signed a Declaration which supported full EMU, and which controversially included a proposal for 'binding minimum taxation rates . . . to avoid tax competition' (CSP, 1990). The Leaders' Declaration from this meeting had been prepared by the CSP working group on EMU, which was attended by Labour's International Secretary. However, the inability of the International Secretary to make commitments that had the full backing of the Labour leader was revealed at the next Party Leaders' Meeting, in Luxembourg on 3 June 1991. At this meeting, Neil Kinnock spoke out against the new draft CSP position: emphasising his party's 'proposals for a democratically accountable Eurofed' and attempting to overturn the commitment to minimum taxation rates (Kinnock, 1991). Although Kinnock could not persuade the rest of the Socialist parties on the taxation issue, the Socialist Leaders' 'Luxembourg Declaration on the IGCs' contained a new commitment for a 'Central Bank accountable to the Council of Ministers' (CSP, 1991a). In the national arena, meanwhile, Labour was still not openly committed to EMU.

By the next Socialist Party Leaders' Meeting, however, Labour's policy was much closer to the European-level positions. In July 1991, the NEC agreed a new policy statement on the IGCs. For this statement, the national working group had taken not only the goals of the previous Socialist Leaders' Declarations, but also the specific language. The new statement fully backed EMU and a single currency, and for the first time used expressions such as 'criteria for economic and social convergence', 'economic and social cohesion', 'the final stage of EMU', and 'the role of Ecophene' (Labour Party, 1991a). One year earlier, most senior Labour figures would not have known what any of this Euro-jargon meant. Moreover, in October 1991 the NEC was even converted to the Socialist leaders' position on the issue of taxation; stating that 'it is all too easy for fiscal interdependence to result in competitive deflation – Monetary Union will therefore require fiscal co-operation' (Labour Party, 1991b, pp. 6–7). Consequently, by the time of the final Socialist Party Leaders' Meeting during the IGCs, in Brussels on 3–4 December 1991 – immediately prior to the Maastricht European Council, on 9–10 December – the British Labour Party was completely integrated into the European Socialist agenda on EMU. In other words, the Socialists' European policy network helped the Labour Party to quickly gain knowledge and expertise on a tricky question in EU politics, and enabled the party to couch the issue in left–right terms (which allowed them to challenge the Conservatives and to minimise internal party divisions).

In sum, there is an emerging network in the Socialist, Christian Democrat and Liberal families for developing common party policies on some of the major issues on the medium- and long-term EU agenda. This network is an on going interaction between the three levels of party organisation in the EU – the national parties, the EP groups, and the party federations. The development from initiation (in working groups), through adoption (by party leaderships), to implementation (in legislative action) is comparable to the policy-making process in any political party in the domestic arena, and particularly to parties in a federal system like Germany. However, the national parties are willing to participate in this network only because it can contribute to a coherence and consistency on problematic issues in domestic party competition. As a result, this network is not used on every issue on the EU agenda. The party families are only able to develop common policy frameworks on socioeconomic issues, such as EMU and environmental and social policies, that are easily transferable into domestic party alignments (Hix, 1995b). In contrast, policies on questions that are more directly related to nation-state sovereignty, such as an EU Common Foreign and Security Policy, tend to be independently developed by each national party.

Party adaptation to a difficult environment

To conclude, therefore, the environment in which political parties operate in the EU is not conducive to the development of classic party competition: where a few parties compete in one main election, and the leaders of the winning party or group of parties form a government. First, the shape of the strategic environment (which was analysed in Chapter 2) suggests that the issue of European integration (the integration–sovereignty dimension) cannot be easily addressed along traditional party lines (i.e., on the left–right dimension), and that the balance of power and overlaps between at least three political blocs in the EU party system prevents the emergence of clear partisan divisions at the European level. This strategic environment consequently undermines the possibility of competition between political parties replacing the existing structure of political competition in the EU between the European nation states. Second, the structure of the institutional environment ensures the persistence of a plurality of organisational forms within each party family, and the supremacy of party organisations and leaders at the domestic level over those at the European level – the EP party groups and the party federations. This consequently prevents the emergence of unitary hierarchical party leadership structures that are geared towards the pursuit of European-level office and/or policy goals. A network for the development of European party policies has begun to emerge, but can only be used to address some of the issues on the EU agenda. All in all, there is an extremely 'low partyness' of the EU system (see Katz, 1986).

However, as pointed out at the beginning of Chapter 2, parties are not completely dependent upon their political and institutional surroundings (Sartori, 1968). Political parties possess significant political and financial resources that enable them to adapt to their surroundings. The main party families – the Christian Democrats, Socialists, Conservatives and Liberals (and to some extent the Greens) – possess their own independent economic bases and channels of communication, have access to the instruments and finances of domestic government, have the almost undivided attention of the media, and are deeply ingrained in the European political tradition. If parties are serious about establishing a party system at the European level, these resources can be used to reduce the strategic and institutional constraints on their behaviour. For example, the main parties have chosen to compete at the European level only on the classic left–right issues of domestic party politics: over policies of socioeconomic redistribution (such as the level of regulation of the EU single market) and sociopolitical value orientation (such as common political and civil rights). Furthermore, parties have increased the level of coordination between their activities in the domestic and European institutions, particularly through the development and implementation of common policies in a number of areas of EU policy-making. Finally, parties have used their resources to introduce the 'Party Article' (Article 138A) in the Maastricht Treaty. The Article was a joint initiative by the presidents of the Christian Democrat, Socialist, and Liberal party federations, with the backing of the national and EP party leaders in several Party Leaders' Meetings between 1990 and 1991. The legal basis of the Article is unclear, but parties may be able to use it to establish a legal and financial framework in the EU that is more conducive to their interests.

A problem, however, is that political parties are not alone in their quest for power and resources in the EU. Parties are but one of the political organisations that want to protect their positions of influence in the EU. First, since the 1980s European-level and national interest groups have established a high level of access to the EU policy process, particularly in the European Commission. Consequently, these interest groups (many of which give funds to political parties) will be reluctant to allow the Commission to develop a more party political identity. Nevertheless, by far the biggest rivals to parties in the control of EU policy-making are the national governments of the EU member states. Governments are made up of politicians who have party political affiliations. Once in government, though, politicians are eager to reduce the influence of their parent parties on their actions. In EU decision-making, moreover, government ministers (in the Council of Ministers and the European Council) are freer from party constraints than they are in the domestic arena. Consequently, governments can use their positions in the EU system to block institutional reforms that may facilitate real partisan alignments at the European level – such as a uniform procedure for direct elections to the EP, the direct election of the Commission President, or the development of a coherent legal framework for 'parties at the European level'. In other words, even if political parties are able to adapt to this difficult environment, it is unlikely that they will be able to reinvent their powerful domestic organisations at the European level.

4

Party Groups in the European Parliament: Election and Formation

We have seen that the prospects of the EU developing political parties of its own rest on the party groups in the EP and the extra-parliamentary federations. The next four chapters will examine how far these have developed the characteristics of political parties, the variables that seem to stimulate their evolution and the factors that hold them back. This chapter will start by looking at the composition and formation of the party groups. It will show how a highly idiosyncratic mix of national and transnational party politics decisively shapes the EP and the whole character of the political representation that it offers the public. This mix, in turn, operates through three stages: the recruitment of MEPs, elections to the EP and post-electoral group formation.

Identifying the party groups in the EP

At the time of writing (1996), there are eight transnational party groups in the EP. The illustration of the hemicycle in Figure 4.1 shows who they are. As MEPs follow the habit common to many European assemblies of seating themselves in a manner that signals their broad political positioning, this diagram is also a convenient way of showing how the groups relate to one another on a left–right spectrum. We can, broadly, divide the groups into three. First are those that are permanent features of the EP. They have existed since the first Assembly of the European Coal and Steel Community convened in 1952 and they have been regularly reconstituted with each new five-year term of the EP. These groups are the PES, the EPP and the ELDR. Second are those that have featured in several parliaments, but are by no means guaranteed a permanent existence. These are the UEL and the Greens. Third are those groups that only came into being in the current parliament, in other words since 1994. These are the EN, the ERA and the UPE. It remains to be seen whether they will be continuing transnational party formations, or just the product of temporary political circumstance.

FIGURE 4.1   Hemicycle of the European Parliament

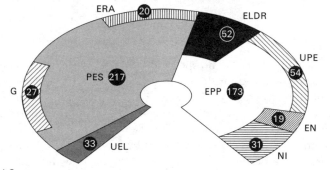

Political Groups

ERA = European Radical Alliance	EPP = European People's Party
EN = Europe of Nations	PES = Party of European Socialists
ELDR = European Liberal and Democratic Reform	G = Greens
UEL = Union of European Left	UPE = Union for Europe
NI = Non-inscrits	

	B	DK	D	GR	E	F	IRL	I	L	NL	A	P	FIN	S	GB	
PES	6	3	40	10	22	15	1	18	2	8	8	10	4	7	63	217
EPP	7	3	47	9	30	12	4	14	2	10	6	1	4	5	19	173
UPE				2		15	7	27			3					54
ELDR	6	5			2	1	1	6	1	10	1	8	6	3	2	52
UEL		1		4	9	7		5			3	1	3			33
G	2		12				2	4		1	1		1	4		27
ERA	1				1	13		2	1					2		20
EN		4				13				2						19
NI	3					11		11			5				1	31
	25	16	99	25	64	87	15	87	6	31	21	25	16	22	87	626

Chairman	PES	– Pauline GREEN (UK)	UEL – Alonso J. PUERTA (E)
	EPP	– Wilfried MARTENS (B)	G – Claudia ROTH (D)
	UPE	– Giancarlo LIGABUE (I)	ERA – Catherine LALUMIÈRE (F)
		Jean-Claude PASTY (F)	EN – James Michael GOLDSMITH (F)

However, we cannot answer the question 'who are the party groups?' without also looking at the national political parties that make them up. MEPs owe their selection and election almost exclusively to national political parties. In addition, most join, leave or change groups as national party delegations and not as individuals. Although such shifts are increasingly determined by the politics of the European Parliament itself, they are scarcely conceivable without the consent of the domestic party leadership and they may be severely constrained by what is happening back home. In the daily politics of the Parliament, national party delegations form as important an organisational focus as the transnational party groups themselves. Whether they are working in their committees or preparing for plenaries, MEPs hold a series of parallel meetings in national party delegations and the success of EP party groups is, paradoxically, often a matter of harnessing national parties to the overall cause of transnational party cohesion. Attempts to deny national party delegations an explicit place in the process of consensus-building at EP level can be counter-productive. Table 4.1 shows how national political parties fit into the party groups. Once again, we can distinguish three types. First, are those that include parties from almost all the EU countries. At the time of writing (1996), the PES group covers all 15 member states; the EPP all but Portugal (its only Portuguese MEP is an independent, whose parent party, in fact, sits in the ELDR); and the ELDR all but two, Germany and Greece. Second are those groups that cover several member states but with certain geographical biases. For example, the Greens are stronger in Northern than Southern Europe (apart from Italy) while for the UEL group things are the other way round, in spite of an attempt to tag on some Scandinavian Greens after the 1995 enlargement. Third are those groups that have only a thin coverage of the member states: EN, ERA and UPE. We will develop some more rigorous ways of measuring the transnational character of the party groups a little later, but for the moment it is worth noting that there is a precise overlap between the size of the groups, their institutionalisation and spread of countries represented. The largest are also the most permanent and transnational.

However, neither transnational positioning on a left–right scale nor national party membership captures the full range of political and social influences that EP groups channel into the making of EU policies and laws. It is, accordingly, useful to examine the age, gender and professional backgrounds of those who make up the party groups,

TABLE 4.1

Composition of EP groups by national party (figures show number of MEPs in each national delegation), as of 1995

	PES	EPP	ELDR	UPE
Austria	Socialists 8	People's Party 6	Liberals 1	
Belgium	Socialists: Flemish 3, Wallon 3	Christian Dems: Flemish 4, Wallon 3	Liberals: Flemish 3, Wallon 3	
Denmark	Social Democrats 3	Conservatives 3	Liberals 4, Radical 1	
Finland	Social Democrats 4	Conservatives 4	Centre Party 5, Swedish People's Party 1	
France	Socialists 15	Christian Dems 4 Republican 5 Social Dems 1 Other UDF 3	Radical 1	Gaullists (Conservatives) 14
Germany	Social Democrats 40	Christian Dems 39 CSU (Bavaria) 8		
Greece	Socialists 10	New Democracy 9		Political Spring 2
Ireland	Labour 1	Fine Gael 4	Independent 1	Fianna Fail 7
Italy	Democratic Left 16 Socialists 2 Independent 1	People's Party 8 Segni 3 South Tirol PP 1	Northern League 6 Republican 1	Forza Italia 27 Independents 2
Luxembourg	Socialists 2	Christian Dems 2	Democrat 1	
Netherlands	Labour 8	Christian Dems 10	Liberals 6, D66 4	
Portugal	Socialists 10	Independ PSD 1	Social Dems 8	Christian Dem 3
Spain	Socialists 22	People's Party 28 Catalan Dem U 1 Basque National Party 1	Catalan 2	
Sweden	Social Democrats 11	Conservatives 5 Christian Dems 1	Centre Party 2 Liberals 1	
UK	Labour 62 SDLP 1	Conservatives 18 Official Unionist 1	Liberals 2	

Table 4.1 *(cont.)*

UEL	GREENS	ERA	EN	NI
	Greens 1			Freedom Party 5
	Ecology: Flemish 1, Wallon 1	Volksunie 1		Front National 2, Vlaams Blok 2
Socialist People's Party 1			People's 2 + June 2	
Left Alliance 1	Green League 1			
Communist Party 7		Energie Radicale (Tapie List) 13	Autre Europe (Goldsmith List) 13	Front National 11
	Greens 12			
Communist Party 2, Synaspismos 2				
	Greens 2			
Communist Party 5	Greens 3 Rete 1	Pannella List 2		National Alliance 11
	Greens 1			
	Greens 1		Calvinist Party 2	
Communist Party 3				
United Left 9		National Coalition Canary Islands 1		
Left Party 1	Greens 1			
		Scottish Nationalists 2		Democratic Unionist 1

together with any information on prior political experiences that may colour their whole approach to party politics and public representation. From Table 4.2, we can draw the following conclusions:

- The EP as a whole has more female representation than most national assemblies in Western Europe. But the probability that any one of its party groups will include women diminishes with movement from the left to the right of the hemicycle. The Greens and the UEL have the most female representation, the EN and the UPE the least, and of the three main party groups the Socialists have more than the Christian Democrats/Conservatives or the Liberals.

- The EP is overwhelmingly professional and middle-class. In fact, just a handful of professions account for almost all of its membership. On the other hand, there are clear differences between the groups in the first-hand understanding of economy and society that their MEPs bring to the task of representation. The few MEPs who have experience as manual workers are concentrated in the PES and the UEL. Business is best represented in the EPP, the ELDR and the UPE, though it is not entirely absent from the PES. Agriculture is surprisingly narrowly concentrated on the Liberals and the parties of the right – the EPP, the UPE and the EN, with very little representation in the PES. The PES, the UEL, and the Greens – all parties of the left- recruit disproportionately from teachers and academics.

- The EP has only a narrow generational base with both the old and the young finding little representation there. Between 65 per cent and 85 per cent of each group were between 40 and 60 years old at the beginning of the 1994–9 parliament. The party groups which best represent the young are those made up of new parties at the national level, the Greens, and before they joined with the UPE, Forza Europa. Low representation of the old confirms the passing from the party groups of the immediate postwar generation with its emotional commitment to European integration, though more recent generations may have an advantage over the 'pioneers' in having had the opportunity to observe a great deal of practical experimentation in differing approaches to common policy-making during their political lifetimes.

Turning to an analysis of the political socialisation of the MEPs who form the party groups, Table 4.3 shows that few arrive in the EP

TABLE 4.2

Age, gender and professional background of MEPs by party group (1996)

	Age profile			Gender	Professional/sectoral backgrounds								
	Under 40	40–60	Over 60	Proportion of women	Education/ Academic	Law	Media	Business	Agric	Public official	Medical/ Welfare	Engineer	Manual
ERA	3.8%	84.7%	11.5%	23.1%	3	4	1	2	–	–	3	–	–
EN	7.7	84.6	7.7	17.3	2	4	2	2	3	3	–	–	–
ELDR	13.5	75.0	11.5	27.0	6	9	2	5	4	3	–	2	–
UEL	6.5	77.4	16.1	38.7	8	1	4	–	1	1	2	1	2
EPP	10.4	71.7	17.9	23.1	32	27	12	19	15	14	13	9	–
PSE	16.2	73.8	10.0	29.4	55	15	19	10	1	14	7	12	12
UPE	11.1	73.6	15.3	19.2	9	5	6	8	3	1	4	12	–
V	24.0	68.3	7.7	44.0	7	2	1	–	3	–	1	–	–
EP average	14.2	72.2	13.6	26.6									

Note: Information on career backgrounds as declared to 'Biographical Notes', European Parliament, PE 177. 792, July 1994.

without a political history. The overwhelming majority begin their careers in national politics and have either held – or continue to hold – an elected position in a national parliament or local or regional government. Many have also served on their national party executive or as local party officials. There are even a few present and former party leaders in the EP (Corbett *et al.*, 1994, p. 53). The overall picture implies a high level of connection with national political parties. It also means that MEPs will be soaked in the assumptions and collective memories of member state politics, which will, in turn, colour their approaches to particular left–right issues and to European integration in general. The role of national or local party service as the main recruitment criterion for MEPs has also been seen as contributing to the political professionalisation of the EP: a condition in which fewer representatives have rich lifetime experiences outside of politics (Westlake, 1994a, p. 105).

Political parties and the selection and election of MEPs

The formation of MEPs into transnational party groups is only the last stage of a lengthy political odyssey that is at every other stage dominated by national party politics. The selection of candidates, the arguments of the campaign, electoral success or failure, and the label under which the MEP is elected are, in most instances, governed by domestic party politics and not EU issues or processes of transnational party collaboration.

TABLE 4.3

Previous political experience of members of the PES and the EPP (%)

	PES	EPP
Government Minister	12.0	10.6
National Parliament	25.5	30.2
Local/Regional Government	42.0	30.8
Party Office	22.9	21.4
No previous political experience declared	20.9	21.4

Source: European Parliament (1994a). Please note that the reliability of the figutes in this table depends upon MEPs providing the European Parliament with an accurate and full account of their previous political experience.

The recruitment of MEPs

The manner in which national political parties recruit candidate
MEPs varies according to the national electoral system. Most member states are single constituencies for the purposes of EP elections.
Proportional representation (PR) is used to count the votes and the
electorate choose candidates from party lists. Party list systems often
give national parties a considerable political hold over existing and
aspirant MEPs. Quite as important as the decision about who is going
to be on the list in the first place is the power to determine the order
in which the party offers candidates to the electorate. Politicians
compete for a top position in the hit parade as a matter of both
personal prestige and political survival. In their role as selectors,
national parties, nonetheless, vary between centralised and partici-
patory decision-making; and between monopolising representation in
the European Parliament for a particular strand of opinion within the
party and attempting a more balanced ticket of inner-party life.
Many even go further and supplement the list with respected non-
party figures, in order to boost credibility and make claims to be
broadly representative of the professions in particular and domestic
society in general. Thus, although Forza Italia (27 members) in the
1994–9 parliament, includes the former head of Berlusconi's publish-
ing group, the president of his football club, the former director-
general of his finance group and his press spokesman, it is more than a
clientelist group (European Parliament, 1994a). To achieve electoral
credibility it also needed to include figures with professional and
political status in their own right. The range of selection styles is
neatly illustrated by contributions to Juliet Lodge's study of the 1994
European elections. Take the examples of the parties in Greece and
the French Parti Socialiste (PS).

> In the case of PASOK, ND and POLA, candidate selection
> remained firmly in the hands of their leaders, reflecting the lack of
> intra-party democracy. In contrast, the Synaspismos balloted all its
> members . . . The KKE's list was apparently drawn up by the
> Central Committee from proposals by the party base. (Verney and
> Featherstone in Lodge, 1996)

The main consideration for the PS in drawing up its list was fairly
to represent the courants (organised party factions). Rocard could

have tried to override the courants and present a party list which represented a new departure for the party, focused upon Europe and representing an 'opening out' to the centrist voters. But overriding the courants was felt to be too damaging to internal unity. (Gaffney in Lodge, 1996)

By contrast, Belgian, British, Irish and Italian MEPs are less likely to be beholden to a national party leadership, and more likely to be concerned with local or regional party sentiments. The UK is the only country with a single-member constituency system, while Ireland has four multi-member constituencies and Belgium and Italy have regional party lists. To the extent that local or regional parties are less well placed than national party leaderships to organise themselves to influence the EP, it is a fair surmise that the more decentralised they are within the domestic arena, the looser will be the constraint of national parties on MEPs and possibilities for transnational party politics in the EP. The UK provides an interesting example. Not only do local parties have few political resources – mainly of information – to keep track of MEPs, they are also faced by a problem of coordination. This is because they are grouped for the purposes of selecting MEPs into giant districts that straddle seven or eight Westminster constituencies, which form the real-life worlds of domestic political organisation in the UK. Even amongst countries that run nationally centralised list systems there are, however, important institutional differences in the extent to which this gives established domestic parties a stranglehold on the selection of the EP, and the subsequent autonomy of its members: first, between those countries where voters are able to alter the order in which candidates appear on the list (Belgium, Denmark, Italy, Luxembourg and the Netherlands) and those where they are not (France, Germany, Greece, Portugal and Spain); second, between those countries that only allow nominations from political parties or other organisations (Denmark, Germany, Greece and the Netherlands) and those (France and Italy) where independent lists are both permitted and sometimes successful (European Parliament, 1994b).

Two of the weaknesses of the EP are the remarkably high turnover of MEPs and absenteeism from plenary sessions. In 1990, Corbett *et al.* calculated the average political life span of an MEP at just three and a half years. Dependence on national parties – and the fact that the EP party groups lack recruitment structures of their own – go some way to explain the very high turnover of MEPs between elections. Some have seen this as a serious constraint on the institutionalisation of the party groups, limiting the growth of stable and experienced parliamentary parties at the European level, making the evolution of the EP more disjointed than it needs to be from one parliament to another, and burdening its groups with MEPs whose sights are never removed from national politics (Westlake, 1994a). For example, a study of French MEPs found that they rarely regard the EP as a career in itself, and that, depending on their age, they variously view it as a nursery school, convalescence ward or retirement home from national politics (Andolfato, 1994). A further problem is that in several countries, the readoption of sitting MEPs may take second place to the payment of domestic political debts, the balancing of party factions and attempts to raise the profile of the list by including senior national politicians, professional leaders and media 'celebrities'. This inevitably increases turnover in the EP. In France and Italy it is common for party leaders to head up their lists, although they will often only take up their seats and attend assiduously if the outcome of the election costs them their domestic party leadership! In France, Ireland, Italy and the UK (Northern Ireland) party selection policies have a tendency to produce MEPs with dual mandates in the EP and national assemblies: even triple mandates if mayoralties and seats on local councils are included. Although membership of more than one parliament seems to be diminishing, there is a pervasive tendency across many other member states for MEPs to retain some foothold in either local and regional government or the national party apparatus, rather than give undivided attention to the EP. That said, individual party groups differ significantly in the degree to which they suffer from high turnover and instability of composition. By comparing the number of MEPs from each group who had some experience of the European Parliament before the 1994 elections with the average for the EP as a whole, Figure 4.1 shows that in terms of personnel the larger groups have had more success than the smaller in ensuring a continuity in their development as parliamentary parties. National parties would seem to have some responsibility for the unstable and sometimes distracted membership of the EP. For a start, they recruit on the basis of very different expectations of how a spell in the EP should fit into an overall political career.

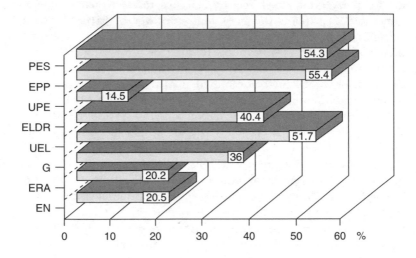

FIGURE 4.2   The proportion of MEPs from each group with service in the EP before 1994

The party politics of election to the EP: the problem of 'second-order' elections

European elections are often said to be second-order in character (Reif and Schmitt, 1980). This means that most electors consider the European political arena to be less important than the national one and that they, accordingly, use their votes in EP elections to express feelings of satisfaction or dissatisfaction with domestic parties or to bring about political change in their own country. Amongst the implications of this hypothesis are the following:

- European elections are not primarily about the institution that is, in fact, being elected: the EP. Campaigns will be dominated by national issues.
- The results of European elections will be governed by the domestic political cycle and not by anything that is happening in EU politics. If Euro-elections are held close to general elections, parties of government will stand a better chance, for they will either be in a honeymoon period of renewed domestic authority, or their core supporters will be reluctant to wound them in the

run-up to a national poll. If, on the other hand, Euro-elections fall in the middle of a national parliamentary term, parties of government will usually suffer from high protest votes.

- As a consequence of the last point, parties of opposition and small parties will tend to do well in European elections.
- Participation in European elections will, on average, be lower than that in national elections, as voters are less motivated to turn out.

Important consequences for the party politics of the EP follow from the weakness of the relationship between what MEPs actually do there and their chances of reelection. Most obviously, it attenuates the political responsibility of MEPs to the electorate as a whole, and deepens their dependence on national parties as selectorates. On the other hand, the second-order pattern both facilitates the construction and operation of transnational party groups in the EP and detracts from any successes in this regard. Cohesion is easier to achieve where elite-level agreements in the EP are unlikely to affect the electoral chances of any national party, even in Euro-elections. Yet, in a sense, the capacity of the EP groups to build a transnational consensus – and sustain it across the several issues that make up a parliamentary term – will not really be tested until this involves the allocation of real electoral costs and risks between national parties.

One obvious question to ask is why political parties do not do more to break the second-order pattern of European elections, most obviously by organising themselves on a more European basis and making their transnational links more explicit. The probable answer is that the second-order pattern has a certain self-perpetuating logic. The irony of European elections is that while they have had only limited effects on the political development of the Union itself, they have had the unintended consequence of reducing predictability and increasing risk in the real heartland of political parties: the national arena. By agreeing to European elections – and by deciding to organise them around the member states – governments inadvertently gave their publics an added opportunity to comment on their mid-term performance. The fact that these are nationwide elections – in most cases the only nationwide polls between general elections – makes it impossible to dismiss popular verdicts too lightly. On the other hand, the absence of a direct threat of a change of power at national level means that governments submit themselves to public judgements that are more than usually volatile. In the four European elections since 1979, outcomes have affected changes of government, cabinets and party leaderships. They have also influenced the entry of new parties to the field of serious political contestation and even limited realignments of national parties. The 1984 election was crucial to the rise of the Front National in France, incidentally as much through the public platform provided by representation in the EP as through the momentum created in domestic politics (Marcus, 1995).

Against such a background, domestic parties have little choice but to compete for as many votes as they can secure. This means that they must field candidates under national party labels that have 'name recognition' and benefit from high levels of inertial or habitual voting; and also that they have to campaign on the issues that are most likely to govern voter choice, which opinion surveys repeatedly show to be mainly national in character. Yet with each European election that is fought on domestic lines, the political parties miss opportunities to aid the development of a 'European public opinion' or a 'European public arena'. There is little evidence, therefore, of what David Held calls a 'developmental democracy', in which each election improves the public's understanding of how the EU's political system works, so enrichening the possibilities for public debate over time (Held, 1987) . This is a shame, because the creation of a demos is a far more demanding task in a transnational political system than in a national one.

The European elections in 1994: an example

Hermann Schmitt and Karlheinz Reif developed the second-order model in response to the first European elections in 1979. However, those elections were for a Parliament that had very few powers. By the time of the 1994 elections there were reasons to expect both voters and parties to treat Euro-elections as more important in their own right. The SEA and Maastricht Treaties had greatly extended the general competencies of the Union and the powers of the EP in particular. In addition to being able to amend legislation (cooperation procedure) or reject it altogether (co- decision), any Parliament elected in 1994 would, for the first time, have the power to confirm the new Commission and its President in office. As the EP gained important new powers, and the role of national vetoes was restricted, a seat on the Council of Ministers would no longer be enough to shape or block the outputs of the Union, even for those political parties whose representatives enjoyed the privilege. By 1994 the public was also more aware of the EU as an institutional framework, whose decisions would shape the distribution of gains and losses for different social groups and countries. In the months running up to the 1994 Euro-elections, the major questions of European integration had burst out of the cosy confines of elite politics to become politicised in the mass arena as never before, and the Maastricht ratification process was widely interpreted as signalling the end of a permissive consensus in which elites would be left to use their own judgement to determine the policies of the Union. With political parties that had greater incentive to compete for seats in the EP, and a public that seemed to be more ready for mobilisation around European issues, the stage appeared to be set for an election that would show some significant departures from the second-order model. Yet this happened only to a very limited degree in the 1994 elections and such change as did occur was differentiated in its impact across national arenas.

- Party federations corresponding to around four-fifths of the total vote (PES, EPP, ELDR and Greens) managed to produce common manifestos and agree elements of a coordinated campaign strategy. Although scarcely precise commitments, the manifestos did state broad policy priorities and they probably did amount to a more differentiated and therefore meaningful set of choices than in previous campaigns (Lécureuil in Lodge, 1996). They were also treated as more binding than before. Whereas in 1989 the PES had only agreed a manifesto by permitting opt-out clauses for particular national parties, the 1994 manifesto was agreed with only one 'footnote' (Smith in Gaffney, 1996, p. 279).
- The firming up of manifestos at the European level was not, however, matched by any significant increase in the use of transnationally agreed programmes in actual political campaigning and debate. On the other hand, Martin Westlake's observation that most Euro-campaigns have one or two common themes that transcend national boundaries probably did continue to hold for the 1994 election (Westlake, 1994b, p. 99). In 1984, the installation of Cruise and Pershing nuclear weapons played this role; in 1989, environmental issues; and in 1994, problems of unemployment.

- Some national parties were more willing than before to differentiate themselves on issues of European integration, indicating that they did see some value in competing on EU questions. Nonetheless, such 'Euro-debates' as there were took two distinctive forms: in some countries, they were concerned with issues of supranational versus intergovernmental integration; and, in others, with left–right problems. Amongst examples of the first, the British Conservatives calculated that they could improve on their opinion poll performance by portraying the Labour Party as 'federalist'; in Portugal, the Christian Democrats saw that there was a constituency of anti-Maastricht opinion that was not adequately represented in the largest two parties – the PS and PSD; and in Italy, the Alleanza Nationale, and elements of Forza Italia, realised that the very solidity of the postwar elite consensus for European integration left a gap in the political market-place for a more 'Gaullist' appeal to national identity. On the other hand, in the Netherlands the parties had a debate of a more 'left–right' kind about the modalities for EU internal and external security policies (Van Deelen in Lodge, 1996).
- In a handful of countries, there were even increased opportunities to vote for political groupings that were specifically organised around the issue of European integration. However, it is difficult to hail this as the first sign of the EU developing parties of its own. First, the new groupings were confined to the Euro-sceptic end of the spectrum, and they cannot, accordingly, be seen as committed to the development of the EU's political system. James Goldsmith's Autre Europe won 12.33 per cent of the vote in France and the Danes were even spoiled with the choice of two Euro-sceptic parties: the People's movement that campaigned to leave the EU altogether and the June movement which merely opposed the Maastricht Treaty. Second, the status of these actors as political parties, as opposed to ephemeral single-issue protest movements, is open to question. Although it is not completely impossible that a Euro-party system should begin with the rise of anti-system parties, or even anti-system protest movements, this is not the most plausible developmental path.
- Survey evidence continued to show that voters were mainly motivated by domestic considerations in their choice of parties. *Eurobarometer*, for example, found that even at the level of asking the public across the Union how people *ought* to vote in European elections, rather than how they *do* in fact vote, 55 per cent

continued to believe that national influences should predominate and only 37 per cent national ones (*Eurobarometer*, No. 41, July 1994). Actual voting behaviour continued to conform to the second-order model, with swings against national parties of government, small and protest parties doing well and participation dropping even from 1989 levels, in spite of Maastricht and the increased importance of the EP.

Although the second-order model is related to the key discontinuity in the EU's party system whereby voters are mobilised around national party attachments while their representatives serve in transnational groupings that are largely unknown to the public, there is one arguably more benign effect. The EP will tend to over-represent small parties and parties of opposition as a consequence of the sensitivity of the European elections to mid-term swings against governments and to 'experimental' voting for new and peripheral parties. At the beginning of the present parliament, for example, 61 per cent of MEPs came from national parties of opposition, and only 39 per cent from parties of government. This can be seen as a healthy – though entirely unintended consequence – of the decision to move to a directly elected EP in a context in which the EU is still treated as a 'second- order' political arena. If voting behaviour in Euro-elections casts some doubt on the extent to which the EP is representative of the public, it increases its capacity to function as a political forum for the parties of Western Europe. The EP gives a whole series of national parties, which would otherwise be totally excluded by the monopoly hold of parties of government on the Council of Ministers, access to an EU institution and to the political debate in the European arena, as well as limited influence on legislation and policy formulation. Moreover, the bias towards parties of opposition in the EP means that it is well-placed to function as a balance and check to the Council. Even if there are no government–opposition relations within the EP, they may exist to a limited degree *between* the Council and the EP.

Group formation, change and composition

Having examined the recruitment and election of the EP, we can now analyse the formation of its party groups. Voting by the public and parliamentary coalition formation are often separate processes in

West European politics. Only in first-past-the-post systems like the UK is there a near-automatic link between voter choice and the formation of parliamentary majorities. However, in most proportional systems with multi-party government, voters do usually know how the parties for which they are voting are likely to team up. Not only does this become an election issue in itself, the post- electoral coalition formation is transparent and widely understood, so any deceptions or unwise decisions can be subsequently sanctioned by the voters. In the case of the EP, however, the transnational party groups to which MEPs adhere once they have been elected under their national parties are almost completely unfamiliar to the public and their composition is rarely debated at election time. The names of the transnational party federations are not, for example, included on ballot papers alongside national party labels. This gives national parties a wide margin for manoeuvre in their choice of an EP party group. On the other hand, parliamentary coalition formation in the EP is for far more limited purposes than in national political arenas. Transnational party groups are not formed to support a government, or to organise opposition, still less to prepare for the mobilisation of votes in future elections. They are, in the main, coalitions formed between national parties to use the powers – and opportunities for political articulation – offered by the EP. As we will see, this can produce some surprising alignments, together with a generally more fluid pattern of majority formation than is common in national parliaments in Western Europe.

It might be supposed that a sufficient explanation for the composition of the party groups is that they simply bracket the national political parties of Western Europe into their preexisting political families – Christian Democrats, Conservatives, Communists, Greens, Liberals and Social Democrats – without changing any of the boundaries between these to allow for the fact that the EP and EU constitute a different political system to any found at the national level. This view would predict what political scientists would call an *exogenous* party system, in which parties – and their relative strengths – are defined outside the institutions they serve and without reference to the rules for exercising power there. In other words, once formed out of the *familles spirituelles*, the party groups in the European Parliament would be expected to remain fairly constant in composition, apart from perturbations caused by changes in the membership of the Union itself, or major realignments in domestic politics of member states, and entries or exits of whole parties from national party systems, the likes of which tend to only occur once in every two or three generations in most West European countries. The exogenous character of the EP party system would also seem to be reinforced by the second-order nature of European elections. The tendency for voters only to vote on national criteria inhibits the entry to European elections of entirely new Euro-parties, organised solely for the purposes of offering the voters alternative EU policy programmes or visions of European integration, and it means that the groups in the EP will not rise and fall at the ballot box on account of their performance in the Parliament itself. In terms of votes, the choice that a national party makes of an EP group is virtually cost-free, and it is only likely to be constrained by elite-level arguments about the party's position on European integration.

An alternative possibility is that the composition of the party groups is partially adjusted to the power structures of the European Union itself and its Parliament; that they are, in political science parlance, *endogenous*. The evidence would, in fact, seem to support two very interesting propositions:

- Until the mid-1980s, the party system in the EP was predominantly shaped by exogenous factors. However, it has more recently shown signs of endogenous development. Before the Single Act and Maastricht Treaties, it was only some of the smaller party groups that came under pressure to adapt their composition to the specific institutional contexts of the Union and the internal rules of the EP itself. Since then, even the larger players have had to contemplate groupings that have caused some surprises in terms of domestic politics and ideological alignments. Simultaneous extension in the competence of the Union and the powers of its Parliament has compelled national parties to reconsider whether their MEPs really are well-positioned to exercise significant influence in the EP. In the new institutional setting, the price of getting this wrong is loss of influence over a significant stage in the making of policies and laws that affect the domestic environment.

- On the other hand, the groups in the EP party system have come under different degrees of pressure to shift from an exogenous to a more endogenous pattern of development since 1986. While the PES still largely defines itself out of national parties from a single political family that has long existed outside the EU's own institutions (exogenous), the recent evolution of the other groups has often been governed by competitive forces and institutional rules specific to the EU and EP (endogenous). Even amongst these others, the analysis which follows will show that the motives and dynamics that govern group formation and composition in the EP vary across the three categories of large, medium and small players.

The politics of large group formation and composition

By the 1994–9 parliament, only the PES remained close to an ideal of linear development. As seen, it has only had to incorporate all the preexisting Social Democratic parties of the European centre left to maintain its position as the largest group in all parliaments since 1979. As its Deputy Secretary-General has remarked, all members of the PES federation are expected to join its parliamentary group and, so far, this has been sufficient on its own to give the PES a lead over all rivals, without any need to search for additional allies or to rule on new applications (Authors' interview with PES official). The only possible exception was the inclusion of members from the Italian Party of Democratic Socialists (PDS) in 1989. With the discrediting of the Communist model, the Italian Communists, who had always been something of a race apart, changed their name to the Party of Democratic Socialists and gained admission to the PES federation, clearing the way for some of their MEPs to enter the group in the Parliament. Nonetheless, this has turned out to be part of a broader domestic realignment in Italian politics in which the PDS now finds itself as the main party of the centre left, some way removed from its Communist roots, and filling the space left by the discredited old Italian Socialist Party. In other words, the movement of the PDS into the PES can be explained by exogenous developments in the domestic political system of one member state and not primarily by the efforts of the group or the national party to maintain influence in the EU's political arena. Indeed, the PDS example illustrates the possibility that parties may, on the contrary, change group in the Parliament in order to improve their position in national politics, perhaps to gain the reputational benefits and governing credibility that are seen to go with transnational affiliations that are perceived as more respectable than others.

The EPP, on the other hand, increasingly resembles an amalgamation of two political families: the Christian Democrats, who were the original group members, and the Conservative parties of Western Europe, many of which have been progressively absorbed in the EPP since the 1980s (Jansen, 1995). The first development in this direction was the decision of the Greek New Democracy Party in 1983 to join the EPP, rather than the now defunct European Democratic Group (EDG). Pre-dating the Single Act as this did, it was a move that showed that endogenous patterns of party system development in the EP can be conditioned by alignment possibilities within and between the groups, and not just by the rules for exercising parliamentary powers. Whilst the EDG was at the time made up only of British and Danish Conservatives, who were too geographically remote from Greece to be a profitable source of partisan alliance, membership of the EPP gave New Democracy access to a close relationship with the Italian Christian Democrats. This would be used in years to come to defend southern and agricultural perspectives at the heart of one of the largest two groups in the Parliament (Authors' interview with Greek MEP).

Between 1989 and 1992, the EPP would progressively absorb the EDG, taking in, first, the Spanish Partido Popular (1989), and then the British and Danish Conservatives in 1992. And when, in 1995, the EU was again enlarged, Swedish and Finnish Conservative parties that might otherwise have joined a more overtly Conservative group also joined the EPP. The EPP group is now more or less evenly divided between MEPs that originate from the two families. This whole process has been facilitated by a general convergence of the Christian Democratic and Conservative parties of Western Europe in domestic political arenas. During the 1980s, Christian Democrats moved to the right on the choice between market solutions and state intervention. They also became more secular in character. Meanwhile members of both political traditions increasingly resembled catch-all parties, mainly interested in a centrist political positioning that would maximise votes and opportunities to participate in government. Nonetheless, for both Christian Democrats and Conservatives, amalgamation in the EPP has also been conditioned by new institutional rules and pressures to compete within the EU's own institutional system. In fact, without such competitive and institutional pressures, the EU would, in many ways, have been an unnatural arena in which to begin a convergence between the two centre-right families. For, whereas these are increasingly alike at the domestic level, at the European they are divided by the traditional enthusiasm of many Christian Democrats for integration and the value many Conservatives place on national identity and domestic self-governance.

A pattern whereby Social Democrats constitute the largest party of the centre left in most member states, while this status is enjoyed in some countries by Christian Democrats and in others by Conservatives, made it almost inevitable that the EPP would peak in the original 'Europe of the Six' and decline thereafter. For, as seen earlier, the distinction between countries that were a part of the first wave of European integration and those which joined after 1973 is largely coextensive with that between states where the centre right has been dominated by Christian Democrats (early members) or Conservatives (late-comers). The decision of most incoming Conservative parties to form their own group, the EDG, meant that the EPP gained only the Irish Fine Gael and Greek New Democracy, in spite of three enlargements and the adhesion of six new states between 1973 and 1987. Meanwhile, the PES was swollen by the British Labour Party, the Irish Labour Party, the Danish Social Democrats and the Greek, Spanish and Portuguese Socialists. This put the EPP under various competitive pressures in the EP. On the one hand, it faced the prospect of becoming a junior rather than an equal partner in the PES/EPP duopoly, its influence not only reduced by failure in the numbers game, but also by the fact that an exclusively Christian Democratic group was condemned to cover a declining proportion of the states in a steadily widening Union, with consequent damage to its claims to be a fully transnational group, representative of the EU as a whole (Authors' interview with EPP official). On the other hand, there was a rather less defined risk that the EPP could even be challenged for second position in the Parliament by another grouping on the centre right. There was talk, from time to time, of the Gaullists joining the UDF in the ELDR, or of the ELDR lining up with the EDG on issues of market liberalisation.

Just as it looked as though a balanced PES/EPP relationship was becoming increasingly problematic, the Single Act and Maastricht changed the rules in a manner that made it more important for many in the EPP that it should be sustained. As mentioned throughout this book, the combination between the extension of the powers of the EP under these treaty changes, and the introduction of a requirement that most powers could only be exercised on an absolute majority of the Parliament's members, and not just of those voting (the absolute majority rule), proved a powerful catalyst to the development of the EP's party system. The PES and EPP have been most directly affected because the absolute majority rule has promoted the party political concentration of the EP by increasing the costs of exclusion from the large groups and providing an incentive for the PES and EPP to expand if they are to maintain their ability to mobilise the absolute majorities that were now needed for the 'big two' to exercise the powers of the Parliament without too much need for outside help. With the introduction of the absolute majority rule, even a 20 per cent level of absenteeism required the PES and EPP to raise their joint membership to 61 per cent of the EP, and a more typical absenteeism of 30 per cent meant that the PES and EPP needed 66.5 per cent of the Parliament to win votes on their own. By contrast, their joint membership in the mid-1980s was only 55 per cent. Indeed, to many in the EPP, the relationship with the PES was not just a matter of self-interest – it was synonymous with the development of an effective EP, and thus a valued part of the overall political construction of the Union. Conversely, the worst possible outcome for the EU's Conservative parties was that the PES/EPP duopoly might just hold, but with the EPP as the weaker partner. This would mean both the continued marginalisation of the EDG parties and that laws and policies would emerge from the Union's institutional complex with a more leftward bias than would have been the case with a broader grouping of the centre right in the Parliament.

Various things may follow from these important changes in the EPP. The group has had to move to the right in order to accommodate Conservative parties and, although its internal cohesion has so far held up remarkably well, it now in effect has three different types of member: traditional Christian Democrat parties; Conservative parties that have joined the EPP party federation; and those that have only joined the parliamentary arm of the EPP. As we will see, the difference between the last two is that those which have not joined the EPP federation do not obtain automatic entry to the parliamentary group. They have to apply to be reaccepted with each new term of the EP. Moreover, the issue of European integration is itself a potential fissure between the three types of party. In addition to the long-standing Christian Democrat/Conservative difference on European integration, Conservative parties which are willing to sign up to the EPP federation are often separated from those who are not by their ability to accept the supranational character of the latter's statute. Both of these factors – the rightward shift and the greater internal heterogeneity of the contemporary EPP – may also affect the functioning of the PES/EPP relationship. Some in the PES have

responded to the Christian Democrat/Conservative merger by signalling that a rightward shift of the EPP must not be allowed to go too
far, for although a grand coalition of the left would be problematic for
the reasons stated below, the PES does possess an option of going it
alone to a degree that the EPP does not (Jansen, 1995). The success of
the opening of the EPP to the Conservative parties may depend upon
the incremental pattern that it has so far shown: the Conservative
parties have only been admitted in ones and twos, largely on terms
acceptable to the original EPP parties and in a manner that has not
upset the embedded assumptions of the PES/EPP partnership.

An example of large group formation: the PES and EPP in 1994

Once the results of the 1994 elections were complete on 13 June 1994,
it was clear that the PES would be well ahead of the EPP in terms of
MEPs who would automatically become a part of the parliamentary
group because their parent national parties belonged to the relevant
federation. Thus, once again, the PES largely defined itself, while
providing a competitive benchmark to which the rest had to respond.
There were two ways in which the PES might have expanded beyond
its core membership: the one presented by the election of several allies
of the French socialists under a list organised by the French business-
man, Bernard Tapie; the other caused by the possible preference of
some Greens – such as the Italian Carlo Ripa de Meana – for
membership of a broad group of the left, rather than a group
specifically devoted to ecological politics. However, Tapie was under
investigation by French magistrates and it seemed better for the PES
to embark on the 1994–9 parliament with the bargaining advantage
of being the one large group that was able to choose on a case-by-case
basis between the EPP/PES duopoly and a coalition confined to its
own side of the political spectrum than to risk the contention within
its own ranks that would have flowed from an attempt to make a
preference for one of these two strategies explicit.

By contrast, the EPP needed to make up its numbers and, ideally,
to form a group that covered all member states. There were, therefore, no fewer than four areas of uncertainty as to its composition in
the 1994–9 parliament: first was the issue of whether the British and
Danish Conservatives would once again be allowed to associate with
the EPP as they had done from 1992–4; second was the question of
whether the entire French mainstream right would enter just one
group, as RPR and UDF voters had been promised when these

parties had run on a single list and, if so, whether that group would be the EPP; third was the problem of what to do with Forza Italia, which was now the dominant party of the Italian right, displacing one of the old mainstays of EPP strength, the Italian Christian Democrats; fourth was the temptation to include the Portuguese Social Democrats, in order to guarantee at least one party from all member states. Cumulatively this added up to a substantial definitional ambiguity on the part of the EPP because it meant that the group could have anything between 130 and 200 members for the start of the new Parliament. It is worth studying the cases in some detail because they tell us a great deal about the considerations that lie behind decisions on group composition.

When the British Conservatives became associate members of the EPP in 1992, they were eager to end their isolation from the European centre right and assert a position at the heart of Europe. There must have been some prospect at the time that the party would move on to full membership of the EPP Federation. However, this was blocked over the coming months by the rise of the Euro-sceptic right and, as long as the Conservatives continue to remain in this rather anomolous position, they will be constrained to reapply for membership of the EPP group with each new European Parliament. There was some speculation that they would be excluded in June 1994 on account of the anti-European tone of some of the party's campaigning and John Major's veto of Jean-Luc Dehaene who was considered the EPP candidate for the presidency of the Commission. Conversely, there were many Euro-sceptics who would probably have preferred Conservative MEPs to keep their distance from the EPP. It is significant, however, that neither of these positions merited serious consideration. The EPP, for its part, needed the 18 votes of the British Conservatives and without their participation it faced the prospect that the UK would only be represented in the group by the Ulster Unionist member. It was, in addition, quick to distinguish between Conservative MEPs and their domestic party. Over the previous two years, the former had been assiduous contributors to the EPP with a good voting record both in plenaries and committees. In addition to representing the more Euro-enthusiastic wing of their party, their collaboration with the EPP was facilitated by a sympathy of views on left–right issues, with the result that the British Conservatives had only fallen out with the group on one occasion in the last two years (Interview with EPP official). The Conservatives for their part were too small to form a group on their own and options such as going in with the French Gaullists or Forza Italia would be either politically embarrassing or even less appropriate on a left–right basis than staying with the EPP. It would, in any case, have left the PES and EPP in continued control of the Parliament and would have thrust the British Conservatives back into a condition of continued isolation from the main power axis in the EP, from which its MEPs had tried for so many years to escape. Indeed, there was a risk of dividing the national delegation, with some choosing to remain with the EPP as individual members.

The politics of group formation and composition amongst middle-sized groups

The last section showed that in all four parliaments since 1979 incorporation into the PES and EPP has remained the dominant strategy for national parties seeking to organise themselves so that they can best influence the powers of the EP. However, not all parties that share this objective can gain – or want to gain – entry to the two largest groups. As many of these are serious parties of government in the national arena, membership of one of the small groups on the peripheries of the EP is not a very satisfying option either. By joining a middle-sized group, they can, on the other hand, pursue one of two strategies: they can either join a group that will be well-placed to make up the numbers of the PES/EPP duopoly on the comparatively frequent occasions that this is unable to mobilise absolute majorities on its own; or, conversely, they can reduce the uncertainties and simplify the logistics of organising majorities based mainly on the left or the right of the Parliament, thus tempting either the PES or the EPP to consider an occasional alternative to the 'grand coalitions' of the political centre that characterise most EP votes. The recent histories of the ELDR and the UPE shows how the increased concentration of the EP around the PES and EPP since the 1980s has compelled others to make competitive responses, with the ELDR, arguably, exemplifying the first of our strategies for achieving influence as a middle-sized group, and the UPE the second.

From the seat figures in Table 6.7 on page 160, it can be seen that the Christian Democrat/Conservative merger has taken the PES/EPP combine from a 50–60 per cent hold on the EP in the 1980s to a 60–70 per cent share in the 1990s. Not only has the position of the ELDR remained stationary at around 8–10 per cent, it has lost some members and been threatened with the haemorrhaging of others as particular national parties have become restless with the group's marginalisation. However, the group has continued to position itself in the EP's mainstream and, as we will see in the next chapter it has voted with the PES and EPP even more frequently than those purported duopolists have voted with one another. In order to maintain its bargaining leverage with the big two, the ELDR has obviously been eager to staunch the decline in its seat share. This has, in turn, required it to look outside the classic liberal tradition for new members. In the 1989–94 parliament it included the Spanish CDS, and in the 1994–9 parliament it has the Italian Lega Nord and two Catalan MEPs in its midst. Although developments such as these threaten to make the group heterogeneous in almost all political dimensions – adding regionalist–nationalist and conservative–radical tensions to the group, and even providing it with a Euro-sceptic tinge – the ELDR enjoys a certain persistence. In 1991, it was even able to survive an attempt by its own leader, former French President, Valéry Giscard d'Estaing, to absorb the whole group into the EPP (Authors' interview with ELDR official). This initiative failed, in part, because many in the ELDR continued to see the EPP as having clericist antecedents, which conflict with their own secular interpretations of centrist politics. But the idea that the ELDR could move *en bloc* into another group was, anyway, misconceived, for many of its members feel closer to the EPP on some issues and to the PES on others. Paradoxically, this creates an inertia that holds the ELDR together. The group may also be sustained by a micawberish hope that something will turn up to improve its fortunes. The position of the ELDR would, for example, be improved by the introduction of the uniform electoral law for the EP stipulated in the Maastricht Treaty. The ELDR is highly exposed to the idiosyncrasies of national electoral law. Because of the first- past-the-post system in the UK, it receives next to no representation for what is, in fact, the largest Liberal Party in Western Europe, while the 5 per cent electoral threshold in Germany means that the FDP has tended to contribute seats to some European parliaments but not to others. Against this, some recent exogenous political trends have benefited the group. It has, in particular, profited from the strengthening of Liberal parties in Belgium and the Netherlands in reaction to the consociational models of politics that have kept Christian Democrats and Socialists in near-permanent government in those countries. The ELDR has also profited from Scandinavian enlargement. Both the EPP and the ELDR have also shown that there are limits to which they are prepared to enlarge just for the sake of maximising numerical strength. For several years, the Benelux Christian Democrats held up the admission of Conservatives to the EPP and, as will be seen, both groups have more recently refused entry to Forza Italia, in the ELDR's case at the instigation of the more left-wing of the Dutch Liberal parties.

The groups formed at the beginning of the 1994–9 parliament remained unchanged for just one year. In July 1995, Forza Europa merged with the RDE to create the new UPE group. This was particularly significant from the point of view of the distinction between endogenous and exogenous party system development. Forza Europa and the RDE were in some ways unlikely allies in terms of their political preferences. Although both were clearly of the right, Forza had, in accordance with the integrationist biases of Italian politics, called for a shift in powers from the Council to the Parliament, a position that was unlikely to be popular with the Gaullists who formed the bulk of the RDE group. During the months in which it had formed a group of its own, Forza had if anything tended to vote more frequently with the EPP and the ELDR than the RDE with which it now proposed to team up. Yet in terms of the structure of EP party politics, rather than the policy preferences of the two groups, the new alliance made sense. By merging, Forza and the RDE transformed themselves from two marginal groups – the first of which was fighting for its survival, as it only just had enough MEPs to form a single country group – into the third largest combination in the Parliament. Indeed, attendance rates of Forza and RDE MEPs in Strasbourg plenaries of only 35 and 40 per cent respectively (see Table 5.2 on page 135) suggested that, prior to merger, these groups were not very optimistic about their chances of affecting the decisions of the EP. In addition, one thing that many of their members had in common was that they were victims of various blockages to the consolidation of the mainstream right in the EP. By summer 1995, Forza Italia had been turned down by both the EPP and the ELDR. Many Gaullists felt torn between recognition of the need for a broad party group of the mainstream right to match the strength of the PES in the EP and what they considered to be the very constraining entry conditions to the EPP. Fianna Fail, the second largest party in the RDE, was prevented from joining the EPP by the prior membership of that group of its main domestic rival, Fine Gael. In this connection, it is significant that the formation of the UPE was accompanied by suggestions that other groups should reflect on the overall organisation of the right in the EP, hints that could be interpreted at various levels: as encouraging the EPP – and even the ELDR – to give more frequent and serious consideration to voting coalitions to their right and rather less to alignments with the PES; and even as enticing some of the more right-wing national parties in the EPP and ELDR to consider defection (*Agence Europe*, 7 July 1995).

The politics of small group formation and composition

Even the composition of the smaller groups reflects the rules and politics of the EP itself. The most obvious reason for this is that the EP prescribes minimum thresholds for group formation, currently 29 if all MEPs come from just one member state, 23 if they come from two states, 17 if they come from three and 14 if they come from four. Unless they can form themselves into groups, MEPs find themselves at a serious disadvantage. Funding and staffing are less generous and, though they do receive speaking time in the plenary, it is rare for them to be allocated committee rapporteurships, which provide MEPs with their principal opportunity for policy formulation. Nor do unattached MEPs have voting rights in the Conference of Presidents, which has an important agenda-setting function in the EP (Corbett *et al.*, pp. 84–6). For these reasons, the minimum thresholds, which are irrelevant to the larger actors in the EP, play a critical role in the formation and composition of the smaller groups. Indeed, the group dynamics of the smaller EP groups are sufficiently distinctive to require their own analysis:

● The small groups are both different amongst themselves, and collectively distinguishable from the large, in the way in which they respond to structural incentives for group formation. The small groups are too marginal to the organisation of the absolute majorities needed for the exercise of parliamentary powers for this to be a significant factor in their formation and composition. In any case, several small groups contain 'anti-system' elements, who are comparatively indifferent to the effective functioning of the EU and EP. In the present parliament, the EN is probably the most 'anti-system' of the groups, with both the UEL and the Greens containing ambivalent national parties, with a potential for both hostility and enthusiasm towards integration. The more marginal groups are to the overall functioning and coalitional structure of the EP, and the less they constitute ideological communities in their own right, the more they are reducible to temporary alliances of convenience to satisfy the EP's own rules for finance and staffing. As it happens, the next point will show that almost all of the small groups contain an element of this problem.

• The small groups often consist of a core that can be identified with a coherent political family, together with a few other MEPs who could quite easily belong elsewhere. These 'extras' will be important beyond their numerical strength, where they hold the whole survival of the group in their hands. Before merging with the RDE, Forza Europa only survived an increase in the minimum threshold for the formation of a single country group by luring an Italian Social Democrat and a defector from Lega Nord (ELDR) into its ranks. Over the last two parliaments, a handful of MEPs have found both the Green group proper and the far left group of the EP to be interchangeable political homes. In the present parliament, the Mouvement Radicale Gauche (MRG), which is an ally of the Parti Socialiste in French domestic politics, has formed a marriage of convenience with a handful of regionalists, who would otherwise have to distribute themselves amongst the main groups (on a left–right basis which would constrain their ability to articulate a regionalist perspective) or accept an unattached status. Nor would the anti-integrationist EN exist if it were not for two Dutch Calvinist MEPs, whom Corbett *et al.* wisely distinguish from the rest of the group on the grounds that their 'inspiration . . . is primarily religious rather than nationalist' (Corbett *et al.*, 1995, p. 84).

The small groups have a far more precarious existence than the large. They are far more exposed to the dangers of disappearing during the course of a parliament or of failing to reconstitute themselves at the beginning of a new parliamentary term. While the second-order character of European elections boosts the overall total of MEPs that belong to the small groups, it also destabilises their composition. The national parties that benefit from protest votes seem to change from one European election to another. Thus the prospects of forming a far right group in the 1994–9 parliament were reduced by the failure of the Republikaner to pass the 5 per cent threshold needed for representation in Germany, while the core of the Green group changed from the French to the German party, as the former, which had held 8 seats between 1989 and 1994, failed to win a single MEP in 1994. In between elections, the small groups are exposed to a series of vulnerabilities on account of the often arbitrary character of their boundaries, low structural incentives to cohere and the attractions of moving to a larger group to gain more influence. For these reasons, they may find it difficult to contain clashes of personality or ideology, or to survive a change in the domestic political costs and benefits that national delegations gain from the choice of one transnational affiliation over another. The turbulent histories of the far left and far right of the EP provide excellent examples. According to Corbett *et al.*, the fissure between revisionist and orthodox communism meant that the Communist group was scarcely on speaking terms and rarely met during the 1984–9 parliament. After 1989, it split into two groups, but the more moderate was dissolved when the Italian PDS joined the PES in 1992. When a single far left group was reconstituted in 1994, it included MEPs from national parties that differed significantly in the extent to which they wanted to disown the communist legacy. Indeed, a far left group was only formed at all after some prevarication as to whether the largest national party – the Spanish Izquierda Unida – should join the Greens or the new UEL. (Corbett *et al.*, 1994, pp. 77–9). Meanwhile, on the far right, the idea of transnational co-operation between nationalist parties proved predictably problematic. Following its success in France in the 1980s, the Front National linked up with the Italian MSI and the Flemish Nationalists, Vlaams Blok, in the 1984–9 Parliament. However, the election of the Republikaner in 1989 led to a spat in which the German far right accused the Italians of repressing the German minority in the South Tyrol, and the Italians accused the Germans of exploiting guest workers from their country. The far right group was, consequently, formed without the Italians, only to find that half of the Germans left in 1992, when their leader complained that the FN and Jean-Marie Le Pen were too racist for his tastes. Cast adrift from the EP group, the Italian party was, in the meantime, entirely free to concentrate on recycling itself at the domestic level as a respectable 'post-fascist' party, under the changed name of Alleanza Nationale (AN). By the time the German Republikaner lost all of its representation in the 1994–9 Parliament, the Italians were no longer available for an alliance with the rest of the far right and that political family, accordingly, failed to form a group at all (Marcus, 1995; Ficschi, Shields and Woods in Gaffney, 1996).

Concluding observations on group formation and composition

To conclude, the group structure in the EP in part reflects the natural distribution of public opinion between the political families of Western Europe. However, the groups have also had to adapt their composition to two institutional rules, specific to the Union itself: first, to the absolute majority rule, which encourages political concentration amongst those who consider themselves to be at the centre of the EP's party system; and, second, to the Parliament's own minimum criteria for group formation that require up to 29 MEPs to get together if they are to gain the benefits of funding, staffing and an assured place in the procedures of the Parliament. The second rule, in effect, represents a barrier to entry to the Parliament's party system equal to 3–4 per cent of the pan-Union vote. Not only is this a level around which several small political movements in Western Europe hover rather uneasily – the Greens, Regionalists, extreme right and radical left – it will also often be the case that protest or surge parties encouraged by second-order Euro-elections will be too specific to domestic political arenas to be easily combinable in the European. All of this will contribute to the somewhat contingent and ephemeral character of the smaller groups. However, we have also noticed one crucial difference between the core groups: of the large groups, only the PES has been able to resist the move towards a more endogenous pattern of development. This is explained by factors that long pre-date the EU and EP, and, in particular, the manner in which the centre left is concentrated in just one party family, the Social Democrats, while the centre right is split between Christian Democrats and Conservatives. But although this pattern arose outside EU politics, it has provided a kind of competitive benchmark of centre-left strength in the EP to which the parties of the centre right have had to adjust, in order to maximise their influence over an increasingly significant source of public policy and law.

Conclusions

Some authors believed that direct elections to the EP, first held in 1979, could provide the institutional catalyst to greater party development at the European level (Pridham and Pridham, 1981). However, in practice, direct elections have tended to entrench the grip of national parties on the selection and election of the EP. If direct elections have had a positive effect on party development in the European arena it has been one of a distinctively paradoxical kind. Because national parties are unlikely to be punished for anything their representatives do in the EP (on account of the second-order character of European elections), MEPs have been free to concentrate on developing a structure of transnational party politics best suited to the development of an effective European Parliament, rather than the garnering of votes. The very failure of elections to catalyse Euro-parties at the mass level may well have been a condition of their successful development at the elite parliamentary level. This is not, however, out of line with previous historical experience of how political parties develop (Duverger, 1954).

If elections have been relatively unimportant in stimulating the development of the party groups in the EP, the configuration of the Parliament's powers has been vital. The secret of the catalyst provided by treaty changes since 1986 is that they simultaneously increased the powers of the EP *and* made those powers more difficult to exercise through the introduction of the absolute majority rule.

However, it was not inevitable that the party groups in the EP should have responded to changed power incentives by improving their capacity to organise themselves transnationally. Some member governments (the French and British) even seem to have believed that they had cunningly framed the Single Act to take back with one hand what they were giving with the other: that any strengthening of the party groups in the EP would fall short of what was required for the frequent mobilisation of absolute majorities and that many of the new powers conferred on the EP would, accordingly, not be used.

The foregoing underscores the developmental relationship between the powers of the Parliament and the effectiveness of its party groups: the parliamentarisation of the EU depends on the capacity of the groups to exercise the powers of the EP without diminishing the overall performance of the Union; on the other hand, transnational party activity would not seem to develop by spontaneous combustion and without the introduction of definite institutional incentives.

Strengthened transnational party activity in the EP is a recent and, therefore, comparatively untested development. But institutional changes since 1979 have tended to pull in different directions. Direct elections have consolidated the power of national parties over the recruitment of the EP, while changes to the powers of the Parliament itself have required MEPs to strive for higher levels of cohesion in transnational party groups. A major question for the future is how far arrangements that require MEPs to respond to the logics of two different party political environments – the national and the European – are functional and sustainable.

5

Party Groups in the European Parliament: Institutional Environment and Inner Workings

Even the observation that the EP groups have only developed as elite-level parliamentary parties, in so far as they have any of the characteristics of political parties at all, begs as many questions as it answers, for there is no uniform model of parliamentary politics in representative democracies. Some parliaments are primarily concerned with forming, supporting and opposing governments; others concentrate on legislative functions; and others still on providing a public forum for political debate. There could, in addition, be very good reasons for going about any one of these tasks in a different way in a developing, as opposed to a fully formed, political system, or in a transnational, rather than a national, setting. Each type of parliament may, in turn, require a different approach to party politics, with the implication that the performance of parliamentary parties can only be judged against the powers and functions that their institution calls upon them to exercise. This chapter will, accordingly, begin with a discussion of the powers of the EP, before exploring the inner workings and political behaviour of its party groups. This will, then, allow us to evaluate the performance of the groups as transnational parliamentary parties in the next chapter.

The party groups and the powers and functions of the EP

The powers of the EP over the Commission and Council of the EU

The EU does not replicate the normal practice in Western Europe of requiring a political leadership to command a parliamentary majority if it is to continue in office. Bearing in mind that the executive powers of the EU are distributed across the Commission, European Council, Council of Ministers and even the Secretariat of the Council, the EP has only very limited powers to authorise the Union's political leadership, or to bring it to account. The Council is, of course, formed in and accountable to national political arenas, while the appointment of the Commission is distributed between the member states. Since the Maastricht Treaty, the EP does, however, have the power to confirm the new Commission in office. In making arrangements for the first use of this power in 1994, the EP attempted to maximise its potential by unbundling it into a three-stage obstacle course stretched over several months: first, the European Council's nomination for the presidency of the Commission was confirmed by a vote of the plenary; then, in an obvious attempt to mimic US Senate hearings, nominated Commissioners were questioned by parliamentary committees corresponding to their expected portfolios; and only at the end of all this was a vote taken on the overall programme and composition of the incoming Commission (Hix and Lord, 1996). However, once confirmed, the Commission can only be removed before the expiry of its five-year term on a two-thirds vote of the EP. Moreover, in the event of the Commission being removed or failing to achieve parliamentary confirmation in the first place, it is not entirely clear what would happen, for the vital power of reappointment lies with the member governments, who could, conceivably, choose to reselect the same Commission. Likewise the principle of Commission collegiality, prized by many in the EP itself, means that the Commission can only be refused a vote of confirmation, or subsequently removed, as a whole. This obviously limits parliamentary authorisation and accountability to a 'take it or leave it' decision that precludes more discriminating choices over the composition and programme of the EU's political leadership.

On the other hand, the EP does have various powers to put the Commission and Council under pressure to explain and justify their policies in public. Questions – both written and oral – can be put to both bodies; the EP can require the Commission or Council to make statements; and the annual reports of the Commission – and the six-monthly programmes of each Council presidency – are presented for debate in the EP. The annual budget of the EU has to be 'discharged' by the EP after a report has been received from the Court of Auditors. The EP is also responsible for appointing an ombudsman to receive complaints about any of the other institutions, and, on occasions, it assumes the role of tribune by taking the Commission or Council to the European Court of Justice on what it considers to be a matter of public interest.

The EP: legislative and financial functions

The rationale for a parliamentary role in legislation is the paradigmatically party political one of ensuring that collective rule-making – which is 'sovereign, without exit, and often sanctionable' – is subject to the debate and scrutiny of those who represent contending societal values (Sartori, 1987). Without an input from the EP, the Union's law-making would be the preserve of a technocratic Commission and a Council that represents only some of the political parties of Western Europe. The only other form of interest intermediation would be that provided by lobbyists. Many of the laws that affect member states are now determined at the EU level and the EP and its party groups must, therefore, be considered a part of the process by which important public rules that govern West European societies are set. The EP must be consulted on all new drafts for legislation before they are forwarded from the Commission to the Council (consultation procedure); in many instances, it has the power to amend legislation (cooperation procedure) and, in some cases, it can reject it altogether (co decision procedure). In addition, the Maastricht Treaty gave the EP the right to initiate legislation for the first time, thereby breaking what had been a monopoly function of the Commission.

It is likewise common for executives to be accountable to elected assemblies for the way in which they tax and spend the voters' money. Rules requiring administrations to renew approval for their plans at frequent intervals have often been used by elected assemblies to lever up their powers and ensure that the process of government is only continued within a framework of broad parliamentary consent. Detailed influence over finance also, of course, confers powers over the allocation of political values and priorities. The EP has undergone an interesting evolution in the use of its financial powers, from an earlier period between 1979 and 1984 in which it twice exercised its right to reject the budget altogether on a two-thirds vote of its membership, to a more sophisticated phase in which its committees and party groups have developed the technical skills and political coordination necessary to negotiate detailed variations of individual budget lines with the Commission and Council. Martin Westlake's assessment is that 'the consensual approach of the inter-institutional agreement has proved more successful than Parliament's previously unilateral and essentially adversarial attempts to increase non-compulsory expenditure' (Westlake, 1994, p. 127).

EP powers over the EU's political development

As Wolfgang Wessels has observed, the evolving character of the EU means that the power to participate in 'system-developing decisions' is more significant than in more settled and fully formed national political arenas (Wessels, 1996). Such decisions concern the membership of the EU and the treaties that define its competencies and internal distribution of powers. One impact of the Single Act and Maastricht Treaty has been to extend the EP's role in deciding the membership and ground rules of the Union. The assent procedure means that all external treaties, associations and enlargements of the EU have to be approved by the EP. This assent procedure also applies to various internal matters, including important mile-posts in the institutionalisation of monetary union, arrangements for a uniform electoral procedure and for Union citizenship. As the EU is likely to be enlarged in several incremental stages, the assent procedure may provide the EP with important leverage in any compromise between the widening of the EU's membership and the deepening of its internal integration. The EP could, for example, press for any extension of majority voting associated with enlargement to be matched by a strengthening of parliamentary accountability at the European level. On the other hand, the EP has had considerable difficulty in securing power over treaty changes. Treaty changes do not need to be ratified by the EP and it has been denied formal representation at all IGCs. The EP has had, therefore, to content itself with a 'think-tank role' in relation to the constitutional development of the EU, with participation in intergovernmental 'reflection groups' that have preceded formal IGCs, and some consultation during the negotiations themselves. Although some national parliaments have, on previous occasions, threatened to link their own ratification of treaty changes to a favourable opinion of the EP, it is unclear whether this is a threat of any meaningful substance, as it is almost always made by those who would ultimately accept half a cake, rather than none at all, in matters of European integration.

The EP as a public forum: the politics of access

Given the low media coverage of its work, in comparison with the attention received by national parliaments, and the communication barriers inherent in a multilingual parliament, the role of public forum would not seem to be a very promising one for the EP. Yet, in spite of this, it is possible to characterise the EP and its party groups as useful intermediators between public opinion, national parties and EU decision-making. Their access to information and understanding of the EU often combines with policy vacuums at the national level to make them important contributors to *domestic* party platforms and public debate, even if the transnational provenance of many of the ideas and arguments that subsequently crop up in national arenas is unacknowledged or little understood. There is, accordingly, a growing recognition that the party groups are not just organised for the exercise of the legislative and financial powers of the EP, or to influence the confirmation of the new Commission. They also exist to formulate and propagate ideas about the EU's political development, and have had some success in structuring their formal and informal relationships with the Commission, Council and party federations of domestic parties, so that they can contribute to agenda-setting and policy innovation (Ladrech in Gaffney, 1996). All of this is important, for in the EU the politics of absence and presence, of who has access to powerful decision-makers and the opportunity to contribute to the Union's agenda, may confer influence, even in the absence of formal power. Various reasons have been given for this: the open nature of the political agenda in what is still in many ways a relatively new political system; the probability that those who make constructive proposals will have a disproportionate influence over the way in which issues and solutions are conceptualised; and the manner in which the institutional compromise in the EU encourages supranational bodies to propose initiatives, even if ultimate decisions have to be taken by intergovernmental councils (Peters, 1994).

The EP and its party groups clearly do enjoy good lines of political communication with several other centres of initiative and influence within the Union. During the plenary sessions in Strasbourg, a

Commissioner and a minister from the country holding the Presidency of the Council are always in attendance in the inner ring of the hemicycle, where they are seated directly next to the leaders of the main party groups. In addition, representatives of the Commission and Council are expected to reply to debates that will normally include a series of statements of the positions of the different party groups. Although the EU is plainly a long way from the model of government conducted from within a parliament, its governing process has at least begun to thicken its contacts with a party-based parliament. Jacques Delors, for instance, established a precedent that the President of the Commission would always be present in person for some part of the Strasbourg session and, as seen elsewhere in this book, a growing tendency for individual Commissioners to see themselves as members of the political families is manifested in an appreciation of the value of dealing with the EP through its party groups. Plenary weeks in Strasbourg are used for monthly meetings between group leaders and Commissioners of the same political persuasion and, for their part, MEPs are increasingly prone to identify party colleagues as 'their Commissioners'. Back in Brussels, the EP is within walking distance of many offices of the Commission and the Council, and a large part of the seating in its specialised committees is reserved for representatives of those two institutions. Indeed, one paradoxical result of the secrecy of the Council may be that it is the monthly cycle of parliamentary committees that provide the focal points for specialised policy communities. That EP committees should be the site and occasion for such get-togethers may be of some benefit in structuring the political debate.

As for communication paths into the European Council and the Council of Ministers, the party groups in the EP enjoy more advantages than is sometimes acknowledged in the interlocking framework of party federations, national governments, parliaments and party leaderships. European parliamentarians, as the policy specialists who are able to give the whole of their time to the consideration of EU issues, free from the absorbing distractions of national politics, may enjoy important informational advantages over domestic party colleagues, even where they are regarded as the junior partners. The fact that the consultation procedure requires the EP's view to be sought before draft proposals are sent to the Council of Ministers means that the transnational party groups are also compelled to take a position in advance of domestic parties. This allows them to take a lead in showing what is possible in terms of transnational party compromise and to provide a series of ready-worked orientations. Party colleagues in domestic politics and the party federations often find it easier to follow these than to waste time reinventing the wheel.

As seen earlier, the EP may also gain an intangible influence through its contribution to the formation and circulation of the elites that run the EU's institutions. It is significant that at the time of writing in 1996 both the last two presidents of the Commission have been former MEPs, Jacques Delors serving from 1979 to 1981 as Chairman of the Economic and Monetary Affairs Committee, an experience that may have shaped some of his later commitment to Monetary Union. Corbett, Jacobs and Shackleton also make the interesting point that the number of Commissioners who have served as MEPs has risen from one out of 13 in the 1970s to seven out of 20 in the present Santer Commission. Whilst there are, as yet, few instances of former members of the party groups reaching top positions in the Council, such as Prime Minister or Foreign Minister (a recent exception was the appointment of the EPP's Abel Matutes to the position of Foreign Minister in the new Spanish government, formed in May 1996), there are significant flows in the opposite direction with 59 ex-government ministers securing election to the 1994–9 parliament, including four prime ministers, one of whom now leads the second largest group, the EPP (Corbett *et al.*, 1995). Although this could, of course, be an instrument for the political capture of the groups by national parties and governments, the evidence seems to be that former national politicians of senior status can also be useful in feeding the perspectives of their groups back into domestic party politics and in avoiding conflict between the two levels. The extent to which the monthly gatherings in Strasbourg are seen as political sites worthy of the attention of even senior government leaders is illustrated by the way in which Kohl and Chirac chose to combine their first meeting as heads of government with a visit to the May 1995 plenary of the EP, where they also met with the President of the Parliament and their own MEPs to discuss the forthcoming IGCs (*Frankfurter Allgemeine Zeitung*, 17 May 1995).

The powers and functions of the EP: what kind of party politics do they require?

Now that we have analysed how the powers and functions of the EP are distributed across the typology of parliaments as government-formers, political system-builders, legislators and public forums, we can be more precise about the kind of party politics that would be most appropriate to the Parliament. Given that the EP does not need to support a government on a continuing basis, the primary challenge to its party groups is one of organising legislative majorities. This is a crucial distinction, for a majority needed to support an effective executive authority has to be a stable one, while legislative majorities can be fluid (i.e., they can include different people at different times). Indeed, in a transnational setting, it is, arguably, better that they should be fluid. An attempt to organise fixed EP majorities could destabilise the Union by producing a 'winner takes all' style of legislative politics that would conflict with expectations that the benefits of integration should be evenly distributed across member states and contending ideological or partisan positions (Dehousse, 1995). Fixed majorities could also alienate key groups and countries from the further development of the EP's powers. To the extent that a combination of low powers of government formation and only partially developed legislative and financial functions gives the Commission and Council little reason to interfere or to organise parliamentary majorities from outside, the EP and its party groups may also have more freedom to shape policy options and debate at a formative stage in the EU's development. The point is well made by Fulvio Attinà:

> The absence of a majority–opposition arrangement and of loyalty ties between the Community government institutions (Commission and Council of Ministers) and the representative institution (Parliament) is not a limitation to the European Parliament because the absence of this requisite renders it free from the binding condition of having a majority subordinate to the political executive branch. The absence of this requisite is rather a liberating element for MEPs who can attempt to influence the European integration process with full autonomy. (Attinà, 1990)

In addition, the need only to organise fluid majorities eases the task of transnational party formation in the EP. The party groups can arrange a kaleidoscope of different legislative coalitions during any one plenary week without there being any danger that a government will fall, or that shifting parliamentary majorities will be equated with instability. On the other hand, the absolute majority rule makes things more difficult. Although it might seem unreasonable that European parliamentary parties, where majority formation is inherently more problematic, should have to pass a higher hurdle than their national counterparts, the requirement can, in fact, be justified by the transnational setting in which they operate. Given that the EU is a multi-country political system, there may be certain arguments in terms of legitimacy and public acceptance that its laws should be passed by oversized majorities that are likely to include more nationalities and parties than simple ones.

However, a further – and much neglected – point is that the powers of the EP do more than test the capacity of the party groups to form absolute majorities of the total membership of the Parliament. They also require the groups to negotiate complex deals with the Commission and Council over long periods of time. Indeed, the politics of the EU are structured around *inter*institutional bargaining patterns that make it increasingly unsatisfactory to analyse the Commission, Council and Parliament as separate processes. A critical dimension to the political growth of the EP in recent years has, accordingly, been its progressive inclusion in a permanent and well-institutionalised dialogue with the Commission and Council. Of growing importance to the coordination of the overall work of the Union are meetings between the presidents of the Commission, Council and Parliament, as well as those between EP committee chairs, directors general from the Commission and officials from the Council Secretariat (Middlemas, 1995, p. 349). A tendency for the Commission to ally with the EP – as the two supranational institutions and out of a perception that a balance of power required the two weaker players to make common cause against the strongest (the Council) – was frequently observed in the 1980s, and, indeed, it was further encouraged by the technicalities of the cooperation procedure (Lodge 1993, p. 28). As John Peterson remarks, 'Under the co-operation procedure . . . the EP could only win a shoot-out with the Council if it was able to convince the Commission to support its proposed amendments' (Peterson, 1996). By contrast, co-decision has tended to deepen EP–Council relations, requiring the two bodies to enter into an elaborate process of conciliation in the event of failure to reach agreement on new legislation. Either way, the main significance of the powers of the EP often lies less in their surface appearance and more in the ability of MEPs to deploy them to the advantage of the Commission or Council, or even one particular group of governments on the Council (Tsebelis, 1994).

All three of the EU's main institutions are somewhat diffuse and cumbrous political actors, open to high levels of penetration by other political processes, and this may make it hard for any of them to agree and sustain a coherent bargaining hand over a long period and under changing circumstances. Whether the EP can negotiate on an equal footing with the Commission and Council will depend on its success in asserting patterns of transnational party politics. Inside the EP itself, this will be necessary to knit together a sustainable absolute majority of the Parliament's membership, and to hold the line against attempts by governments represented on the Council to 'nobble' particular national party delegations. Outside the EP, transnational party coalitions have a potential to cross-cut the institutional division between Parliament, Commission and Council, so reducing the significance of the EP's relative weakness in any 'straight fight' with either of the other two bodies. Once again, the point is well made by John Peterson, this time in relation to the workings of the co-decision procedure:

> The co-decision procedure fosters competition between alliances of member states linked to EP factions. Usually, the EP will seek allies on the Council who may have agreed with reluctance to the terms of a common position. The EP then tries to 'peel them off' from the rest of the Council. When this strategy works, policy choices will tend to be less determined by intergovernmental bargains and more reflective of compromise between broad political tendencies (Socialist vs Christian Democratic). . . In other words, the co-decision procedure may act to enhance the development of socio-political cleavages at the European level. (Peterson, 1996)

The party groups and the Committees of the EP

Shaun Bowler and David Farrell have argued that if the EP has managed to 'assert itself in an age of parliamentary decline' it is because of the distinctive combination of parliamentary procedures and party politics that have been developed in Brussels and Strasbourg. There would, indeed, seem to be a link between the effective internal organisation of the EP and its ability to make the most of its powers, especially where these require it to mobilise the expertise needed to negotiate on a par with external bodies like the Commission and Council (Bowler and Farrell, 1995). The work of the EP is arranged around monthly cycles. For two weeks every month, MEPs divide up into specialist committees which meet in Brussels. During the third week, they meet in their party groups – also in Brussels – to decide positions and tactics for the plenary session of the EP in Strasbourg, held during the fourth week of the cycle. Much of the coordination of this cycle is handled by a 'Conference of Presidents', comprising the chairs of each party group, thus underscoring the centrality of the latter to the smooth workings of the Parliament. Across the range of the EP's powers and functions, the working method is much the same. An attempt is made to reconcile an enormous volume of work, much of it requiring specialist knowledge, with the right of all MEPs to participate in every decision of the EP, by delegating to the committees the preparatory work of drafting detailed proposals, which are then sent as reports for the approval of the whole Parliament. The group weeks act as political filters between the committees and the plenaries, but this should not blind us to the fact that the politics of the party groups are crucial at every other stage of the process. Only by showing how they help nurse reports from conception in the committees to agreement in the plenaries can we understand how the groups are the main sites for political bargaining and coalition-building in the EP, and evaluate the extent to which they reproduce the key role of conventional parliamentary parties in providing coordination and coherence across issues, time, and complex multi-stage procedures.

The overall party political balance of the Parliament shown in the illustration of the hemicycle on page 78 of Chapter 4 is replicated in all of the 19 committees, which usually have a membership of between 50 and 60 MEPs. However, only six of the 101 national party delegations have the minimum of 19 MEPs necessary even to attempt to spread themselves as full members across all of the EP's committees. This may be a factor that encourages the transnationalisation of party activity, for, if a matter of particular political sensitivity arises on a committee on which a national party has no representation, it may only be able to gain access to both debate and decision through sympathetic members of the group from other countries, or by begging the group to absent a full member of the committee so that one of its own MEPs can attend as an alternate. Opportunities to draft reports are allocated to particular committees by the Conference of Presidents and, within the committees, reports are assigned to individual MEPs, known as rapporteurs, once again on a basis of proportionality to party strength. The party groups even agree a points system for weighting the importance of each report they are assigned and, in the case of disagreement, simply hold an auction to see which group is prepared to make the highest bid to attain the report for one of its members (Corbett *et al.*, 1995, pp. 128–9). The party groups will, in addition, appoint a spokesman for each committee, whose task it is to articulate the group position in debates, and a coordinator, who will function as a whip, checking the attendance of group members, making sure that substitutes are called upon where full members cannot be present, and negotiating procedural and substantive bargains with other groups and the committee chair. The chairs are also distributed between the groups – on a basis of strict proportionality! – with the groups using their choices to signal political priorities and an intention to lead on certain issues.

Some students of parliaments might recognise at least two features here that could, in other circumstances, be used to supplant the role of party politics. These are, first, the assignment of some key agenda-setting roles to individuals – rapporteurs and committee chairs – and, second, the functional fragmentation of the Parliament as a whole into a series of specialist committees. There is a risk of giving rapporteurs disproportionate personal influence over the framing of policy-options and of conferring on committee chairs the power to use their control of procedure to influence decisions of substance. This would, for example, follow from the famous finding of game theory that, in a context of just those complex group decisions that are commonly found on committees, preference orderings are almost always indeterminate, and almost any alternative can 'win', depending upon the order in which the chair chooses to put questions to the vote. The overall organisation of the Parliament into committees could, on the other hand, very easily lead to an all- absorbing division of labour with MEPs becoming narrow policy specialists, inclined to substitute the mind-set of the technician or single-issue lobbyist for the defining role of the party politician as a generalist, concerned to apply a range of political values to the whole gamut of public issues. Such a risk is underlined, first, by patterns of self-selection for committee memberships with MEPs eager to show off a professional expertise or to ride a personal political hobby horse and, second, by the fact that 80 per cent of members only get an opportunity to sit as full members on just one committee (Corbett *et al.*, 1995, p. 110).

It has, indeed, been suggested that, in the peculiar conditions of transnational politics, the EP can only ever be a parliament of strong committees and weak parties, much on the model of the United States Congress. Informational advantages over those not represented on particular committees, will, it is argued, normally allow well-organised committee members to dominate discussion of their own reports in the relatively chaotic conditions that characterise full party group discussions, and prevent the latter from straying too far from the committee line. Once a position is agreed in a committee, its defenders often enjoy a kind of escalation dominance, by which it becomes increasingly difficult to undo a committee line the further it progresses through the parliamentary process. This is underscored by procedural arrangements, time constraints, the cost of recontracting agreements that have already been made, and the ability of the agenda-setter to dominate the manner in which problems are constructed in the political imaginations of busy colleagues. Indeed, a report that has been agreed by a respectable margin in committee often enjoys an edge over counterproposals because it is *known* to be capable of interparty agreement. This is an enormous asset in a Parliament in which time is the scarcest resource and key decision rules require an absolute majority of the membership, not just of those voting. The following, for example, is the analysis of two senior MEPs, one from the EPP and the other from the PES:

> In the EPP, if there is a consensus amongst the group members on the committee, the matter will not normally go to the full group at all. A good spokesman, who can hold our people on the committee together, will be trusted by the rest of the group, and his proposal for the whip will normally be accepted without much argument. In ten years, as a spokesman on various committees, I have not lost one vote in the group on my recommendation for the whip. (Authors' interview with member of EPP)

> Unless there is a conflict between two committees, you can normally expect the committee line to carry the group as a whole. It would be intolerable for the group on the basis of ignorance to overturn the position of a committee. One good thing about a committee-based Parliament is that it allows for the construction of a real expertise. The committee has to be made to work and then to lead the Parliament. (Authors' interview with member of PES)

However, on closer inspection, party group cohesion and committee solidarity tend to be mutually dependent in the case of the EP. We will look more deeply at the reasons for this at the end of the section on party group plenaries, but for the moment it is sufficient to observe that the party groups are key units for bargaining and aggregation on the committees themselves, and it is only those reports that enjoy a considerable consensus within and between party groups on the committees that are unlikely to be unpicked elsewhere in the Parliament. A report that is known to have sparked partisan controversy within a committee, or even to have ridden roughshod over a minority view within a group, will be a sitting duck to subsequent challenge. A senior MEP, with experience as chair of one of the working parties for resolving arguments between EPP members on various committees, argues that all concerned know that the penalty of not settling at the lowest possible level is that disputes will be put to a majority vote of the entire group. There is even a further danger that the full group discussion will be too inconclusive or acrimonious for a majority vote to be possible, and that the group will, accordingly, find itself unable to issue a whip for the plenary. This can lead to the group losing the initiative in the EP, or to chaotic and inconsistent decision-making if several other groups are unable to agree a line (Authors' interview with EPP member).

Wise rapporteurs and coordinators will probably want to negotiate an oversized majority on the committee, minimise the number of groups opposed and get all committee members from their own group on their side. This is confirmed by the evidence of a senior PES coordinator:

We have never reported back to the committee without a consensus or overwhelming majority of the coordinators. If we can get agreements with all the other party groups on the committee we can usually carry these over into the plenary. Everyone is in the habit of working together, so the norms are well worked out. (Authors' interview with PES member)

Even casual observation of the committees reveals that the role of the rapporteur is conceived as one of attempting to sum up a consensus. Rapporteurs are expected to listen to much debate before and after preparing a draft, to amend their drafts in the light of feedback and to approach the whole exercise with a view to synthesising as many views as possible. Some even call themselves '*suiveurs*' (followers), rather than rapporteurs. Major reports may also be proceeded by a series of minor reports and/or be co-authored by rapporteurs from more than one group (the Martin (PES)/Bourlanges (EPP) report on the position that the EP should take in the reflection group prior to the 1996 Intergovernmental Conference is a classic example). Attempts to impose a personal point of view and to short-circuit the normal painstaking process of consensus-building within and between party groups on the committee will almost always come unstuck and set MEPs back in the ambition most of them share to move up the scale from small- to large-time rapporteurships. Indeed, group co-ordinators have even removed rapporteurs, rather than allow them to take a risk on pushing a report through a committee on a slender majority (Corbett *et al.*, 1995, p. 132). Questions of procedure are also subject to a consensual style of interparty group management that limits opportunities for manipulation by individuals. The chair of each committee has to work with three vice-chairs, each of whom is usually drawn from different groups, and, together with coordinators drawn from all the party groups, these form a bureau that normally decide procedural matters.

Group weeks: decision-making within the groups

The generous allocation of a whole week every month for MEPs to get together in their groups reflects both the political difficulty of building consensus in transnational parliamentary parties without centralised disciplines, and the functional importance of the groups in providing a connecting mechanism between the committees and the plenaries. On the first point, agreements cannot be rushed and there is no easy alternative to elaborate mechanisms for allowing all MEPs and national delegations to review the range of parliamentary business before the formation of group positions. On the second, effective preparatory work within and between the groups can ensure that the limited time available in a plenary can be given over to matters on which absolute majorities are likely and that the Parliament is, therefore, ready to proceed to the effective use of its powers.

Table 5.1 shows how the two main groups, the EPP and the PES, organised a typical group week in April 1995. One point of crucial importance to our later analysis is that neither of the large groups attempts to blot out national party delegations as 'rival' political forms to those of the transnational party groups themselves. The timetable is structured to allow national delegations to meet on their own and the television screens of the Parliament regularly display full details of who amongst them are going into private session and when, thus providing some indication for all to see of where political difficulties are brewing amongst the national delegations. Even when the PES and EPP come together in full session, their Presidents will on many critical issues allow debates to be structured along national lines by asking national delegation leaders to state their positions in turn. One new arrival to the EPP records being struck by the extent to which its president seemed in this way to legitimise the role of the national delegation in either giving or withholding consent to group decisions. A further point, to which we will return, is that even when the groups are not in full session, their bureaux contain one MEP from almost all national delegations, thus, once again, maximising the opportunities for the positions of all national parties to be anticipated in the group line.

However, it also needs to be noted that the national delegations themselves tend to vary in the extent to which they choose to harmonise a position before discussion in the group as a whole. This choice will be influenced by the size of the national delegation, the

TABLE 5.1

How the PES and EPP organised a group week, 11–15 September 1995

	Party of European Socialists	European People's Party
Monday	Greek and Portuguese national delegations	Meeting of full group 1 working party Irish delegation
Tuesday	Bureau of group 5 working parties PES committee coordinators British, German, Greek, Italian, Spanish and Portuguese delegations	Meetings of working parties A–E Austrian, British, German, Greek delegations
Wednesday	Bureau 7 working parties Austrian, British, Danish, Dutch, French, German delegations Meeting of full group	Meeting of full group 1 working party Dutch delegation
Thursday	Meeting of full group contd SPD seminar	British delegation Executive EPP Women
Friday	Greek delegation	Irish delegation

extent to which its MEPs identify with the transnational group as much as their national party, the distance of median national party preferences from the average position of the transnational group and the likelihood of a group line emerging that will cause domestic problems for a national party. Large national party delegations are often tempted to organise closely because their numbers give them the opportunity to be influential in intra-group bargaining through unity in voting and coherence in argument. Conversely, national party delegations are less likely to coordinate prior positions where they can reasonably expect the eventual consensus of the group to be close to their own priorities. This, for example, is the explanation that the prominent Belgian MEP, Fernand Herman, gives for why his fran-cophone Christian Democrats scarcely ever meet as a national party delegation, and would not even seem to have bothered to elect a leader (Authors' interview). By contrast, the British Labour Party, whose position is still fraught with political difficulty in terms of the minefields that consensus-building in the PES could trigger in domestic party politics, often engages in a frenzied round of national delegation meetings during group week, culminating in a monthly visit to Brussels by the domestic party's General Secretary, whose task it is to anticipate the domestic impact of agreements that seem to be emerging in the PES and to caution Labour MEPs if necessary.

Apart from the task of keeping national delegations and transna-tional group in tandem, the other major challenge of group week is to filter the work of 19 different committees into overall party positions. From Table 5.1, it can be shown that the PES and EPP differ in how they do this. The EPP coordinates the work of its representatives on the 19 EP committees through five working parties, while the PES prefers a more 'open plan' in which coordinators from all the committees get an opportunity to work on suggestions to be put to the group as a whole. Needless to say, there are advantages and disadvantages in both approaches. Specialised working parties may allow those national delegations who are not represented on parti-cular committees to gain an input to recommended group positions and they do ensure that the process of mutual surveillance is carried out by those who know most about each thematic area of the EU's activities. On the other hand, even organisation into five working parties may perpetuate artificial institutional divisions in the con-sideration of issues, and fail to utilise to the full the function of party politics as a coordinating mechanism for reducing inconsistency across different parts of the policy-making process.

In both the PES and the EPP, group week culminates in meetings of all their MEPs. These are impressively attended and may last for several hours as the recommendations of working groups or coordinators are debated and decided. The key question is, of course, what decision-making rule will eventually determine the group line for the plenary. Most of the time, the groups seem to converge on a qualified supranationalism in their own internal decision-making: national delegations accept that the group line may ultimately be decided by majority vote, on condition that:

- Every effort is first made to decide matters by consensus and without a vote, hence the elaborate arrangements for group weeks described in foregoing paragraphs.
- Even when national delegations have been outvoted in their own groups, they reserve the right not to support the common line in the plenary, so long as their dissent has been openly explained and reasonably justified to the rest of the group beforehand.
- Efforts should even be made to facilitate reasonable dissent; first, as just suggested, by clarifying limits beyond which it may be in everyone's interests not to insist on political loyalty in all circumstances; and, second, by taking pressure off potential dissidents by ensuring that groups can always call on alliances across the political divide to compensate for votes lost in their own camp. A key issue is whether groups allow a conscience clause to individuals, as opposed to whole national party delegations unable to follow the transnational party line – and under what circumstances. This, for instance, would seem to be a key difference between the PES and the EPP, with the latter insisting on tighter group disciplines.

Relationships between domestic parties and national party delegations

Group weeks provide the most obvious intervention point for domestic political parties that are interested in affecting the EP's treatment of a particular issue. Only when draft reports emerge from committees will national parties be able to consider the exact detail of what is being suggested, and the precise political package deals or trade-offs that are being proposed. This raises two questions: first, whether national parties have developed the technical capacity to follow the EP process and make effective interventions during group week; second, whether they can best secure their objectives by 'instructing' their MEPs to take certain positions during group week, or by trusting them to use their own judgement. The arrangements made by the two main British political parties can be used to illustrate the first point. The Conservative Central Office has a full-time liaison officer posted in Brussels and Strasbourg, while, as we have seen, the Labour Party's General Secretary frequently attends group week discussions on the positions that the national delegation and PES will take in plenary.

On the question of the autonomy of MEPs there have been some notable attempts by domestic parties to instruct their national delegations on how they should vote. This would seem to be fairly widespread on questions of fundamental political importance, such as the membership of the Union (i.e., use of the assent procedure) and the confirmation of the Commission. However, there would seem to be only two major examples of domestic parties attempting to 'mandate' MEPs on a more regular basis: the French Socialists in the early 1980s and the British Labour Party since 1994. That domestic parties do not make more frequent and assiduous attempts to instruct their MEPs may reflect the following factors:

- There is little to be gained from instructing national party delegations because most of these are tiny in relation to the Parliament as a whole. Of the 101 national party delegations presently in the EP, the average size is just six members, and only six of them have more than 20 members, or 3 per cent of the Parliament. Moreover, a further advantage of the fluid patterns of majority formation in the EP is that it is difficult for one national party delegation to manoeuvre itself into the position of being the critical source of votes on any particular issue. Should it threaten to withhold its support, other votes can usually be found else-where.

- There are, conversely, considerable incentives for a national party delegation to remain within the consensus-building process, given the emphasis that is placed on accommodating as many national partisan positions as possible. However, for a national party to do this it must be prepared to justify its position and participate in a wider process of package-dealing and horse-trading. Domestic parties may, therefore, have little to gain from 'instructing' their MEPs to take positions that will simply condemn them to being outvoted, and something to lose by denying them the flexibility to negotiate their way into winning coalitions.

- Although there plainly are occasions when national parties would prefer their MEPs to be honourably defeated, rather than implicated in a transnational party compromise that will cause domestic embarrassment, we have also seen that national parties are unlikely to be punished in elections for anything their MEPs do. This will increase the attraction of leaving EP votes to the discretion of national party delegations.

Committees and party group weeks: patterns of decentralised consensus-building

Now that we have looked at how group weeks work, we can explain more fully the hypothesis that the committees and party groups of the EP are closely related ingredients of a viable transnational parliament. To see why this is so, it is useful to draw on Giovanni Sartori's decision-making theory of democracy, which predicts that a committee-style approach to policy-making will help to reconcile preexisting elites to a new institutional structure – in our case national party elites to the operation of a transnational parliament that has some role in the making of laws that will affect all member states. Whereas adversarial modes of decision-making tend to force political choices into a zero-sum mould of winners and losers, Sartori argues that committees usually (i) have a commitment to decision-making by consensus; (ii) concentrate on settling questions by means of package deals that give everyone a little of what they want; (iii) focus on detailed problem-solving, rather than rhetorical clashes, thus allowing for the formation of convergent coalitions in which actors are able to reach a common position from many different ideological starting points; and (iv) tend to disguise the identity of winners and losers by avoiding formal votes. By committee-style decision-making, Sartori means any group that comes into frequent face-to-face contact to exercise political functions, in the knowledge that they will all have to carry on working together, whether they like it or not, for years to come (Sartori, 1987; also Higley *et al.*, in Olsen and Marger, 1993). Thus both the formal committees of the EP and the meetings of its party groups are committees in the Sartori sense. And, the interplay between them is crucial, for the party groups provide a coordinating mechanism between the 19 functional committees; they institutionalise sensitivity to the problems of particular national parties; and they act as both 'market-makers' and 'bankers' in the art of political compromise. They construct the complex package deals that are needed to reconcile several interests at the same time and without which many political trades would not happen. They keep a tally of the political credits and debits that accrue in the course of bargaining.

Conference of Presidents

As seen, the key link between committees, group weeks and plenary sessions of the EP is provided by the Conference of Presidents, where the agenda for the plenaries is negotiated and decisions are taken on which reports are 'ripe' for decision in terms of technical preparation, partisan consensus and external demands on the EP to reach conclusions. The impossibility of running the Parliament on any other basis than negotiation between its party groups, and the claim that the EP is ultimately a party-based parliament, is illustrated by changes that have had to be made in recent years to the Conference of Presidents. Originally, a gathering of the committee chairs made the crucial decisions about the EP's work programme. But it proved impossible to set the overall agenda of the EP without the participation of the presidents of the party groups. So these were, first of all, brought into an enlarged Conference of Presidents, and in the 1994–9 parliament the committee chairs were dropped altogether from the process. The Conference of Presidents is crucial in the one area that has so far been neglected in our analysis – the need for some body to decide how questions requiring parliamentary decision are to be distributed between the committees, and the order in which completed reports are going to be considered by the plenaries.

Assessments of this development are mixed, with some taking the view that the Conference of Presidents has the potential to impose a new, centralised mode of party politics, reversing the complex, bottom-up processes of coalition-building that has been portrayed in this chapter. Implicit in this view is a prediction that the transnational groups are converging on a conventional pattern of party politics in which leaders will in the future have sufficient hold over their followers to be able to negotiate on their behalf in a permanent directoire of party Presidents. Thus one MEP goes so far as to warn against the development of a 'supreme Soviet', perhaps under a misconception that if there is to be a powerful Parliament in an ambitious Union, the EP will have to sacrifice the slow processes of decentralised consensus-building that have previously allowed it to reconcile its internal political complexity with its collective effectiveness (Authors' interview with EPP member).

Others argue that their own experience of attending the Conference of Presidents is that it still follows rather than leads patterns of coalition-building in committees, national delegations and group memberships and that there is simply no point in attempting to force the pace by putting matters to plenary before a consensus has been allowed to mature within the committees and the groups (Authors' interview with ELDR member). Another benign assessment is that, once things have been allowed to work their way through the committees and the groups in the normal manner, the Conference of Presidents simply finalises the coalition-building between the groups, adding speed and efficiency to the identification of potential majorities. All groups, it is argued, gain better information from the Conference about the ways in which others intend to vote, and because the politics of the Parliament discourage strategic deception, these indications can usually be trusted. Those seeking to break their word – or to be wrong in their appreciation of the balance of views in their own group – may pay a price in their political reputation as reliable partners and so reduce their capacity to make future deals.

An intermediate assessment is that the Conference of Presidents may in the future attempt to preempt more decentralised forms of consensus-building, only to find that centralisation is, in fact, inefficient and that the old methods possessed a peculiar logic in spite of their seemingly impossible complexity. An example of such dysfunctional centralisation may have been provided by the attempt of EPP President, Wilfrid Martens, to speed the Bourlanges/Martin report, designed to prepare the EP's position for the IGC reflection group, through the Institutional Affairs Committee (IAC). At the April 1995 meeting of the IAC, Martens seemed to indicate that an EPP/PES majority was ready to steam-roller the report through the EP. Quite apart from this threatening to preempt the internal political process within his own group, the other groups were so outraged that they tabled a total of 657 amendments, which they insisted on voting one by one in what almost became an all-night sitting of the IAC on 4 May 1995. In addition to taking over more decentralised forms of consensus-building, the last example shows how the Conference of Presidents could also become one more site for the deployment of the EPP/PES duopoly, more or less subtly disguised by the apparent implication of other group presidents in decisions dominated by the larger groups. However, once again, there is nothing inevitable to this development and, from another perspective, the Conference of Presidents tempers the iron law of PES/EPP oligarchy by giving each party President a voice on behalf of his or her group, regardless of size. By some accounts, efforts are, indeed, also made to make decisions on the Conference of Presidents by consent and without recourse to weighted voting of the groups.

The party groups in the plenaries of the Parliament

Full meetings of the group continue to be called at sometimes frequent intervals during plenaries. This underlines the collective style of group decision-making and the limited authority of group leaders to react to events and strike bargains without consulting the full membership. It is, of course, in plenary sessions that the party groups face the central challenge of organising the absolute majorities needed to exercise the EP's powers. Indeed, plenaries present the groups with a fourfold political task, each element of which we will examine in more detail in the sections that follow:

- to articulate a coherent political message;
- to mobilise as many of their MEPs as possible for the sessions;
- to maximise their own internal cohesion in both debates and votes;
- to cultivate winning alliances with other groups.

Articulation

The articulation of coherent group positions is facilitated by the structure of EP debates and by the controls that the groups themselves exercise over access to speaking-time in the plenaries. Most plenary debates are relatively short – between 60 and 120 minutes – and during this restricted time the eight group presidents will almost always be called upon to state their party positions. After committee chairs have also had their say, there may be only a few minutes per debate to allocate to ordinary members and, as this precious commodity is distributed by the groups themselves, there is a temptation only to give speaking-time to those most likely to argue the group line. In one recent set of proposals within the EPP, it was even suggested that no time should be given to those who were not prepared to represent the line agreed during group week, that records would be kept of how well speakers had supported the group line and that future allocations would also be linked to good attendance in both plenaries and committees (Authors' interview with EPP member).

Participation

The overall attendance rate of MEPs at the Strasbourg primaries is in the region of 70 per cent (*Financial Times*, 10 May 1994). However, not all who in are in attendance will be available for all the votes, and some may choose to be discreetly absent rather than vote against their group line. Tapio Raunio estimates that during the 1989–94 Parliament only around 48 per cent of members bothered to vote even on more important occasions (Raunio). As Table 5.2 shows, there are also significant variations in the degree to which the party groups mobilise their members to take part in plenary votes. It is tempting to conclude that these differences in turn- out are proportional to the size of the groups and their varying scope to influence outcomes. Thus the best voting scores – of between 65 and 68 per cent – are achieved by the PES and the EPP. With nearly two thirds of the seats – and a considerable tendency to vote together – MEPs from these groups have good prospects of taking part in winning majorities and have, accordingly, every incentive to participate. Yet variations in participation are not strictly proportionate to size. For example, Forza, the Greens, the UEL and the RDE were almost identically sized groups over the period that the calculations were made – with between 25 and 31 members – yet their participation in plenary votes ranged from roughly 35 (Forza) to 55 (Greens) per cent. Additional factors that may affect participation are belief in the value of the EP and, in particular, that its work should be supported as a means to fill the democratic deficit of the Union; the number of MEPs in the group who hold dual or even triple mandates – those who continue to hold national or local office – may find that their attendance at Strasbourg suffers: and the seriousness with which MEPs take the task of civic representation.

Cohesion

To ensure their own internal cohesion most parliamentary parties operate a whipping system. This, in turn, consists of two elements: an agreed guidance for voting and a system of political sanctions and

TABLE 5.2

Participation rates of MEPs from different groups in the plenary votes of the EP (calculated from sample of 66 votes between June 1994 and September 1995)

Group	Participation (%)	Size
ERA	33.4	19
EN	40.1	19
ELDR	54.5	54
FE (now part of UPE)	35.3	29
UEL	46.4	31
EPP	67.8	173
PES	69.0	221
RDE (now part of UPE)	41.0	25
G	54.4	26

rewards that is clearly linked to the loyalty of individual members. Although much criticised as discouraging independence of political thought and behaviour, it is hard to see how parliamentary parties could function without agreed orientations for voting. For, without some mechanism to maximise the proportion of members who will follow an agreed line, a parliamentary party ceases to be a meaningful site for processes of political aggregation. MEPs are no different from representatives the world over in facing a trade-off whereby they may have to accept constraints on their voting in specific cases, if they are to ensure the broad success of their political preferences over some long-term average of political choices. As legislators, they are contributors to the governing process and thus have to meet public expectations that they will show consistency and coherence over time. As party politicians, they compete with others to maximise their influence over the distribution of political values, and will not want to lose out through organisational underperformance.

One EPP member claims that it has recently become practice in his group to indicate the importance of a vote to the group with the number of exclamation marks after its description on the voting sheets handed to each group member. Another claims that MEPs who transgress too often, without good cause or prior notification of the group, are likely to find themselves 'without help from the group when they need it'. This could affect their access to political opportunities, such as influential committee positions, speaking-time in plenaries and, above all, choice rapporteurships that give MEPs opportunities to make their reputations in the Parliament and beyond. For less elevated souls, the groups also have travel and distinctions within their gift and some may even fine their members for non-attendance (Authors' interview with EPP members). The complex structure of political choices in the plenary of the EP – with most MEPs being called upon to vote long lists of detailed amendments and specific clauses to several reports which they have not seen at the committee stage – means that the whip will often be valued as a source of political guidance: as a necessary simplification to the decision-making process and a means of dealing with information overload.

But, it is also important to recognise the limitations of group whips. The group whips are strong as mechanisms of political communication and coordination, but they are weaker than national party whips in terms of rewards and sanctions. MEPs have considerable scope to defy the whip, should they be minded to do so. Only a small proportion of votes is recorded, with the result that it is simply impossible to check how group members have voted. Thus whips often have to content themselves with just making sure that their people turn up to vote, without there being any guarantee that they will, in the event, vote the right way. In addition, group rewards and sanctions may only be effective in relation to MEPs who plan to develop their careers within the Parliament on a long-term basis. Those who regard their stay in the EP as just a stage in a national political career may be more concerned that loyalty to the transnational group line should not damage their prospects in domestic party politics. Moreover, as one Conservative MEP, claiming to have introduced 'whipping along Westminster lines' to the EPP has pointed out, whips cannot have 'extensive power and patronage in the absence of a government to defend or bring down'. Nor are group whips effective against whole national delegations as opposed to individual MEPs (Letter to *Financial Times*, 27 February 1994). To proceed with sanctions against the former, or to exclude any national delegation from the distribution of appointments or benefits within the group, would upset the whole delicate balance of transnational cooperation. As we have seen, provisions for whole national delegations to dissent are well-institutionalised in group procedures.

Alignments

The varying success of the groups in ensuring cohesion in plenary votes is fully examined in the next chapter and, at this point, the reader may find it worthwhile to look ahead to the 'indices of agreement' achieved within each group. These are set out in table 6.2 on page 142. For the moment, our concern is, however, to observe that there is a critical relationship between the internal cohesion of particular groups and the alignments that they form with others. On the one hand, the study of consensus-building within groups can never give us a complete understanding of the party politics of the EP: no one group commands enough votes for a simple majority of the Parliament – let alone the absolute majority that is required to exercise many of its powers. On the other hand, the deals that are made *between* groups may, of course, strain unity *within* them, or, conversely, take some of the pressure off the groups, allowing them to ease up on a search for complete unity and permit a degree of internal dissent in the knowledge that this will be compensated by cross-group deals. Table 5.3 on page 139 illustrates the frequency with which the different groups vote the same way in plenaries. A few patterns stand out:

- The dominant voting pattern in the EP is a 'centrist alliance' across the left–right divide, implying that it is the parties belonging to the PES, the EPP and the ELDR that gain most from the exercise of the Parliament's powers, and the 'outliers' on the left and right wings that are most likely to be excluded from winning coalitions. The sample of the votes in the table does, indeed, suggest that the 'big three' groups vote together around 75 to 80 per cent of the time.

- The next most frequent voting pattern is a bipolarised one of left–right voting. ERA, UEL and the Greens on the left are, for instance, much more likely to vote with one another than with the RDE, Forza and the EN on the right. Likewise, both the EPP and PES are slightly more likely to vote with the smaller groups on their own side of the political spectrum than with those who adopt contrasting left–right positions. There has been some talk of a red–green alliance of the left (PES, ERA, G and UEL) challenging the normal pattern of alliance-building across the left–right divide, though, as we will see, this is often only practical on votes that do not require absolute majorities.

- After coalitions of the centre and bipolarity, the next most frequent voting mode is that almost everyone votes the same way. Most other groups find that they are able to vote with the dominant PES/EPP/ELDR axis around a third to a half of the time.

- There are a few occasions on which 'polar opposites' vote together, such as the UPE and the EN on the right, and the UEL, the Greens and the ERA on the left. Sometimes this is because of grand coalitions of the whole Parliament; at other times, it reflects a protest of the excluded, a 'convergent coalition' of those who object to an alliance of the centre, albeit from contrasting left–right perspectives.

The above alignments are best explained by a combination of institutional rules, political preferences and the ability of groups to make themselves critical to the success or failure of different approaches to majority formation. It is often observed that the absolute majority rule gives the PES and EPP a considerable incentive to vote together. Given the interest of those two groups in maximising the existing powers of the Parliament – and laying claim to further extensions to its role – collaboration is the simplest way of ensuring that absolute majorities of the Parliament will be mobilised on a predictable and sustainable basis. Yet even the PES/EPP combine may be insufficient, once absences and dissent are taken into account, and it will often be necessary to widen the process of consensus-building beyond the two largest groups, if absolute majorities are to be achieved. However, the smaller groups are by no means equal in their potential or desire to form profitable alignments. This may, in turn, be a function, first, of their distance from median preferences on particular issues, with those occupying extreme positions on a left–right scale, or holding opinions most sceptical of European integration, finding it hardest of all to participate in winning coalitions; second, of the arithmetic of particular parliaments; and, third, of differences to which the varying national subcomponents of the groups constrain political bargaining at the European level.

Conclusion

This chapter has revealed how parliamentary parties are both similar and different in the transnational and national political arenas. On the one hand, there are important similarities of function. Both are sites of political aggregation and consensus-building; both facilitate coordination across a range of institutional processes and allow politicians to compete to apply different sets of social values to law-making and governance. On the other hand, there are key dissimilarities of form.

TABLE 5.3

Alignments between the party groups in the EP

	ERA	EN	ELDR	FE (UPE)	UEL	EPP	PES	RDE (UPE)	G
ERA	–	18.6%	69.5	35.6	56.0	64.4	76.3	33.9	64.5
EN	18.6	–	32.2	33.9	35.6	32.2	33.9	47.5	25.4
ELDR	69.5	32.2	–	49.2	54.2	74.6	81.4	44.1	57.6
FE (UPE)	35.6	33.9	49.2	–	37.3	64.4	52.5	49.2	37.3
UEL	56.0	35.6	54.2	37.3	–	45.8	57.6	30.5	67.8
EPP	64.4	32.2	74.6	64.4	45.8	–	74.6	50.9	44.1
PES	76.3	33.9	81.4	52.5	57.6	74.6	–	45.8	61.0
RDE (UPE)	33.9	47.5	44.1	49.2	30.5	50.9	45.8	–	30.5
G	64.5	25.4	57.6	37.3	67.8	44.1	61.0	30.5	–

Note: Data based on sample of 59 randomly selected plenary votes between June 1994 and July 1995, before the FE and RDE merged into the UPE. Those two parties are, therefore, indicated separately.

The party groups in the EP are less directly linked than national parliamentary parties to mass electoral politics, or to the executive functions of government. They are also less structured internally, with few party disciplines or political resources with which to reward or sanction their members. This may mean that they possess less autonomy in relation to sub-party political groupings: in their case, national delegations. But it is also possible that the need to negotiate – rather than impose – a consensus improves the quality of decision-making. It is to questions of effectiveness that we now turn.

6

Party Groups in the European Parliament: An Evaluation of Their Performance

Now that we have identified the party groups, given an account of how they work and examined the kind of party activity that is called for by the powers of the EP, we can meaningfully evaluate the performance of the party groups in the EP. In order to do this, we will, first, test the cohesion of the *individual* party groups and, second, examine whether they *collectively* constitute a coherent and stable party system.

Cohesion of the Party Groups

By the cohesion of the party groups we mean their ability to achieve internal unity and make decisions without excessive outside interference. It therefore amounts to a measure of how they have emerged as institutions in their own right, for any failure to achieve cohesion would indicate domination either by component national delegations or by bodies external to the EP itself (March and Olsen, 1984). We saw in the last chapter that there is one feature of the EP that takes some of the presssure off the groups to develop as cohesive transnational parliamentary parties (the absence of any need to form stable majorities capable of supporting governments in office) and another that increases it (the rule that many of the powers of the Parliament

140

can only be exercised on an absolute majority of the membership, rather than of those voting). There are also reasons to expect transnational parties to find it more difficult than national ones to achieve cohesion. Their subcomponents are not merely factions or tendencies, but fully formed political parties in their own right, with proud histories as self-governing organisations in the national arena. Conflicts of 'national interest' will cross-cut the transnational parliamentary groups and several will, at any one time, be divided between national parties of government and opposition. Given that it is difficult to make sense of the notion of 'parliamentary power' unless the EP can make the Council do things that it would not otherwise do, the party groups need to have the cohesion to take positions unwelcome to member governments, even though many of their MEPs come from national parties of government, and their political careers are vulnerable to sanctions in the domestic arena. The extent of this problem is illustrated in Table 6.1, which shows that the fissure between national parties of government and opposition cuts across four of the groups, representing about 85 per cent of the total membership of the present parliament. On top of all this, there are factors specific to the EP itself, which may strain group cohesion. Some MEPs feel stronger loyalties to committee than party group positions and, in addition, the practice of forming intergroups, which deliberately bring together MEPs with like values and interests from

TABLE 6.1

Domestic cleavages of government and opposition across the main party groups of the EP (measures taken at start of the Parliament, June 1994)

	PES	EPP	ELDR	UPE
MEPs from domestic parties of Government	52	97	15	21
MEPs from domestic parties of opposition	146	76	27	34

Notes: By dividing MEPs from each group into 'yes' votes, 'no votes' and abstentions and calling each a modality, it is possible to calculate an index of agreement as follows (Athinà, 1990):

$$\text{Index of agreement} = \frac{\text{Highest modality} - \text{sum of other two modalities} \times 100}{\text{Total votes cast by group}}$$

Any positive figure means that more than half of the group votes the same way. Any negative figure means that the group splits its vote without any one of the three modalities commanding more than half its membership.

across the party political divide, may provide a focus for the organisation of cross-party dissent as much as consensus. At the moment there are around forty or fifty such intergroups that concern themselves with a variety of subjects from the institutional development of the EU to welfare issues, the interests of particular economic sectors and consumer problems.

The simplest way of measuring the cohesion of parliamentary parties is to look at the frequency with which their members vote as a block. 'Roll-call' analysis can be used to calculate 'indices of agreement' for each group. Table 6.2 illustrates the indices of agreement for the groups in the 1984–9 parliament and the first year of the 1994–9 parliament.

From this evidence, we can attempt a series of conclusions about the cohesion, and broader political behaviour, of the party groups.

● The figures imply that individual party groups manage to achieve average levels of cohesion that in no case fall below 80 per cent and in some exceed 90 per cent. On the other hand, these figures are somewhat lower than those for national parliamentary parties, where levels of cohesion approaching 98 or 99 per cent are not uncommon.

● Cohesion has tended to rise with time. In particular, the PES has done a great deal to improve its cohesion since the 1980s and, had the EPP not also improved an already impressive performance

TABLE 6.2

Indices of agreement: levels of voting cohesion for the party groups in the EP, 1984–9 and July 1994–December 1995

1984–9		July 1994–December 1995	
PES	62.2	PES	89.00
EPP	84.1	EPP	90.21
EDG	82.9	ELDR	80.14
Communist	71.2	UEL	83.84
RDE	75.7	RDE (UPE)	93.19
Rainbow	67.8	Forza Europa (UPE)	81.29
European Right	96.1	Greens	85.21
		ERA	100.00
		EN	70.7
		NI	74.13

Note: Attinà (1990) for the 1984–9 figures; authors' own calculations for 1994–5, based on randomly selected sample of 121 votes.

between 1984–9 and 1994–5, the PES would have closed the entire gap between the two giants of the Parliament. Political socialisation, and the gradual emergence of the party groups as policy communities in their own right, might be grounds for saying that this was only to be expected. On the other hand, the groups have strengthened their cohesion in recent years in the presence of a series of perturbing factors that could easily have threatened their smooth political development. Prominent amongst these have been the enlargement of the Union and the amalgamation of two different political families – the Conservatives and the Christian Democrats. Since the early 1980s, the groups have had to adjust to three enlargements of the Union, a process that has brought in six new countries and nearly doubled the number of national party delegations that have to be accommodated in any successful consensus-building within the groups from 51 to 95 (although there are 101 national parties in the EP, there are only 95 in the groups, because 6 parties are unattached). National delegations from new countries will not have experienced previous processes of group socialisation and may be unfamiliar with some of the norms of transnational cooperation.

- Cohesion shows some interesting variations across issues and parliamentary powers. This illustrates two important themes in the development of European parliamentary parties which have been stressed elsewhere in this book. First, the party groups may have to make policy choices along several different issue dimensions – left–right, intergovernmental–supranational, north–south and so on – with each of these holding out different possibilities and limits to transnational party unity; and, second, the constitutional complexity of the EU requires different issues to be decided under different legislative procedures. At the time of writing (1996), there are more than twenty different procedures for passing a law through the EP. To the extent that the voting figures show varying degrees of transnational party unity across issues, this may have as much to do with the pressures different procedures put on the groups to cohere than levels of agreement within the groups on the substance of the issues.

- The politics of cohesion are very different amongst the larger and smaller groups. The incentive to cohere is very high amongst the former, whereas members of the latter know that they have very little chance of being able to influence parliamentary outcomes. Indeed, the relatively good cohesion figures that several of the smaller groups achieve is less impressive that it appears at first sight as several of them are dominated by just one or two national delegations. In addition, these groups suffer from remarkably low participation rates in plenary votes, which suggests that many of their members may dissent by not voting at all (see Table 5.1).

• We need to be careful of the conventional assumption that party groups in the EP are likely to become less cohesive as they become more transnational. For instance, the EPP, which has always been one of the most transnational of the party groups, enjoyed a slightly higher index of agreement in both the 1979–84 and 1984–9 parliaments than the now defunct EDG. What is stranger still is that the EDG itself had a marginally higher index of agreement in the 1984–9 parliament when it was a three-party alliance of British, Danish and Spanish Conservatives than in the 1979–84 parliament when to all intents and purposes it was a single-party group (with just two of its 63 members coming from the Danish and the rest from the British Conservatives)! Likewise, the improvement in the cohesion of the PES has taken place over a period in which it has become more transnational. Indeed, the large groups, which are in many ways the only ones with reasonable transnational credentials, tend to have slightly higher indices of agreement than several of the smaller groups.

In the view of one senior member of the PES, the success of the large groups in achieving respectable levels of agreement from around 20 parties from 15 countries is 'one of the wonders of the modern world' (Authors' interview with PES member). Amongst more mundane explanations we might, however, consider the following.

Happy political families?

Some of the earlier literature argued that the political families of Western Europe were afflicted by considerable cross-country variations on the same ideological themes. Socialism, Conservatism, Christian Democracy and Liberalism were differently conceptualised across the member states and would not, therefore, prove 'additive' in any pan-European context. According to one political science joke, the first thing Socialists nationalise is socialism. However, by referring back to Tables 2.1 to 2.10 in Chapter 2 we can show that one possible explanation for the cohesion of the groups in the Parliament is that their component national parties do not, in fact, cover particularly demanding spans of the ideological spectrum. Table 6.3, accordingly, shows for each of the six party groups where meaningful statistics are available the range betweeen the most left and most right national party in the group, and that between the most pro- and most anti-European. With the possible exception of the ELDR, the groups are relatively compact on a left–right scale. On this measure, it should, for example, be no more difficult to cooperate in the PES and EPP that cover a range from 3.5 to 5.25 and 5.71 to 8.33 respectively (on a 1 to 10 scale) than it is to work in many of the domestic party coalitions that characterise West European politics. The pro–anti European scale might appear more problematic, until it is remembered that this measure runs from -100 to $+100$; that none of the main groups contains an overtly anti-European party in its ranks; that European Parliamentary elites are likely to be both more enthusiastic and consensual on European integration than the average of their national parties; and that the national parties that are problematic – such as the Danish Social Democrats and the British Conservatives – tend to be outliers within groups that are otherwise homogenous on European integration.

However, the difficulty with any attempt to explain party group cohesion in terms of ideological compactness is that MEPs are often required to follow group lines that are the result of negotiation across – and not merely within – transnational parties. The ideological span of the most typical of these alignments – that between the PES and the EPP – runs, for instance, from 3.5 (Italian PDS) to 8.33 (Swedish Moderata Samlung). This makes it difficult to attribute cohesion to high levels of ideological homogeneity.

Post-ideological explanations of political cohesion

It has become fashionable amongst some to announce the end of political ideology. One possible implication of this is that even wide intergroup differences in political values, such as those between the left of the PES and the right of the EPP, are no longer relevant. However, it is hard to attend sessions of the EP without being struck by the extent to which ideological positions are clearly stated. Indeed, this may be encouraged by the absence of executive domination of the Parliament and the presence of incentives to ensure that one's own value preferences are embedded in the formative stages of what are new policies and institutions. A more sophisticated 'post-ideological' account of group cohesion in the Parliament might, however, begin

TABLE 6.3

Range of opinion within party groups on (i) left–right issues and (ii) European integration, as measured by Chapter 2 estimates of positions of component national parties

	1 Most left party in group (scale 0–10)	2 Most right party in group (scale 0–10)	3 Range, 1–2 (maximum possible 10)	4 Most pro-European (scale −100 to +100)	5 Least pro-European (scale −100 to +100)	6 Range 4–5 (maximum possible 200)
PES	3,5 (PDS, It)	5.00 (PSI, It)	1.5	+81 (PvDA, N)	+21 (SD, Swe)	60
EPP	5.71 (CVP, Bel)	8.33 (MS, Swe)	2.62	+95 (PCS,L)	+34 (Con, UK)	61
ELDR	4.8 (D66, N)	8.3 (DP, L)	3.5	+88 (VVD, N)	+59 (VLD, Bel)	23
UEL	1.8 (KKE, Gr)	3.63 (PCP, P)	1.83	+68 (SYN, Gr)	+19 (PCF, Fr)	49
UPE	5.8 (FF, Ire)	7.88 (RPR, Fr)	2.08	+79 (PSD, P)	+54 (RPR, Fr)	25
G	1.78 (GL, N)	4.28 (G, Swe)	2.50	+70 (G, Lux)	+40 (G, Ger)	30

with the observation that ideology may not be a self-sufficient predictor of rational political behaviour in an institutional context such as the EP. For example, imagine you are a national party that takes a relatively distinctive position on the left–right or pro–anti European scale, say 7.5 on the former. Your support is crucial to the formation of a winning coalition to your left, perhaps spanning an ideological space of 4.0 to 7.5 with a mean position of 5.7. On the other hand, a majority could also be formed by bringing in some more left- wing parties, maybe reducing the mean of the winning coalition to 5.5. Your choice is therefore, one between insisting on ideological purity and getting an outcome of 5.5 or joining in the politics of compromise and obtaining an agreement that is in fact closer to your ideological preferences – at 5.7. Rational political behaviour may well dictate the second.

The idea that it is rational even for the ideologically disparate to cohere – and that this is for most no more than an extension of the domestic political experience – is a point that is often emphasised by MEPs themselves. Most members of the PES and EPP, in particular, come from 'catch-all' political parties in domestic politics, compelled to maintain a broad church if they are to compete electorally, and from parties that see themselves as organised for government rather than ideological posturing. This, of course, requires compromise to form coalitions and to meet the constraints of practical governance. Of the 41 parties in the PES and EPP 32 are classified as follows in Michael Laver and Ben Hunt's study of how West European parties trade off the opportunities of office and ideological purity: 19 are 'parties most interested in office', 11 are parties that 'balance office and policy' and only two are 'parties most interested in policy' (Laver and Hunt, 1992, pp. 56–8). The importance of this consideration is underscored by the recruitment patterns of MEPs, who are almost never drawn direct from party activists – the group most likely to be concerned for the purity of party ideology – and are almost always ex-members of national or local assemblies and governments. In other words, they are almost always preselected for their ability to keep to party disciplines and accept the compromises that go with the formation of winning coalitions.

In addition, we have already encountered two further features of the EP that may make cohesion rational even in the face of diversity. The first is the need to establish divisions of labour and mechanisms of coordination in the face of an overload of decision-making. The advantage of functioning in a transnational party group is that particular MEPs and even national parties can leave others to look after particular issues in the expectation that they will fight for the application of broadly similar political values to their own. The advantage of following a group whip is that it represents an informational economy. An attempt to research every possible issue – clause, sub-clause and amendment – and to calculate an optimal position on each would be self-defeating. It would exceed the time available. On other hand, MEPs can usually expect the group whip to average out with political pay-offs that are broadly satisfactory from a personal point of view. An interesting implication of this analysis is that it implies that cohesion is partly a product of the very complexity of the Parliament and politics of the EU, and that party groups that are seriously concerned to influence outcomes may even feel themselves under pressure to expand until they are capable of an effective division of labour, covering all the processes of the EP. Again, there is evidence to support this with even the ELDR considering itself to be stretched with 54 members (Authors' interview with ELDR member).

The second factor is that the EP is united by external environmental pressures, even where it is divided by internal ideological

ones. Even for those with no long-term career interests in building up
the powers of the Parliament by proving the capacity of its party
groups for cohesion, there is a natural politician's interest to maximise
influence over particular day-to-day issues. Large sections of the
Parliament feel themselves to be engaged in permanent competition
with the Commission and Council to shape new policy and legislation. Not only is this a game that the EP can only win if its parties are
capable of mobilising absolute majorities of the EP's membership;
committees and plenaries are also continuously requested to reach
consensus and expedite business if the Parliament is to maintain
influence in an inter-institutional dialogue with bodies that many of
its members consider to be stronger than the EP itself. A perceived
interdependence between the performance of the party groups and
the powers granted to the EP means that MEPs are under continuous
pressure to prove that transnational parliamentary parties can work,
if their institution is to be given more power. Given the present
'permanent revolution' in EU institution-building – with three IGCs
already since 1996 – the struggle to prove that transnational parties
are capable of supporting the further parliamentarisation of the
Union without diminishing its overall performance casts a long
shadow over group behaviour in the EP. This motive for cohesion
is not, however, without its problems, for it implies that MEPs are
more interested in uniting to maximise the powers of their own
institution than in dividing to articulate and represent all the
conflicting values that European publics have in integration. This is
a difficulty to which we will return.

Leadership structures and command systems

According to this explanation, the groups achieve respectable levels of
cohesion because they are not as different from conventional political
parties as is commonly believed and may, in particular, mimic some
of their internal hierarchies and disciplines. Each of the groups does,
indeed, possess an elaborate leadership structure which, as Table 6.4
shows, implicates anywhere between 15 and 40 per cent of members
in their overall success, arguably tilting their sense of identity in
favour of the group and deepening their commitment to do everything possible to build consensus on tricky questions. The fact that
less than half of MEPs tend to be reelected members of the previous
parliament – only 42.5 per cent in 1994 – means that a high

proportion of these individuals, who are also likely to be key opinion-formers at least in the first half of each parliament, will be absorbed in the group leadership structures. As seen, the bureaux of the groups tend to include one leading figure from each national party delega-tion, thus facilitating the development of common positions by means of continuous communication and adjustment between the group and its national parts. On the other hand, we have also seen that, although the groups issue whips, they only have very limited capacity to play snakes and ladders with their members' careers. This must limit any explanation of cohesion based on the notion that the groups have replicated features of hierarchical parliamentary parties.

A symbiotic relationship between the national delegations and group cohesion

Another possibility is that the dual character of EP party politics – the survival of both the national party delegation and the transna-tional group as organisational foci – has been surprisingly conducive to cohesion. The practice of meeting in national delegations and representing the leader of each of these on the bureaux of the groups will often simplify processes of bargaining and consensus-building. Several national delegations issue their own whips in parallel with those of the group as a whole, and these may prove the more

TABLE 6.4

Leadership structures of the party groups and percentage of member-ship participating in leadership positions (1994)

	Group leader	No. of vice-presidents	No. of bureau members	Other officers	% of group in leadership
PES	Green, Lab – UK	15	16	1	15.0
EPP	Martens, CVP – Belgium	6	25 Full	1	34.1
ELDR	De Vries, VVD – Neth.		25 Alternates		
UEL	Puerta, IU – Spain	3	15	1	39.2
FE	Ligabue, FI – Italy	7	3	1	35.4
RDE	Pasty, RPR – France	2	5	1	31.0
G	Roth, G – Germany	5	–	2	30.7
ERA	Lalumière, ER – France	2	–	1	20.0
EN	Goldsmith, Autre Eu –	–	6	1	42.1
	France	3	1	3	42.1

persuasive of the two for those whose sights are so fixed on national
party advance as to be unaffected by the capacity of EP party groups
to dispense rewards or sanctions.

For those 50 per cent of MEPs who on past performance will leave
the EP at the end of each parliament, the prospect of a reputation for
disloyalty seeping back into domestic politics is assured by a whole
series of factors: the presence in national delegations of some MEPs
with dual mandates (France, Italy and Ireland), the presence of
liaison officers from the domestic party bureaucracy (almost all
countries), the high number of MEPs who hold some kind of party
office at home, and even the presence of some party leaders in the
Parliament. Whether an MEP wishes to continue in the EP, seek
future office at home, or just make a splash while in the Parliament, it
will be important to follow the whip of the national party delegation.
The national party delegation is, in fact, the key intermediating force
between the individual and the group in the apportionment of
political opportunities in the EP itself. Not only are offices and
rapporteurships distributed on a proportional basis to the transnational groups. Most groups also attempt an equitable subdivision
between their national party delegations. As shown in Chapter 4,
loyalty to national party delegations is also reinforced by the use of
list systems for most European elections, with intense competition
from politicians to secure the highest possible place on their party list.

Thus so long as most of its national delegations can be accommodated, a transnational group will often be able to 'piggy-back' on
national party disciplines. Contrary to the asssumption that transnational party groups will only begin to work once MEPs show an
undivided commitment to the integrationist ethic and blend imper-
ceptibly into the groups irrespective of their national origins, low
levels of cohesion in the groups may, in fact, be the consequence of a
malfunctioning of key national party delegations. During the 1980s,
for example, the PES was dogged by infighting between factions of
the French Socialist Party, while the British Labour Party MEPs
reproduced all the domestic battles between pro- and anti-EC
tendencies, Bennites and anti-Bennites. This led to frequent chal-
lenges and counter-challenges for the leadership of the European
Parliamentary Labour Party, and to a level of introversion and
personal bitterness that limited the ability of the Labour delegation
to contribute to transnational group unity (Abelès, 1992; Corbett *et
al.*, 1995, p. 91).

Core–periphery relationships in the groups

The limited elements of internal hierarchy reviewed in the last two sections may also interact with distinctive patterns of political concentration to make the groups more cohesive. Table 6.5 shows the cumulative proportion of each group covered by its first and second largest national parties (concentration measures) and the average size of the remaining parties (fragmentation measures). It is immediately apparent that although the PES and EPP include an enormous number of national parties, just two parties account for just under a half of each group. A pattern of two dominant parties around which a whole lot of smaller players then have to cluster is even more marked for the smaller groups with the exception of the ELDR.

While the uneven mix that is present in most of the groups between a handful of large national parties and a profusion of small ones has the disadvantage of making them somewhat less transnational in character, it may have the advantage of aiding consensus-building. A half of most groups are often united merely by virtue of peer group

TABLE 6.5

Concentration and fragmentation measures in the party groups (1994)

	PES	EPP	ELDR	UEL	RDE (UPE)	G	FE (UPE)	ERA	EN
Concentration measures:									
Largest party	LAB	CDU	PSD	IU	RPR	Grünen	FI	ER	AuE
	UK	Ger	P	Sp	Fr	Ger	It	Fr	Fr
Seat share (%)	28.0	27.2	15.4	29.0	53.9	48.0	93.1	68.4	68.4
Second largest party	SPD	PP	D66	PCF	FF	Verdi	Ind	SNP	Juni
	Ger	Sp	Neth	Fr	Ire	It	It	UK	Den
Share of 1st + 2nd (%)	46.1	42.8	26.9	51.5	80.9	64.0	100	79.0	79.0
Fragmentation measures:									
No. other parties	16	21	16	7	2	9	0	3	2
Ave. seat share of other parties in group	3.4	2.7	4.6	6.9	9.5	4.0	–	7.0	10.5

Note: (i) concentration measures = proportion of groups covered by first and second largest national parties; (ii) fragmentation measures = average seat share of remaining national parties in each group.

disciplines within their core national delegations, while the remaining half consists of national delegations that are so small that they have every incentive to anticipate the centre of political gravity amongst their larger counterparts and to concentrate on facilitating its evolution on terms acceptable to themselves, for the only alternative to this may be marginalisation in the group and the Parliament. Put in more formal terms, group cohesion is a collective good that allows the Parliament to function and take effective decisions. However, there is always a danger that particular national delegations will choose to 'free-ride', hoping that they will be able to enjoy the benefits of majority formation while opposing the consensus of their group, perhaps in order to resolve domestic difficulties. A not implausible story of how cohesion works in the EP groups is that their core national delegations are few enough in number to monitor and trust one another not to free-ride by producing less than their fair share of consensus-building behaviour, while the peripheral national party delegations are sufficiently small and fragmented for free-riding behaviour to be punishable by marginalisation (Lord, 1994).

The analysis of one PES member of how his group works in the 1994–9 parliament is that the British Labour Party and German SPD (combined share 46 per cent) 'hold the key. Once these decide to do something this counts for more than consensus across the board' (Authors' interview with PES member). In previous parliaments, the German and Italian Christian Democrats were in a like position to assume a leading role in the EPP, underpinned by their common enthusiasm for European integration. Even in the 1994–9 parliament, where the occupancy of first and second positions in the EPP by a Christian Democratic party (German CDU/CSU) and a Conservative party (Spanish PP) might have produced less agreement amongst the larger players, many have been surprised by the priority the PP has given to consensus-building. Amongst smaller national parties in the Parliament, many MEPs also confirm the law of anticipated reactions hypothesised above, emphasising a tendency to combat the threat of marginality not through obstruction of the efforts of larger players to take a lead in building consensus, but careful footwork to ensure that the larger national delegations are aware of their views in advance (Authors' interview with EPP member). Cohesion based on the policy leadership of the larger national party delegations will only be possible where (i) these delegations have the political skills and experience to assume such a role, and the support of their domestic political parties for the objective of building a cohesive party group in the EP, (ii) there is unity within and between the larger delegations, (iii) the larger groups are sensitive to the needs of the smaller and (iv) agreements can be made by upgrading the common interest and by avoiding conflicts of 'national interest'.

The party groups and rule-based methods of cooperation

The previous three explanations of group cohesion in the EP stress the conventional disciplines and hierarchies of party politics. However, many MEPs argue that they have only had limited success in reproducing these command structures in the context of transnational parliamentary parties and that this has, in a sense, been their good fortune. They claim to have discovered almost by accident that it is possible to reverse Michels' 'iron law' that the inner life of political parties must be 'oligarchic' (Michels, 1949). They have done this by grounding an ambitious collaboration on nothing much more substantial than the willing compliance of group members with a series of political conventions that cannot, in the final analysis, be enforced. Amongst the informal rules of the game that MEPs mention as governing their group behaviour are the following:

- A tolerance of majority voting within the groups, on the understanding that this will only occur after all national parties have had an opportunity to express their opinions, and every possible effort has been made to proceed by consensus. According to some, a mixture of commitment to go on talking until consensus is reached, and of a background threat that majority voting will be used in the event of failure, is usually sufficient to ensure that formal votes will not in fact be needed and that 'whole months can go by without votes being taken' (Authors' interview with EPP member). Indeed, there is a shared interest in taking decisions without votes once discernible majorities emerge, as this obscures the identity of winners and losers.
- Full and frank communication. If members have problems with the group line, they should indicate what these are well in advance to give the rest of the group every opportunity to find some formula that will meet their objections. Thus even where dissent occurs, it is organised according to precisely defined rules.
- Commitment to compromise. As one MEP has put it, an immense sense of commitment to making an awkward transnational political system work pervades the EP, as is often the case with

the other EU institutions. It is simply not considered *'communautaire'* to disagree too long or too often and most 'colleagues feel
that they are honour-bound to accept a common position if they
feel that it is 'eighty per cent right' (Authors' interview with EPP
member).

- Avoidance of conflict. We have already seen that the conventions
of party politics in the EP do everything to obfuscate the
distinction between winner and losers and to redefine political
choices as positive rather than zero-sum in nature. Votes and
vetoes are traded, so that most MEPs can claim that there is at
least some element of the final package that meets their needs.
One experienced committee chair claims that most agreements
are made by party groups, and national delegations within them,
conceding particular clauses of legislation and resolutions to one
another, so that all concerned gain something of what they care
about most, or avoid outcomes that would be truly damaging to
their partisan interest (Authors' interview). By methods such as
these, the EP can make decisions that do not just 'count'
preferences, but weight them according to the intensity with
which they are held (Schmitter, 1996). Great efforts are made
to avoid concentrated political damage or embarrassment to a
particular national party or its constituents. Tricky questions are
often held over to allow as much time as possible for creative,
problem-solving approaches to resolve differences.

Some studies of the Parliament imply that the formation of norms
of cooperation is facilitated by the powerful socialising effects of the
party groups. Reversing the normal argument that national diversity
will be a barrier to party political cooperation on transnational
ideological lines, Marc Abelès argues that MEPs cling all the more
to their party groups in order to temper the disorientation many feel
as a consequence of removal from the familiarities of domestic
politics. The groups allow MEPs *'une maison commune'* in which they
can live with those of 'similar political principles, even if they are
inheritors of different histories':

MEPs are along way from their country of origin. It is often
difficult to comprehend all the tasks they are expected to perform.
The group offers a reassuring environment and familiar ideological
points of reference. . . It offers not only a material infrastructure of
services, but a horizon of coherent choices for the new MEP. . .

Deterritorialised, the MEP searches for new solidarities. . . Without a doubt, the group plays the role of cocoon. (Abelès, 1992,
pp. 148–55)

Others are more sceptical, suggesting that the informality of the EP
groups is the product of their remarkably undemanding political
environment. We should not, it is argued, be fooled by the inner
complexity and diversity of the groups, for in reality they are united
by the simplicity of their situation. Without having to consider the
demands of either mass electoral politics or government, they are free
to concentrate on the limited task of building legislative coalitions.
Moreover, few resource implications follow directly from the exercise
of the EP's legislative power. As Keith Middlemas has put it, the
fractiousness of party politics in the US Congress finds no parallel in
the EP, 'because it does not have the pork barrel in its own hands'
(Middlemas, 1995, p. 360). A further problem with explanations that
stress the consensual methods of the groups is that measures of their
cohesion can easily become tautological: if the EP often only proceeds
to votes in the plenaries once agreement has been reached within and
between its dominant groups, there is little way of knowing whether
roll-calls test their capacity as political actors, or merely disguise a
high incidence of lowest common denominator decision-making or
even 'non-decisions'. It is to problems with using roll-call analysis
that we now briefly turn.

Problems with roll-call measures of party group cohesion in the EP

Useful though it has been in expanding our understanding of the
political behaviour of the party groups, we need to note that there are
inherent limits to the value of roll-call analysis in the case of the EP:
first, roll-calls are only used for a minority of votes and the decision to
request a recorded vote is itself a political act, restricted to particular
conditions that may make roll-calls unrepresentative of normal party
political behaviour. Knowledge that an MEP's voting behaviour is
going to be published will, in addition, influence the way he or she
will vote. We thus have a classic social science problem of finding
some independent statistical test that does not change the very thing
it is supposed to measure; second, there is a problem of interpretation
in making a linkage between roll-call scores and the success of the
party groups as sites for consensus-building and majority-building.
Whereas the extremes of no statistical relationship in votes and

indices of agreement of nearly 100 per cent would allow firm conclusions to be reached, intermediate possibilities are of ambiguous political meaning. For example, very stable patterns of consensus *between* the groups might create more freedom for dissent *within* the groups. Yet this would, quite unreasonably, show up in roll-call analysis as a drop in the cohesion of party politics in the EP.

The coherence and stability of the party system in the European Parliament

It would be a great mistake just to look at the party groups in the EP one by one, or to treat them as mere emanations from the separate national party traditions in national politics. Parties have to compete and parties have to cooperate. The groups in the Parliament exist in a force field in which it is impossible for any one of them to make decisions without anticipating the reactions of at least one of the other groups. The importance of analysing the party groups as a system, rather than separate entities, is underscored by the absolute majority rule and a general predisposition to settle matters by oversized majorities, in order to maximise the persuasive force of the Parliament. Factors such as these put a premium on intergroup alliance-building.

Numbering the parties in the EP system

An obvious starting point for a party system analysis of the EP is with the question of how best to count its component groups and classify it as a multi-party system. A striking feature here is that the number of groups has remained remarkably steady since 1979, never exceeding 11 and never falling below seven. This has been in spite of an expansion of member states from nine to 15 and a near doubling of the number of national party delegations that have to be squeezed into the transnational party groups, from 51 in 1979 to 95 in 1995. However, a crude count of the number of party groups does not in itself yield a satisfactory system analysis for the obvious reason that it neither weights the groups according to size, nor attempts to identify the extent to which the Parliament is governed by core–periphery relationships between dominant large groups and marginalised small ones. Luciano Bardi has, accordingly, used a measure of the 'effective' number of parties in a political system to reach the conclusion that the EP is, in essence, a four- to five-party system (Bardi, 1996).

How transnational is the party system in the EP?

Benefits for the democratisation and political integration of the Union predicted by some of the theories outlined above depend upon the overall system of groups in the Parliament attaining a transnational character, rather than specific groups developing in such a direction. In assessing the degree to which the Parliament has developed a transnational party *system* – and not just a few transnational groups – we need to count how many countries are covered by each of the party groups, work out the proportion of each group covered by its largest national parties, bear in mind the general cohesion of the group and then weight each group according to its seat share. We would be wrong to be impressed by the transnational credentials of a group that covered all 15 member states were we to discover that just one or two national parties were in a position to dominate its decision-making. We would, likewise, be wrong to be impressed by the transnational credentials of a group that assembled a balanced membership of parties from many countries, only to find that they were unable to act together.

The suggested indicators of the transnational character of the groups are summarised in Table 6.6. Only the three largest groups covering about 70 per cent of the Parliament – the PES, the EPP and the ELDR – would seem to be genuinely transnational in the number of countries covered. On the second measure – the proportion of each group covered by its largest national delegations – the PES and the EPP come out less well. They both have just one national party delegation that can, on its own, throw a little less than 30 per cent of the group's votes into the political balance, for or against a proposition, and, in both cases, three national delegations can command a majority within the group. The ELDR, on the other hand, is internally much more diffuse, but it does not cover all the member states, and, even where its transnational credentials appear sound on paper, its coherence as a cross-country ideological coalition is more suspect. Beyond the PES, EPP and ELDR, the smaller groups have only weak transnational credentials. Only two – the UEL and the Greens – cover slightly more than a half of the member states. Four out of six are effectively two-party coalitions with just two national party delegations holding around 80 per cent of the seat share of the group. The UEL is geographically curious with a predominance of French and southern European members, and just a few Scandinavians attached, largely in response to the 1995 enlargement. More than half the Greens are made up by the German Grünen; more than two-thirds of the EN by James Goldsmith's Autre Europe list which ran in France in the 1994 elections to the European Parliament; and most of the ERA by Bernard Tapie's Énergie Radicale, also from France. One possible problem is that the minimum thresholds for group formation have not been changed frequently enough or proportionately with the progressive enlargement of the EP from 410 members in 1979 to 626 in 1995, with the result that the institutional spur towards transnationalisation has been relaxed, at least for the small groups.

Defining the core of the EP party system

A further concept used by political scientists that can aid our understanding of the party politics of the EP is that of the 'system core'. This has been used in two senses: the one suggesting that particular parties and alignments are so important that they define the political character of the institution in which they exist; the other focusing on combinations of parties that can dominate over all others, and the consequent likelihood that a party system will have a single equilibrium, multiple equilibria or no equilibrium at all. Gordon Smith, for

TABLE 6.6

Measures of the transnational character of the party groups (1994)

	Number of countries represented in group	Percentage share of two largest parties in group	Cohesion of group (%)	Weight in party system (%)
PES	15	46.1	89.0	35.5
EPP	15	42.8	90.21	27.6
ELDR	13	26.9	80.14	8.3
UEL	8	51.5	83.84	5.0
FE (UPE)	1	100.0	81.29	4.2
RDE (UPE)	4	80.9	93.19	4.7
G	9	64.0	85.21	4.0
ERA	5	79.0	100	3.0
EN	3	79.0	70.7	3.0

example, suggests the following three tests for the core of any party system:

- the presence of a party or parties that over a substantial period have been in leading positions;
- the presence of parties that have been especially influential for the functioning of the political system or institution in which they exist;
- the existence of party alignments, especially coalitional line-ups. (Smith in Mair and Smith, 1990, p. 161)

According to these tests, the EP does, indeed, possess a robust and persistent core, consisting of just two groups, the PES and the EPP. Table 6.7 shows the proportion of the EP covered by each of the political groups since 1979 with the combined share of the PES and EPP highlighted. Since direct elections in 1979, the two main groups have persistently accounted for anything between 50 and 70 per cent of the EP. They have also tended to vote together on around three occasions out of four (Table 5.3). The PES/EPP axis has often been the thread of coherence that runs the whole way through the work of the EP, combining a range of political processes and bargains into a regular stream of policy outputs. It would even seem that collaboration between the two main groups is underpinned and partially institutionalised by explicit memoranda of understanding, which help to prolong cooperation from one parliament to another (Arndt, 1992). In Chapter 4 we also showed how the PES and EPP have in recent years been prepared to make significant adjustments to their own composition, in order to maintain their role in the system as a stable core and to adapt it to changing rules for the exercise of the EP's powers. Even though appearances of parliamentary duopoly can be galling to the remaining groups, the voting figures in Table 5.3 show that any hegemony is benign to the extent other groups vote with the big groups as often as they vote with one another. Indeed, only the EN votes with the PES and EPP conspicuously less than half of the time.

Some predict that if the EP wins its battle for fuller powers, the PES and EPP will switch out of a collusive role and into one of bipolarised left–right conflict; and that the political maturity of the EP will not be properly tested until it can sustain groups that are both transnationally coherent and fully politicised with a capability to make choices that involve real conflicts (Ladrech in Gaffney, 1996).

TABLE 6.7

Seat shares of the party groups, 1979–95 (%)

	1979	1984	1986	1989	1992	1993	1994	1995
PES	27.5	30.0	33.2	34.7	34.7	38.2	34.9	35.5
EPP	26.1	25.3	23.0	23.6	31.3	31.3	27.7	27.6
PES + EPP	**53.6**	**55.3**	**56.2**	**58.3**	**66.0**	**69.5**	**62.6**	**63.1**
EDG	15.6	11.5	12.2	6.6				
Communist	10.7	9.9	8.9					
ELDR	9.8	7.1	7.9	9.5	8.7	8.8	7.6	8.3
RDE	5.4	6.7	6.6	4.2	4.1	3.9	4.6	4.2
Technical	2.7					3.9		
Arc en Ciel		4.4	3.9	2.7	2.9	3.1		
European Right		3.7	3.1	3.3	2.7	3.1		
UEL				5.4	5.4		4.9	5.0
Left Unity			3.3	2.5	2.5			
G				5.6	5.4		4.1	4.0
Forza						4.8	4.7	
ERA						3.4	3.0	
EN						3.4	3.0	
Non-inscrits	2.7	1.5	1.4	2.7	2.3	4.1	4.7	4.9

We saw in the last chapter that there is some evidence that left–right bipolarisation is the second most frequent mode of parliamentary behaviour. There are, however, good reasons for believing that a consensual bipartisanship of the PES and EPP will, for the foreseeable future, continue to be the dominant mode. To see why this is so, let us imagine in Table 6.8 what would be needed for more adversarial left–right politics to function in the 1994–9 parliament. The table lines the groups up into conceivable coalitions of the left and right. The ELDR is included as a possible partner in either camp given the broad range of left–right views to be found within that group and, thereafter, it is assumed that the coalitions are widened to the left and to the right until a majority is obtained. Bearing in mind that the absolute majority rule requires 314 votes for many of the powers of the Parliament to be exercised, the PES and EPP conceivably could build grand coalitions of the left or the right as an alternative to collaborating between themselves.

But this pattern would present three major problems. First, such strung out coalitions of the left or the right would only be able to afford a combined rate of dissent and absenteeism of just 1–9 per cent

TABLE 6.8

Alternatives to a PES/EPP duopoly? Possible left–right coalitions in a bipolarised EP

Left coalition	Group size	Cumulative total	Right coalition	Group size	Cumulative total
PES	221	221	EPP	173	172
ELDR	52	273	ELDR	52	225
G	25	298	RDE (UPE)	26	251
ERA	17	315	F (UPE)	29	280
UEL	28	343	EN	19	299
Left Non-Inschs	0	343	Right Non-Inschs	31	330

before the absolute majority rule blocked all action. By contrast, a PES/EPP coalition, with 394 seats, can afford to lose up to 20 per cent of its support in these ways. Second, the strategic players, whose support would be critical at the margins for agreements in a bipolarised parliament, would be the groups of the far left and far right, or even the unattached members. On the right, in particular, these groups contain anti-system elements, opposed to the whole structure of the contemporary EU and to much of the project of European integration. Third, the ELDR might be an unstable partner if forced to choose between a broad left or a broad right. Some of its members incline to the right on the issue of markets versus intervention. Others take a more Social Democratic view. Likewise, many ELDR members who are on the right on socioeconomic issues incline towards the PES on ethical and personal issues, preferring not to align too closely with Christian Democratic elements. It might be objected that this analysis is founded only on figures for the 1994–9 parliament. But the factors that yield a parliamentary party system in which it is difficult to find stable alternatives to PES/EPP coalitions of the centre are deeply rooted. The social cleavage structures that underline voting habits have proven remarkably stable throughout Western Europe, and the fact that 14 of the 15 member states use proportional representation to elect members of the European Parliament means that such shifts as do occur are likely to be muted in their effects. In addition, the 'second-order character' of European elections means that there are no 'uniform swings' in elections to the European Parliament, and that sharp movements to the left or the right in particular member states are often cancelled out by cross-currents in others. The combined effects of the absolute majority rule and the PES/EPP duopoly are centripetal and stabilising: they encourage the EP to conclude its political bargains at the centre of politics and to avoid sharp left–right alternations. Not only does this correspond to the normal distribution of most public political preferences, it also seems to be most appropriate to a Union in which dominant trends in public opinion are at any one time to be found on the centre left in some member states, but on the centre right in others. An attempt to exercise the Parliament's collective rule-making functions from an exclusively 'leftist' or 'rightist' perspective could be damaging at this stage in the Union's development. It would mean that member governments – with strong preferences of their own on a left–right scale – would be taking more of a gamble in supporting the extension of the Parliament's role.

The stability of the EP party system

Even if we could have been more optimistic that the Parliament had developed a fully transnational party system, we would also be interested in its stability or persistence. If transnational parliamentary parties are to have a role in the development of the EU as a political system, we want to be sure that they have themselves bedded down to a definite form: that they are neither so fluid nor ephemeral that their efforts to shape political choices for the Union fail to accumulate from one period to another. The case for the prosecution is that several of the groups still seem to be somewhat *ad hoc* formations. A sense that the boundaries between the groups are porous, and that they have failed to define hard-edged clusters of political values or interests in the EU political arena, is seemingly underscored by the fact that, in recent years, more seats have changed hands as a result of MEPs switching groups during the lifetime of a parliament than as a consequence of changing electoral preferences, expressed through the ballot box (Bardi, 1992).

Figure 6.1 provides a graphic illustration of recent fluidity in the party politics of the EP. In fact, around one in ten of the MEPs reelected in 1994 had once sat in another group and one in five members of the PES and EPP came from national party delegations that once did so. There are grounds for believing that a European party system, initially formed by just aggregating domestic party systems, was always going to be less stable than the latter, at least until it could encourage some parties to regroup to take account of the specific politics of the EU. Whereas many national systems have one or two peculiarities – more than one large mainstream party on the left or right, a Liberal 'outlier' – the EP has at one stage or another inherited the full range of these idiosyncrasies from its component national systems. Above all, the schism of the European centre right between Conservatives and Christian Democrats was scarcely noticeable in national arenas – where just one of these parties usually holds sway. It only became a problem once these parties came together in a transnational system.

In an ideal world, a fully stabilised party system might be characterised as one without gaps or overlaps on key political dimensions, such as left–right choices. One with gaps would encourage new entrants and one with overlaps would be open to regroupings. Figure 6.2, drawn from some of the data in previous chapters, shows that the EP's party system covers most of the political

FIGURE 6.1 Main changes in group composition between elections, 1989–95

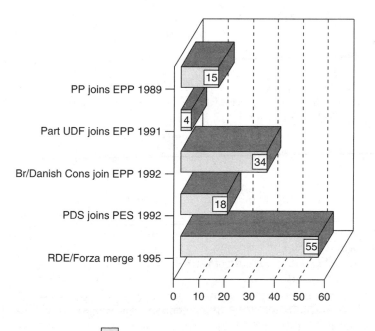

Seat changes

FIGURE 6.2   Left–right range of party groups

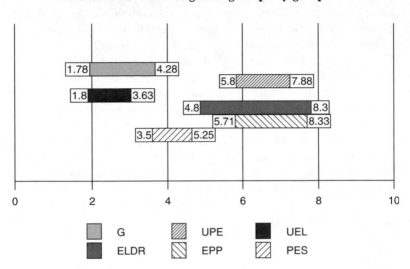

spectrum. In fact, it may be even more complete than appears at first sight. This is because the far right does coordinate its activities, even though it has not been able to satisfy the formal requirements of group formation in the 1994–9 parliament. If the EP party system is largely without gaps, it does, on the other hand, still have overlaps, and these have historically been significantly more pronounced on the right than the left, hence the merger of Conservatives and Christian Democrats and, more recently, of Forza and the RDE.

Pulling some strands together and opening up a few others, we might observe the following about the overall stability of the EP party system:

- Changes in group membership since 1986 may be evidence of system maintenance, and not of instability: individual national parties have changed group in a way that has allowed the system as a whole to remain unchanged. The PES and EPP have always provided the dominant core of the EP party system. However, this could only continue after the Single Act effectively introduced oversized majorities to the Parliament (by requiring the EP to organise absolute majorities of its members if it was to exercise its powers) if the PES and EPP enlarged themselves to include more national parties.

- Luciano Bardi has pointed out that the party system in the EP may be subject to a five-year cycle of concentration and partial fragmentation. Efforts by MEPs to arrange themselves into concentrations that facilitate absolute majorities are subject to interruption each time the second-order pattern of EP elections sucks new protest or 'surge' parties into their midst (Bardi, 1995).
- The EP party system is more tidily organised on the left than on the right. The right has yet to resolve substantial overlaps on a left–right socioeconomic scale between the EPP, ELDR and UPE (Figure 6.2). What may, however, keep the three groups distinct is the multidimensionality of their relationship: the ELDR differs from the EPP on ethical questions and elements of the UPE disagree with it on the issue of intergovernmental or supranational integration. Prospects for the final consolidation of the centre right in the EPP may, therefore, depend on a complex convergence.
- There are also some incongruities between national party systems and that of the EP which could, conceivably, cause some problems in the future. There are cases of parties that collaborate in the EP, even though they compete in the national arena and, conversely, of those who compete in the EP, even though they are coalition partners at home. One implication of the British Conservative presence in the EPP and Labour membership of the PES is that these parties, which come from the most adversarial domestic system in Western Europe, often vote together in the EP. Meanwhile, the Gaullists and the UDF are both part of the majority that supports the French government in Paris. Yet in Strasbourg, they vote in three different groups, the EPP, the ELDR and the UPE.

Conclusion

The indicators we have developed here would suggest that transnational party formation is by no means a hopeless task, at least at the parliamentary level. The groups in the EP are capable of respectable levels of cohesion and institutional autonomy. They also form a party system that would seem to be centripetal and relatively stable for this stage in the Union's development, even if it is not quite as transnational as appears at first sight. What cannot, however, be known is whether they would be able to sustain these qualities in a more

normal – and challenging – context of party competition, characterised first by a clearer linkage between the work of MEPs and mass
electoral politics, and second by relationships of government and
opposition in the Parliament. Any development in the transnational
dimension of electoral competition would place a premium on the
groups' extra-parliamentary links. These are mediated through the
party federations, to which we now turn.

7

Parties Beyond the Parliament

In this chapter we turn to the emergence of parties at the European level outside the European Parliament. The main extra-parliamentary structures in the EU are the party federations. Since their birth in the mid-1970s, the internal mechanisms of the party federations have become more complex and regularised, and the external links between the party federations and the EU institutions have strengthened (particularly through the emerging role of the Party Leaders' Meetings). As a result, party organisation beyond the EP has evolved from 'transnational party cooperation' for coordinating the European election campaigns to 'nascent Euro-parties' that attempt to extend party activities to the main agenda-setting arena in EU politics (the European Council).

Three phases of party development beyond the Parliament

The development of parties outside the EP has three distinct phases: a period of optimism, from the birth of the party federations in the early 1970s to the first EP elections in 1979; a period of stagnation, from the aftermath of the first elections to the 1989 elections; and a period of renaissance, from the start of the negotiations on the Treaty on European Union, in 1990, to the time of writing in 1996 (Hix, 1996).

Optimism: birth of the party federations

The catalyst for the formation of party organisations outside the EP was the decision to hold direct elections to the EP at the December

1969 EC summit in the Hague. In 1957 the Socialist International (SI) had created a Liaison Bureau for cooperation between the EC parties, and on 5 April 1974 the SI transformed the Bureau into the Confederation of the Socialist Parties of the EC (CSP). Also following the Hague summit, the 1972 Congress of the Liberal International (LI) asked the party leaders to examine ways of deepening cooperation between the EC parties. However, the Federation of Liberal and Democratic Parties in the EC (ELD) was formally founded on 26 March 1976 independently of the LI. Similarly, at the 1973 EUCD Congress in Bonn, a working group was set to draft a statute for a 'European Christian Democratic Party'. The statute was ready by February 1976, but the establishment of the European People's Party: Federation of Christian Democratic Parties in the EC (EPP) was delayed until 29 April 1976 because of a prolonged dispute over the name.

Although no more party federations were set up prior to the first EP elections, several other party families established transnational links. The PCI and PCF held several summits, but rejected any formal organisational connections. In 1978, a number of Regionalist parties established the European Free Alliance (EFA). There was also limited cooperation between Green parties, and some informal contacts were made between extreme right parties. Consequently, the only other formal party organisation created in this period was the European Democratic Union (EDU), which was established in Salzburg in April 1978. However, the EDU was never meant to be anything more than a loose grouping of all the elements of the centre right, including non-EC parties, and did not play a role in the EP elections.

There was considerable optimism about the future of the party federations. Leading academics and politicians openly predicted that these new party structures would launch a new democratic phase of European integration. These hopes were summed up by Leo Tindemans, the former Belgian Prime Minister and the President of the EPP, when he proclaimed that, 'only European political parties can bridge the gap between the hopes of public opinion and the powerlessness of governments to turn these expectations into proposals for concrete policies' (Christian Democrats, 1976).

Stagnation: no clear role for the federations

However, these predictions collapsed with the reality of the first EP elections. The party federations began with the lofty ambition of adopting detailed manifestos for the European elections. In the build-up to the first elections, however, the EPP was divided over the place of 'Christian' principles in the programme, and between parties who wanted an anti-Socialist bloc and the parties in domestic coalitions with Socialists. The Liberal parties agreed only to be bound by the (few) sentences in the manifesto in bold type; and the difficulties of adopting a common Socialist manifesto were so great that the project, and the 1977 Electoral Congress, were abandoned in favour of a shorter political declaration by the party leaders and an Appeal to the Electorate. After this experience, the parties settled for vague statements of principle in the 1984 elections.

Furthermore, despite the efforts of the party federations, the EP elections were fought within the member states, by the domestic parties, with domestic candidates, and on domestic issues. With rudimentary organisational structures, the transnational parties could be nothing more than clearing-houses: providing information and campaign materials, and organising (poorly attended) conferences. Most voters and party activists were unaware of the work of the federations, despite the use of some of the federation symbols. (Menke and Gordon, 1980; Niedermeyer, 1984, 1989).

A fundamental problem for the party federations was that they did not have a clear role beyond the adoption of European election manifestos. Their only attachment to EU decision-making was through the groups in the EP. After the elections, however, the EP groups had the financial and political resources to survive independently of the party federations. Consequently, any further development of party organisation outside the EP would have to be on the initiative of the national parties. As Dick Toornstra, the Secretary-General of the CSP, told the Socialist Parties' International Secretaries: 'parties are finally called upon to make a choice, whether they want a Confederation with some political power or just a European Socialist Post Office box' (letter from Dick Toornstra to the CSP International Secretaries, 27 June 1979).

However, by the end of the 1980s, there were some indications that further development was possible. In the 1989 elections all three federations agreed common manifestos without much difficulty, and for the first time there were two truly supranational issues in all the national campaigns: the environment and the single market. Moreover, on 1 April 1984 the European Coordination of Green Parties (ECGP) was inaugurated. Finally, and most significantly, new partisan organs emerged in each of the party federations that provided a real voice for national parties in the European arena: the Party Leaders' Meetings.

Renaissance: towards 'parties at the European level'

A new phase of party development outside the EP was ushered in by the negotiation and ratification of the Treaty on European Union in the Intergovernmental Conferences (IGCs),beginning with the Rome European Council of 27 October 1990, which set the agenda for the IGCs. The EPP party leaders met on 25 October, and unanimously agreed to support a fixed timetable for EMU in the European Council. The British Conservative Government had already stated that it would oppose any such move. However, the use of qualified majority at the Rome summit for setting the IGC agenda enabled the Christian Democrats to secure their goals with the support of the Socialists. The British press consequently proclaimed that the British Prime Minister had been 'ambushed' by the Christian Democrats. Margaret Thatcher later admitted that her advisers had under-estimated the importance of the EPP meeting:

> What I did not know was that behind the scenes the Italians had agreed with a proposal emanating from Germany and endorsed by Christian Democrat leaders from several European countries at an earlier caucus meeting. (Thatcher, 1993, p. 765)

Copying the EPP leaders' strategy, the Socialist and Liberal leaders also arranged their meetings to coincide with the IGC timetable and agenda.

Moreover, when the Treaty on European Union was finally adopted at the Maastricht European Council in December 1991, it surprisingly contained an article stating that:

> Political parties at the European level are important as a factor for integration within the Union. They contribute to forming a European awareness and to expressing the political will of the citizens of the Union. (Treaty on European Union, Article 138A)

In response to this so-called 'Party Article', the Secretaries-General of the Socialist, Christian Democrat and Liberal federations presented a joint paper on the 'Political Follow-Up to Article 138A', which called for a 'European Political Party Statute'. By 1995, the EU Party

Statute was still in the pipeline. Meanwhile, in November 1992 the Confederation of Socialist Parties was transformed into the Party of European Socialists (PES); in June 1993 the Green Coordination was dissolved and the European Federation of Green Parties (EFGP) was established; in December 1993 the Federation of Liberal, Democratic and Reform Parties became the European Liberal, Democratic and Reform Party (ELDR); and in October 1995 the European Free Alliance (EFA) – of regionalist parties – adopted new articles, and begun calling itself a 'party at the European level' in accord with Article 138A.

By 1995, there were four extra-parliamentary party organisations at the European level, with member parties in nearly all the EU member states. The organisation of Party Leaders' Meetings around the European Council had also become a new party political dynamic in the EU system. The party federations had at last found an institutional point of focus beyond the EP and had created a set of incentives for national parties to provide financial and political resources to sustain their development. As the next two sections show, this evolution combined an (internal) institutionalisation of the party federations as the main organ of extra-parliamentary activity at the European level, and a growing (external) connection between these organisations and the European-level institutions.

Internal institutionalisation of the party federations

There is a dramatic difference in the complexity and coherence of decision-making rules between the original statutes of the party federations in the mid-1970s (or in 1984 in the case of the Greens) and the new statutes that were adopted in the early 1990s.

Socialists

- *Confederation of the Socialist Parties of the EC, 1974*

The first statutes of any extra-parliamentary party organisation within the framework of the EC were the 1974 Rules of Procedure of the CSP (CSP, 1974). The basic aim of the CSP was 'to strengthen inter-party relations and, in particular, to define joint, freely agreed positions on problems raised by the existence of the EC' (Article 2). Although there was thus an explicit link to the institutional structure of the EC, the organisation of the CSP was the European extension of the Socialist party organisations in the domestic arena and not of the Socialist representatives in the European institutions. This was reflected in the full voting rights of the national party representatives in the main decision-making bodies, as opposed to the consultative status of the EP group representatives and the Socialist Commissioners. Moreover, the CSP was subservient to the global party 'International': Article 1 stated that the party federation only existed as a regional organisation under the statutes of the Socialist International. Finally, the decision-making authority of the organs of the party were considerably weak. The Bureau and Congress could adopt non-binding 'recommendations' to the national parties (and not to the EP group) by a simple majority. Binding decisions could be adopted by unanimity in the Bureau and two-thirds of the Congress delegates, but the CSP had no means of enforcing these decisions as there were no provisions for fining or expelling member parties.

- *Party of European Socialists, 1995*

Consequently, the contrast with the structure of the PES in 1995 is striking (PES, 1995). The PES now had a more specific set of aims (Article 3): to strengthen the Socialist movement in the Union and throughout Europe; develop close relations between the national parties, the national parliamentary groups, and the PES group in the EP; define common policies for the EU; engage individual members in its activities; promote contacts with European trade unions and professional associations; and adopt a common manifesto for the elections to the EP. These aims are thus similar to the traditional aims of a party in any political system: to secure political office for party representatives; pursue policies through the institutions of the system; provide channels of cooperation and communication for the various party office-holders; involve the party membership; and establish links with the traditional groups in civil society.

In addition, PES decision-making is much more complex. The constituent elements of the PES include the Full Member Parties (of which two, the Norwegian DNA and Cypriot EDEK, are not from EU member states), the Associate and Observer Parties, the Socialist Associations (such as the EC Organisation of Socialist Youth (ECOSY)), and the PES groups in the EP and the Committee of the Regions. The PES also has a new decision-making organ: the Party Leaders' Conference. Party leaders of the member parties had met unofficially since 1974, but the Leaders' Conference was formally instated in the inaugural statutes of the PES in November 1992 (PES, 1992a). Under the new statutes, the Party Leaders' Conference is the only organ that can make recommendations to the member parties and the EP group. Furthermore, the right to take binding decisions on the member parties was removed from the Congress and given to the Leaders' Conference. Finally, the statutes provide for party leaders to adopt decisions by a qualified majority in all areas where majority voting is used in the EU Council of Ministers (Article 9.4). If a member party it is unable to implement a decision by a majority vote it must declare so before the vote is taken. Moreover, although it has not been used in practice, the PES can enforce these decisions by financial sanctions or expulsion of a member party.

Christian Democrats

- *European People's Party: Federation of Christian Democratic Parties of the EC, 1976*

Compared to the CSP, however, the first statutes of the EPP outlined a more developed party organisation at the European level (EPP, 1976). Unlike the CSP, from the outset one of the central aims of the EPP was to 'support, coordinate and organise the European activities of its member parties' (Article 3.d). Also in contrast to the CSP, the EPP had a programmatic aim: 'to participate in, and support the process of, European integration and cooperate in the transformation of Europe into a Federal Union' (Article 3.c). Decision-making was split between three organs: the Congress, the Political Bureau, and the Executive Committee; and the EPP already had provisions for 'observer parties'. The first EPP statutes did not contain any provision for the adoption of binding decisions, but a member party could be expelled by a majority of the Political Bureau (Rule 15.b). Nevertheless, whereas all CSP decisions were officially taken by a consensus, all EPP positions could be taken by a simple majority (Articles 6.i and 7.h).

- *European People's Party: Christian Democrats, 1993*

Like the PES, the story told by the 1993 EPP statutes is more complex than the original tale (EPP, 1993a). An obvious difference was the establishment of three new official organs. First, the Executive Committee had been replaced by the Presidency, which involved: the EPP President, the Vice-Presidents, the Secretary-General, and the President of the EPP group in the EP with full voting rights; and a

Christian Democrat Commissioner, the Secretary-General of the EPP group in the EP, the President of the European Union of Christian Democrats (EUCD) and the President of the EPP group in the Council of Europe Assembly with consultative status (Article 11). The explicit purpose of this gathering of the European-level elites is to ensure the 'permanent political presence of the EPP' (Article 11.c). The second new organ, the Office of the Secretary-General, had existed under the original statute, but was not an official organ with a detailed set of functions. The post now covers a broader range of tasks, including supervising cooperation between the General Secretariats of the domestic parties and the EP group (Article 14). The new statutes hence envisage the EPP Secretariat as the apex of a Christian Democrat party bureaucracy stretching from the domestic members to the EP group.

Like the PES, moreover, the third new EPP organ is the Conference of Party Leaders and Heads of Government. This was first installed as an official organ of the party federation in the 1990 statute reforms (EPP, 1990). Although officially the EPP Leaders' Conference is lower than the EPP Congress, in reality the Leaders' Conference is the dominant body of the EPP. Like the PES, the EPP Leaders' Conference is the only body where decisions are made collectively by the Christian Democrat elites from the European and domestic arenas: the national party leaders, the Christian Democrat prime ministers, the Christian Democrat Commissioners, and the President of the EP group. Consequently, decisions of the EPP Leaders' conference are more legitimate than those of the Congress or the Political Bureau, and have a more direct effect on the actors in the domestic and European institutions. However, whereas the EPP Political Bureau is instructed to make all decisions by an absolute majority of those present (Article 9.c), the EPP statute does not establish any formal voting rules for the EPP Leaders' Conference.

Liberals

● *Federation of Liberal and Democratic Parties in the EC, 1976*
The decision-making structure established by the first statutes of the ELD was more like the CSP than the EPP (ELD, 1976). The ELD had only two official organs: the Congress and the Executive Committee. The ELD aims were more organisational than programmatic: 'to seek a common position on all the important problems affecting

the EC' (Article 2). Also, the statutes stated that the Liberal federation would 'act within the framework of the Liberal International [LI]'. However, unlike the CSP, parties did not have to be members of the LI to be full members of the ELD. They simply had to accept the statutes and programmes of the Congress (Article 3). Like the EPP, moreover, the Liberal group in the EP was a central component of the extra-parliamentary Liberal organisation from the outset (Article 10). The ELD statutes did not establish any provisions for making decisions binding on the member parties. However, unlike either of the other transnational party organisations, the Executive Committee was instructed to make all decisions by majority votes.

- *European Liberal, Democratic and Reform Party, 1993*
Again, the obvious contrast between the ELD and the statutes of the 1993 ELDR Party is in the level of complexity (ELDR, 1993a). The aims of the ELDR were expanded to include a programmatic commitment (to 'strengthen the liberal, democratic and reform movement in the EU and throughout Europe') and a more detailed organisational aim (to 'develop close working relationships among the national parties, the national parliamentary groups, the ELDR Group in the EP and the Liberal, Democrat and Reform-Group in other international fora' (Article 3)). Moreover, rather than two main decision-making organs, the 1993 statutes provide for four. The activities of the Congress remained practically the same as under the original statutes. The Executive Committee was replaced by the Council, and two new organs were created. First, like the EPP Presidency, the ELDR Bureau was established to bring together the key European level figures – the President, Vice-Presidents, and the Treasurer with full voting rights, and the Secretary-General and the President of the EP group with consultative status – and is responsible for the management of the day-to-day activities of the ELDR.

Second, as with the PES and EPP, the ELDR Party Leaders' Meeting was established as an official organ. The ELDR Leaders' Meeting was not formally instituted into the statutes until 1993, although the Liberal leaders had met informally almost every year since the creation of the party federation. The official institutionalisation of these meetings confirmed the position of the ELDR Leaders' Meeting as the central decision-making organ in the Liberal party federation. Although the Congress can make recommendations to the member parties, the decisions of the ELDR Leaders' Meeting are in practice more legitimate because of the authority of the participants.

Nevertheless, whereas under the statutes of the PES and the EPP, the party leaders may adopt positions by a majority, the ELDR statutes explicitly state that: 'in all the organs of the ELDR Party, efforts shall be made to establish the broadest possible measure of agreement among the member parties' (Article 16). This is thus in stark contrast to the majoritarian intentions of the old statute. It is a recognition, however, that whereas the old ELD was insignificant for the member parties, the ELDR Party can make important decisions about domestic and EP group policies towards the EU.

Greens

- *European Coordination of Green Parties, 1984*
The fourth extra-EP transnational party organisation within the framework of the EC system was the European Co-ordination of Green Parties. However, as the inaugural statutes show, the ECGP was different to the three main European party organisations (ECGP, 1984). Full membership of the ECGP was not restricted to parties from the EC member states. The ECGP had only one decision-making organ: the twice-yearly Meeting of the Green Co-Ordination. However, this gathering was similar to the CSP Bureau, the EPP Political Bureau, and the ELD Executive Committee: its aim was to coordinate the activities of the member parties on European policy questions; and day-to-day decisions could be taken by majority decisions whereas policy decisions needed unanimity. Moreover, although the statutes did not officially mention a Congress of the Green Co-Ordination, a biannual Congress was held; and like the other transnational parties, the activities of the ECGP were organised by a Secretary-General.

- *European Federation of Green Parties, 1993*
However, it was not until the inaugural statutes of the EFGP that the Green parties established a real 'party federation' (EFGP, 1993). The central aims of the EFGP are similar to the other three parties: 'to assure a close and permanent co-operation among the Members in order to accomplish a common policy' (Article 2). Nevertheless, the institutional structure of the EFGP is more like the other party federations under the early statutes. The EFGP only has three decision-making organs – the Congress, the Council, and the Committee – and there are no provisions for meetings of the Green party leaders outside the Congress. However, the Committee of the EFGP is

similar to the EPP Presidency and the ELDR Bureau: as an ongoing body that brings together the key political decision-makers. And, without a party leaders' meeting to resolve disputes at the highest political level, the EFGP has established a novel procedure for tackling such problems: an Arbitrage Committee.

Nevertheless, there is a further fundamental difference between the EFGP and the other three EU party organisations: the EFGP is not EU-specific. The membership of the party is open to any European Green party, and a majority of the member parties are from non-EU states. Also, the EU as an institutional system is not mentioned anywhere in the statutes, and the official seat of the EFGP is in Vienna (whereas the seats of the other three parties are in Brussels). Furthermore, the Greens have held most of the Congresses in non-EU member states. However, this does not necessarily mean that the EFGP is not part of the 'EU party system'. The EFGP still seeks to get Green representatives elected and nominated to offices in the EU institutions, and seeks policy outputs from the EU system. The EFGP statutes also provide for specific cooperation within the framework of the Green party federation among the member parties from the EU member states (Article 7). Consequently, the expansion of the membership of the EFGP beyond the boundaries of the EU is less a rejection of the EU system as a whole than a reflection of the ideological commitment to a wider European construction. As the statutes state: 'The Federation devotes itself to an open, active, constructive and critical approach to the ongoing integration process in Europe towards a world wide cooperation' (Article 2). Overall, the EFGP is part of the EU party system, but is an anti-system party in that it does not accept the territorial boundaries of the political system in which it operates.

In sum, therefore, the changing 'official stories' reveal that the party federations have established considerably more complex organisations since their creation. There has also been a clearer definition of when and why different voting procedures should be used: majority votes for day-to-day management, and unanimity for medium- and long-term policy objectives. Finally, in the three main party federations, Party Leaders' Meetings have emerged as the main organs for coordinating policy on European issues in the domestic and European arenas. However, the EFGP does not fit this pattern. On the one hand, the Green federation is at the level of development of the other federations in the 1970s and 1980s. On the other hand, the EFGP is a

fundamentally different type of party organisation altogether: based
on the coordination of Green parties inside and outside the EU (like a
Socialist or Liberal International, or the EUCD).

External links to the EU institutions

Turning to the external organisation of parties beyond the Parliament, the party federations have moved away from a single focus on
the EP groups to additional links to the actors in the Commission, the
Council of Ministers and the European Council. The relationship
between the party federations and the actors in the European
institutions is a two-way channel: representation of the party members holding European political office in the organs of the party; and
the control of the behaviour of these actors by the party organs. This
development is summarised in Tables 7.1 and 7.2.

Party-institution linkages in the 1970s and 1980s

As Table 7.1 shows, in the early phases of party development the only
real linkage to the European institutions was through the party
groups in the EP. In terms of representation of party actors in the
extra-parliamentary organs, the EP groups had full voting rights in
the EPP and ELD Congress and executive bodies, and consultative
rights in the CSP and ECGP organs. As for controlling the EP
groups, however, all the party federations were able to make recommendations to their MEPs, but these could not be enforced. Only the
EPP made any effort to enforce policy decisions: through the Action
Programmes adopted by the EPP Congress at the beginning of each
new EP term; and only the ELD required that the Executive
Committee had to be consulted in the selection of candidates for
the European elections.

   As for the party actors in the other European institutions, the
Commissioners had full voting rights in all ELD organs and in the
EPP executive bodies, and consultation rights in the CSP executive.
Concerning the Council of Ministers, however, only the EPP made
any provisions for the participation of Christian Democrat government Ministers in party meetings. Finally, the party leaders (including the heads of government) participated in the work of the party
federations through the informal CSP, EPP and ELD leaders' meetings. There were, however, no provisions for the delivery of party

TABLE 7.1

Party–institution linkages in the 1970s and 1980s

Parties		European Parliament	Commission	Council of Ministers	European Council	All EC institutions
				Institutions		
Socialists, 1974	Representation:	Medium	Low	–	Low	Low
	Control:	Low	–	–	–	–
Chr. Dems, 1976	Representation:	High	Medium	Low	Low	Medium
	Control:	Medium	–	–	–	Low
Liberals, 1976	Representation:	High	High	–	Low	Medium
	Control:	Medium	–	–	–	Medium
Greens, 1984	Representation:	High	–	–	–	Low
	Control:	Low	–	–	–	Low
All parties	Representation:	High	Low	–	Low	Low
	Control:	Medium	–	–	–	Low

Notes: '–' means that the party actors in an institution are not represented in any party organs, or that there are no mechanisms for making party demands on the actors in that institution; 'low' means that the party actors in an institution have *ex officio* rights in the party organs, or that recommendations can be made to the actors in that institution but not enforced; 'medium' means that the party actors in an institution have full voting rights in some party organs, or that there are some provisions for enforcing party decisions on these actors; and 'high' means that the party actors in an institution have full voting rights in all party organs, or that there are provisions for the enforcement of party decisions on these actors.

decisions to the party actors in these other EC institutions. Overall, therefore, under the first statutes, the level of participation of European level party actors in the work of the party federations was low, and the ability of the party federations to influence the behaviour of these actors was practically non-existent.

Party-institution linkages in the 1990s

As Table 7.2 illustrates, however, the situation in the early 1990s was substantially different. The only element of continuity was the relationship with the EP groups. In terms of participation, in the 1990s the MEPs were fully active in all the organs of the main party federations – with the EP group leaders also participating in the new Party Leaders' Meetings. In return, party federation control over the EP groups increased slightly: with official recognition in the Internal Regulations of the three main EP party groups that they are the 'Group of the PES', 'Group of the EPP', and 'Group of the ELDR'. As a result, the party federation leaders' meetings are required to approve which parties and individuals sit in their EP groups. In fact, in 1994, the posts of EPP Party and EPP Group President were held by the same person – Wilfried Martens. The only countervailing fact was that the relationship between the EFGP and the Green group in the EP was reduced formally (with no rights of participation in the EFGP Congress independently of the domestic parties) and informally (with the EFGP less dependent on the resources of the Green group after the transfer of the 'Official Seat' of the EFGP to Vienna).

In contrast to the stability of the relationship with the EP groups, the links to the other European institutions significantly increased between 1974 and 1995. The Commissioners are full participants in the ELDR Congress, Council and Bureau, and *ex officio* in ELDR Leaders' Meetings. They are also full participants in the EPP Congress, Political Bureau, and Leaders' Conference, and ex officio in the EPP Presidency. The Commissioners are *ex officio* in the PES Bureau and Leaders' Conference. In return, however, there are hardly any provisions for influencing the actions of the Commissioners. Only the PES has begun to establish a way of introducing partisan influence into the work of the European Commission: through the launch in January 1995 of an informal 'Socialist Caucus', of the nine Commissioners from PES member parties.

Party actors in the Council of Ministers have also increased their involvement in the work of the federations. The Council of Ministers

TABLE 7.2

Party-institution linkages in the 1990s

Parties		European Parliament	Commission	Council of Ministers	European Council	All EU institutions
				Institutions		
Socialists, 1995	Representation:	High	Medium	Medium	High	Medium
	Control:	Medium	Low	Medium	Medium	Medium
Chr. Dems, 1993	Representation:	High	High	Medium	High	High
	Control:	High	–	Medium	Medium	Medium
Liberals, 1993	Representation:	High	High	Medium	High	High
	Control:	Medium	–	Low	Low	Low
Greens, 1993	Representation:	Medium	–	–	–	Low
	Control:	Low	–	–	–	–
All parties	Representation:	High	Medium	Medium	High	High
	Control:	Medium	–	Low	Low	Medium

is formally mentioned in all the party statutes: Christian Democrat ministers are full participants in the EPP Congress; a representative of the Liberal ministers can attend ELDR Party Leaders' Meetings; and the President of the Council of Ministers (if he or she is from a Socialist party) can participate in PES Leaders' Conferences. Moreover, ministers are increasingly involved in party federation business in an informal capacity. On several occasions government ministers and opposition party spokespersons have come together under the auspices of the party federations to discuss current issues in the Council of Ministers, and junior ministers and party spokespersons are increasingly involved in the party federation working groups. Finally, through the work of the Party Leaders' Meetings, the activities of ministers have begun to be constrained by the policies of the party federations. The clearest example of this was at a PES Party Leaders' Meeting in March 1996, where the leaders undertook to:

> investigate how Socialist Finance Ministers at the recent ECOFIN Council had prevented the adoption of measures in favour of employment, despite: 1) the expression of complete support for these measures by their respective party leaders; and 2) a favourable opinion by a Socialist pre-meeting to the Council, of Socialist Ministers and Alan Donnelly (PES group spokesman on employment). [PES, 1996]

However, only the PES has explicit provisions for attempting to bind the actors in the Council of Ministers, by requiring that a majority vote is taken on any issue where a qualified majority is used in the Council of Ministers.

The most significant change from the early statutes, nevertheless, has been in the relationship between the party federations and the European Council. The institutionalisation of the Party Leaders' Meeting means that the heads of government have the most powerful position in the party federations. Indeed, the 1993 EPP statutes explicitly state that in the Conference of Party Leaders and Heads of Government there is a special role for all 'members of the European Council belonging to a member party'. This thus includes the prime ministers, the foreign ministers and the Commission President and Vice-President from the EPP member parties, even if they are not a party leader. This is not formally stated in the PES or ELDR statutes, but in reality they practise the same procedure. However, the level of control over the actions of party representatives in the European Council remains low.

In conclusion, therefore, the external structure of the extra-parliamentary organisations has evolved from a single link to the EP groups towards a more general connection to all European-level party actors. This shift is particularly highlighted by the role of the participants in the European Council in the Party Leaders' Meetings. There has also been an increase in the influence of the party federations on the behaviour of the actors in the EU institutions, but the overall level of party control remains low. Nevertheless, the party federations have sought to maximise their limited influence by deliberately organising Party Leaders' Meetings around the European Council, as the next section discusses.

Party Leaders' Meetings and the European Council

Two further developments have resulted from the institutionalisation of the Party Leaders' Meetings as the main organs of extra-parliamentary activity at the European level. First, the quantity and quality of the leaders' meetings has fundamentally changed. And, second, they have begun to influence decision-making in the European Council. An important question, however, is whether the internal changes have resulted from the ability to influence the European Council, or whether Party Leaders' Meetings were only able to influence the EU agenda because of their internal evolution.

Quantity and quality of the Party Leaders' Meetings

The complete list of all the meetings of the Socialist, Christian Democratic and Liberal party leaders is shown in Table 7.3. From the first informal leaders' meetings in the mid-1970s to their new role within the party federations in the 1990s, the Party Leaders' Meetings have experienced a quantitative and qualitative development.

On the quantitative side, as the table shows, the number of leaders' meetings increased: from an average of two meetings a year for the EPP and PES and one a year for the ELDR up to the mid-1980s, to an average since 1989 of three a year for the EPP and PES and two for the ELDR. Nearly 50 per cent of all the Party Leaders' Meetings from 1974 to 1995 were held in the last six years of the period. Also,

TABLE 7.3

Dates and venues of the Party Leaders' Meetings

Yr.	Date	Party Family	Venue	Yr.	Date	Party Family	Venue
1974	26 Nov.	Socialist*	The Hague	1989	10 Feb.	Socialists+	Brussels
1976	18 Jan.	Socialists	Helsingor		11–12 Mar.	Greens+	Paris
	26–7 Mar.	Liberals*+	Stuttgart		10 Apr.	Liberals*	Copenhagen
	5–7 Nov.	Liberals+	The Hague		28–9 June	Socialists*	Paris
1977	18–20 Nov.	Liberals**+	Brussels		14 Nov.	Socialists+	Lisbon
1978	6–7 Mar.	Chr. Democrats+	Brussels	1990	8–9 Feb.	Socialists+	Berlin
	23–4 June	Socialists**+	Brussels		17 Feb.	Liberals	Potsdam
	2–3 Dec.	Liberals*+	London		23–4 Mar.	Chr. Democrats	Pisa
1979	11–12 Jan.	Socialists	Brussels		5 June	Socialists**	Vienna
	22–3 Feb.	Chr. Democrats+	Brussels		6–8 June	Liberals***+	Dublin
	29 June	Socialists*	Brussels		25 Oct.	Chr. Democrats*	Shannon
1980	15–16 Feb.	Liberals+	Paris		15–16 Nov.	Chr. Democrats+	Brussels
	24 Feb.	Chr. Democrats	Strasbourg		23 Nov.	Liberals	Dublin
	3–4 Mar.	Socialists+	Luxembourg		10 Dec.	Socialists*	Berlin
	1–2 Sep.	Chr. Democrats+	Cologne	1991	20 Jan.	Socialists	Madrid
1981	27 Apr.	Socialists	Amsterdam		7 Apr.	Greens+	Zurich
	12–14 June	Liberals+	Copenhagen	1992	**13 Apr.**	**Ch. Democrats**	**Brussels**
1982	7–8 May	Socialists+	Venice		3 June	Socialists**+	Luxembourg
	12–13 Nov.	Chr. Democrats**+	Paris		6–7 June	Liberals**+	Poitiers
	6–8 Dec.	Liberals	Paris		21 June	Chr. Democrats**	Luxembourg
1983	20 Apr.	Liberals	London		3 Dec.	Liberals*	Brussels
	3 Oct.	Chr. Democrats	Brussels		3–4 Dec.	Socialists*	Brussels
	26 Nov.	Chr. Democrats*	Brussels		6 Dec.	Chr. Democrats**	The Hague
	9–10 Dec.	Liberals**+	Munich		14 Feb.	Chr. Democrats*	Brussels
1984	22 Jan.	Liberals	Stuttgart		5 June	Socialists+	Lisbon
	8–9 Mar.	Socialists**+	Luxembourg		15–16 June	Liberals+	Copenhagen
	31 Mar.	Greens+	Liège				
	2–4 Apr.	Chr. Democrats	Rome		2–3 July		

Year	Date	Party	Venue
	12–13 May	Liberals+	Brussels
	1 June	Socialists*	Brussels
	23 June	Liberals*	Rome
1985	22 Mar.	Greens+	Dover
	9–10 Apr.	Socialists*	Madrid
	13 Apr.	Liberals	Copenhagen
	23 Apr.	Chr. Democrats	Luxembourg
	5–7 June	Liberals+	Groningen
	19–20 June	Chr. Democrats**	Rome
	9 Nov.	Chr. Democrats	Brussels
1986	1 Mar.	Chr. Democrats	The Hague
	10–11 Apr.	Liberals+	Catania
	10–12 Apr.	Chr. Democrats+	The Hague
	3 Oct.	Liberals	Hamburg
1987	4–5 Mar.	Socialists+	Lisbon
	27 Mar.	Greens+	Stockholm
	1–3 Apr.	Liberals+	Lisbon
	30 May	Chr. Democrats	Brussels
	23 Oct.	Socialists	Paris
1988	8–9 Apr.	Greens+	Antwerp
	14 May	Liberals	Turin
	30 May	Chr. Democrats	Bonn
	10 June	Socialists*	Rome
	19 Oct.	Chr. Democrats	Brussels
	6–7 Nov.	Socialists	Berlin
	7–8 Nov.	Chr. Democrats	Luxembourg
	3–9 Nov.	Liberals*+	Luxembourg

Year	Date	Party	Venue
	25 Sep.	Chr. Democrats	Brussels
	10 Oct.	Socialists*	Brussels
	9–10 Nov.	Socialists+	The Hague
	14 Nov.	Chr. Democrats+	Athens
	4 Dec.	Chr. Democrats*	Brussels
	7 Dec.	Liberals*	Brussels
	9–10 Dec.	**Socialists****	**Edinburgh**
1993	2 June	Chr. Democrats*	Brussels
	16 June	Liberals**	Copenhagen
	18–20 Jun.	Greens*+	Helsinki
	19–20 Jun.	Socialists**	Copenhagen
	4–5 Sep.	Socialists*	Arràbida
	5–6 Nov.	Socialists+	Brussels
	9 Dec.	Ch. Democrats***+	Brussels
	9 Dec.	Socialists**	Brussels
	9–10 Dec.	**Liberals*+**	**Torquay**
1994	22 June	Chr. Democrats*	Brussels
	22–3 June	Socialists**	Corfu
	7–8 Dec.	Socialists**	Essen
	9 Dec.	Chr. Democrats*	Brussels
1995	6–8 Mar.	Socialists+	Barcelona
	24–5 June	Socialists**	Cannes
	25 June	Chr. Democrats**	Cannes
	5–7 July	Liberals+	Stockholm
	6 Nov.	Chr. Democrats	Madrid
	11 Nov.	Socialists*	Madrid
	23 Nov.	Liberals*	Bonn
	8 Dec.	Chr. Democrats*	Brussels
	14 Dec.	Socialists**	Madrid

Note: A meeting with one asterisk was held close to (in the week before or after) a European Council; and with two asterisks was also in the same venue as a European Council. A meeting with a cross was held during a party congress. The meetings in bold were the first as the main organs of the party federations, under the new party statutes.

whereas most of the meetings in the early period were held alongside party congresses (as indicated by the crosses in the table), in the 1990s the majority of the EPP and PES leaders' meetings were held independently as the number of congresses decreased (to one every two years). This consequently parallelled the shift of decision-making power away from the party congresses towards the Party Leaders' Meetings. Furthermore, in the 1990s, the Green party leaders started to meet, although these gatherings were not yet recognised under the EFGP statutes. The Party Leaders' Meetings hence evolved from *ad hoc* events to regular fixtures in the EU timetable and in the annual calendars of the Brussels press corp.

An increased volume of Party Leaders' Meetings may be a necessary condition for influencing EU decision-making, but it is not sufficient by itself. However, the quality of the Party Leaders' Meetings has also changed in ways that impact on the EU agenda. First, the number of national party leaders who attend the leaders' meetings has increased significantly. When a leaders' meeting is held, party leaders can choose to send another senior party official instead. When there are pressing matters in the domestic arena, there is little point in wasting a day or two at a party federation meeting, unless it can clearly contribute to a party leader's competitive position. As a result, between 1980 and 1988, the average attendance of the national party leaders (and not their junior staff) at the party federation meetings was 65 per cent for the Socialists, 73 per cent for the Christian Democrats, and 52 per cent for the Liberals. Between 1989 and 1994, in contrast, the average attendance of party leaders was 75 per cent for the Socialists, 85 per cent for the Christian Democrats, and 58 per cent for the Liberals.

The second major qualitative change is the organisation of Party Leaders' Meetings specifically around the meetings of the European Council. The internal agenda of the Party Leaders' Meetings began to focus on the issues in the European Council. In the 1970s and the 1980s, the leaders' meetings did not really have fixed agendas and hence tended to discuss a wide range of issues which were not directly related to the European institutions. For example, several Christian Democrat meetings discussed the development of Christian Democracy throughout the world (and specifically in Latin America), and a series of Socialist meetings in the 1980s debated the issues of unemployment and structural change in Europe. In the 1990s, in contrast, a detailed agenda for each Party Leaders' Meeting is prepared by the federation secretariats, and approved by the executive committees (of the national party International Secretaries and the EP group leader). The items on these agenda are usually the exact issues of the previous or following European Council, as the titles of some of the declarations indicate: 'EPP Position on the Dublin Summit'; 'Socialist Leaders' Declaration on the IGCs'; or 'European Council in Essen: the ELDR Position'.

Linked to the organisation of the agenda of the meetings, the Party Leaders' Meetings are increasingly held in the week immediately before or after a European Council, and sometimes even in the same place as the EU summit. The rationale of meeting before a European Council is that the non-governmental parties can put pressure on the party actors participating in the European Council. The incentive for governmental actors, on the other hand, is to form alliances with like-minded actors prior to the European Council bargaining. Similarly, by meeting immediately after a European Council, the participants in the European Council are forced to defend their positions to their fellow 'European Party' members. In Table 7.3, the Party Leaders' Meetings held 'close to' a European Council are marked with a single asterisk, and those also held in the same venue as a European Council are marked with two asterisks. Before 1990, the timing of the Party Leaders' Meetings was not systematically linked to the European Council timetable. Only a few leaders' meetings between 1974 and 1989 were held close to a European Council, and these were almost entirely by coincidence (such as the Socialist leaders' meetings as part of the first EP election campaign in 1978 and 1979). In contrast, over 70 per cent of the meetings between 1990 and 1995 were held immediately before or after an EU summit. Moreover, since 1991, the Socialists have tried to hold all their leaders' meetings on the day before a European Council and in the same venue. Finally, until 1989 over 50 per cent of all European Councils did not have any 'close' Party Leaders' Meetings, and only one had more than one meeting close to it. In contrast, since 1990, about three-quarters of all European Councils have had at least two Party Leaders' Meetings close to them; and about one-third have had all three groups of party leaders meeting in close proximity.

However, these quantitative and qualitative developments only really hold for the Socialists and Christian Democrats. The Liberal leaders do not meet as often, do not attend so frequently, and rarely meet close to many European Councils. Nevertheless, this counter-vailing experience of the ELDR fits with the suggestion that the other parties only developed because they had the potential of influencing

the European Council. Whereas the Socialists and Christian Democrats together had over two-thirds of the participants in the European
Council between 1990 and 1995 (eight heads of government, five or
six foreign ministers and the Commission President) the ELDR had
only one prime minister and three foreign ministers. Moreover, the
Liberal foreign ministers were from coalitions where the 'European
policy' of the governments was dominated by the parties holding the
prime minister's offices (the Christian Democrats in Germany and the
Conservatives or Socialists in Denmark). It is not surprising, therefore, that the Liberals have begun to arrange for party leaders to meet
only at the ELDR Congress and to organise special ELDR Councils
close to every European Council instead. This way, recources would
not be wasted on meetings with a low attendance of the national
leaders, and the ELDR would still be able to issue declarations (with
the prior support of the party leaders) on the issues on the European
Council agenda.

In general, therefore, there is considerable evidence to show that
the Party Leaders' Meetings have developed as they have established
a link to an institutional arena (the European Council). However,
simply organising around the European Council does not necessarily
mean altering the EU agenda. In fact, one could argue that the
agenda of the leaders' meetings changed, that party leaders began to
attend, and that the European media began to take notice of the
meetings only because the meetings began to be held close to a
European Council. In other words, the European Council influenced
the leaders' meetings, and not vice versa. The reality, however, is a
balance between dependence and independence: Party Leaders'
Meetings needed the European Council to raise their profile and
status; but have subsequently been able to structure the options of the
national governmental leaders on some of the issues already on the
agenda. This latter point is hence the subject of in the next section.

Influencing the European Council

In the 1990s, party leaders have been most active around the
December European Councils. This is more than coincidence since
these meetings are traditionally used as an overview of the previous
year (of both Council Presidencies) and a discussion of the agenda for
the coming year. An analysis of party activity around, and the
outcomes of, the four December European Councils in 1991, 1992,

1993 and 1994 hence illustrates the impact and limitations of the new organisational strategies of the Party Leaders' Meetings. In this analysis, however, we focus only on socioeconomic issues. As discussed in Chapter 2, parties at the European level can only compete on issues where they are coherent across national boundaries (i.e., the left–right positions that define the transnational party families).

• *Maastricht, December 1991: the Treaty on European Union*
The main issue on the agenda of the European Council at Maastricht on 9–10 December 1992 was the final agreement on the Treaty on European Union. On this subject, the Liberal party leaders had met on 3 December in Brussels, and had called for: EU citizenship; co-decision powers for the EP; a uniform European election procedure; and full EMU, with convergence criteria for 'price stability and budget deficits' (ELDR, 1991). The CSP leaders met on 3–4 December, also in Brussels, and highlighted the need for an EU 'social dimension' (more economic and social cohesion and EU social policy), and convergence criteria for EMU based on 'social indicators' (such as levels of unemployment) (CSP, 1991b). Finally, the EPP heads of government and party leaders met on 6 December in The Hague, and agreed to support co-decision powers for the EP, more majority voting in the Council of Ministers, and new European competences in a number of policy areas (EPP, 1991).

In other words, the Christian Democrats focused on institutional questions, and the Liberals and Socialists took opposing positions on the economic issues in the treaty. However, the EPP was also at a clear advantage because there were six Christian Democrat prime ministers at the European Council, (Martens (CVP), Kohl (CDU), Andreotti (DC), Santer (PCS), Lubbers (CDA) and Mitsotakis (ND)), and the EPP party leaders had been able to discuss their proposals directly with the drafter of the Maastricht Treaty and the Chair of the EU summit, Ruud Lubbers (*Agence Europe*, 7 December 1991 and 9–10 December 1991). As a result of these factors, the outcome of the Maastricht European Council was very close to the EPP position, and contained only the CSP and ELDR issues that coincided with the aims of the EPP (i.e., the ELDR position on 'economic' convergence criteria, and the CSP position on economic and social cohesion). The Socialists and the Liberals were only able to secure one joint aim that had not been on the EPP agenda: the provisions on EU citizenship. Nevertheless, the Socialists had failed to prevent convergence criteria for EMU based purely on economic targets, and the Liberals had failed to secure an agreement on a uniform electoral procedure for the EP.

The Treaty on European Union adopted by the Maastricht European Council also contained a new Article (138A) on 'parties at the European level'. The idea for a 'Party Article' originated in a series of joint meetings between the presidents of the three party federations (Martens (EPP), Willy De Clerq (ELDR) and Guy Spitaels (CSP)). (Joint meetings of the three presidents of the party federations were held on 18 September 1990, 12 December 1990, 17 June 1991 and 2 October 1991.) The party presidents argued that:

> Without the contribution of European parties, Union is neither thinkable nor viable . . . [and] this essential contribution should be recognised explicitly in the new treaty on Political Union, in order to make possible, in the medium term in a way similar to national policy, European legislation that provides for a working framework for European Parties. (*Agence Europe*, 19 June 1991)

The federation presidents also cited Article 21 of the German Basic Law as a possible model for an EU Party Article. (Article 21 of the German Basic Law states: 'Political Parties shall participate in the forming of the political will of the people'.) Opposition from several national governments meant, however, that this provision was absent from the Luxembourg 'non-paper', the Luxembourg Draft Treaty and the first Dutch Draft Treaty. Nevertheless, by the Maastricht summit, the position of the party federation Presidents had been endorsed by the national party leaders. The second Dutch Draft Treaty hence made a commitment 'to include an article on parties at the European level', which was adopted by the Maastricht European Council, and the precise wording was decided before the Treaty was formally signed in February 1992. This was the first clear indication of the party federations attempting to alter the institutional environment for their own ends.

● *Edinburgh, December 1992: Denmark, subsidiarity, enlargement and employment*

The next European Council when three Party Leaders' Meetings were held beforehand was in Edinburgh, on 11–12 December 1992. The packed agenda included the Danish referendum against the Maastricht Treaty, a clarification of 'subsidiarity', when to open EU enlargement negotiations, and EU finances. The EPP party leaders met on 4 December in Brussels, and urged the European Council to uphold the Maastricht ratification timetable, increase EU transparency, launch enlargement negotiations 'immediately', and adopt a common approach on unemployment (EPP, 1992). The Liberal leaders subsequently met on 7 December in Brussels, and also called on the European Council to reject a renegotiation of the Maastricht Treaty and to democratise the EU, but 'insisted that the only path to economic recovery is through free and fair trade' (ELDR, 1992). Finally, the inaugural PES Party Leaders' Meeting was held on 9–10 December in Edinburgh, and called for a coordination of national economies to stimulate economic recovery, a European works programme, and an increase in the cohesion funds (PES, 1992b). Again, the parties were united on the institutional agenda (i.e., Maastricht ratification and the subsidiarity provisions), but were divided on the economic issues: with the Christian Democrats caught between the free market position of the ELDR and the interventionist position of the PES.

A further important event at the PES leaders' meeting was a confrontation between Franz Vranitzky (the SPÖ Chancellor of Austria) and Felipé González (the PSOE Prime Minister of Spain). González arrived in Edinburgh prepared to veto the opening of enlargement negotiations if the European Council would not significantly increase the finances available under the new Cohesion Fund. Vranitzky insisted, however, that EU enlargement was paramount for European Socialists; and that Austrian, Finnish, Swedish, and Norwegian membership would lead to more economic transfers to the less prosperous regions. Vranitzky apparently also pointed out that under the new statutes of the PES, a majority of the Socialist leaders could impose their wishes on the Spanish party. Under this PES pressure, González agreed to back down.

Including the prime ministers and foreign ministers, at the Edinburgh European Council there were eight Christian Democrats, eight Socialists, four Liberals, and five from centre right parties that were not members of any party federation. Compared to Maastricht, therefore, the Christian Democrats were no longer in ascendance. Nevertheless, in cooperation with the Socialists, the Christian Democrats managed to secure a European Council 'Declaration on an Economic Recovery in Europe', which was a surprising development given the initial agenda of the summit. However, some of the ELDR agenda for financial propriety was included in the Delors II budgetary package. It was partially due to the PES leaders' meeting, moreover, that the European Council agreed to launch the enlargement negotiations at the beginning of 1993, without any opposition from González.

- *Brussels, December 1993: the European Employment Initiative*
After the Edinburgh Declaration on Recovery, the European Commission began to draft a White Paper on Growth, Competitiveness and Employment. However, by the time the White Paper was ready for adoption at the Brussels summit on 10–11 December 1993, the balance of power in the European Council had shifted, to ten PES, six EPP, four ELDR, four non-attached centre right leaders, and one independent. However, not only were the Socialists now the largest group in the European Council, but they had begun preparing for this meeting before the other parties. On 4–5 September 1993, the PES leaders held their first private and informal 'Conclave', in Arrábida in Portugal, where they set up a working group on state–economy relations in Europe, chaired by Allan Larsson, the former Employment and Finance Minister of Sweden (PES, 1993a). This was the first working group of personal representatives of the national party leaders, which increased the legitimacy of the final report. The Larsson Report on The European Employment Initiative was subsequently adopted at the PES leaders' meeting on 9 December, in Brussels (the day before the European Council), and included a detailed list of EU interventionist measures (PES, 1993b).

Meanwhile, the Christian Democrat leaders also met on 9 December in Brussels, alongside the EPP Congress, and approved the draft EPP Manifesto for the 1994 EP elections (EPP, 1993b). On the subject of EU policies on employment, the EPP Manifesto advocated a mixture of free market economics with the use of some state intervention to facilitate economic recovery. In addition, the Liberal leaders met on 9 December alongside the Electoral Congress of the ELDR, in Torquay, and approved the ELDR Manifesto for the 1994 EP elections (ELDR, 1993b). On economic policy, the ELDR Manifesto advocated strict adherence by the member states to a stable monetary policy and a reduction of budget deficits and the tax burden. In other words, the positions of the parties on economic issues at the European level had solidified: with the Socialists advocating EU policies to promote cohesion, investment and infrastructure, the Liberals advocating deregulation and fiscal restraint, and the Christian Democrats somewhere in between.

The December 1993 Brussels European Council consequently approved the Commission White Paper, which included some of the proposals from the PES's Larsson Report (such as new procedures to coordinate national initiatives for the long-term unemployed). However, the bulk of the European Council's proposals were free market-oriented: stable monetary policies to combat inflation; a further opening-up of international trade; and the creation of a low-tax environment to encourage small and medium-sized enterprises. Nonetheless, the European Council refused to address the ELDR demands for a democratisation of the European institutions in parallel with the employment strategy (*Agence Europe*, 12 December 1993). In other words, despite the Socialists' numerical superiority, the outcome was between the EPP and the ELDR. The Christian Democrats were still pivotal, but they now needed an alliance with the Liberals and the non-attached parties of the right to oppose the Socialists: the British Conservative Government's submission on the Commission White Paper was fairly similar to the final outcome (HM Treasury, 1993).

- *Essen, December 1994: towards the 1996 IGC*

However, the position of the EPP would be further put to the test at the Essen European Council on 9–10 December 1994, where the balance had shifted further towards the Socialists: eleven PES, five ELDR, three EPP, and six non-attached centre right leaders. The wide-ranging agenda for the Essen summit included the implementation of the employment initiative, macroeconomic coordination in EMU, and the agenda of the 1996 IGC. With the backing of the Liberal party leaders, a special meeting of the ELDR Council was held in Paris on 6 December, and called for a democratisation of the EU institutions and an economic strategy based on market liberalisation (ELDR, 1994). The PES leaders met on 7–8 December in Essen, in the same building as the European Council of the following day (to the annoyance of Chancellor Kohl), and called for an EU investment programme, an expansion of social services, cooperation between the social partners, and a common policy to combat racism and xenophobia (PES, 1994). And for the first time, the Committee of the European Federation of Green Parties issued a statement from a special meeting in Essen on 8 December 1994, calling on the European Council to reform the EU in the interests of 'democracy' and 'peace', and to protect the environment and reduce unemployment (EFGP, 1994). Although there would be no Green representatives in the Essen summit, this was the first EFGP declaration directed specifically at a European Council, and hence a copy of the strategy of the more established Euro-parties.

Finally, the EPP leaders also met on 8 December in Brussels, but decided to have an open exchange of views on the agenda of the EU without the pressure of adopting a position on the forthcoming Council (like the Socialist leaders' Conclave at Arrábida). As the official minutes reveal, the EPP leaders were concerned about the small number of Christian Democrats in the European Council. In response to particular concern of the Dutch and Italian parties, however, Kohl, Santer and Dehaene promised that the positions taken by their governments in the 1996 IGC would be closely coordinated with the policies of the EPP party.

However, the increased strength of the PES did not enable the Socialist federation to impose its views on the outcome of the Essen European Council. The summit ignored the Socialist agenda for a broad EU investment and employment policy, and reaffirmed the long-term commitment to fiscal temperance. This consequently confirmed a shift in the dynamics of the EU party system, away from the triangular relationship between the EPP, ELDR, and PES of the Maastricht and Edinburgh meetings, and towards a new centre right bloc of the EPP, ELDR and non-attached parties of the right.

In sum, therefore, when the party federations pursued a deliberate organisational strategy (of holding leaders' meetings close to European Councils) they contributed to setting the medium-term (i.e., pre-legislative) agenda. This impact reflected the shifting alliances between the partisan forces on the main socioeconomic issues on the EU agenda. This is illustrated in Figure 7.1. In the Maastricht and Edinburgh European Councils in 1991 and 1992, the core of the EU party system was a 'triangular' set of alliances between the Christian Democrats, Liberals and Socialists (see Hix, 1993). The issues on each side of this triangle were adopted in the European Council: the ELDR–PES alliance on 'democracy and rights' (such as the EU citizenship provisions, and the increased powers of the EP); the EPP–PES alliance on 'social justice' (such as EU social policy provisions and the inclusion of the social partners); and the EPP–ELDR alliance on the 'free market' (such as the strict 'economic' convergence criteria for economic and monetary union and the White Paper proposals on competitiveness). In the Brussels and Essen European Councils in 1993 and 1994, however, the EU party system began to shift towards

FIGURE 7.1 Shifting socioeconomic alliances in the European Council

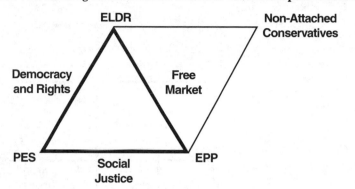

a two-bloc system: with an enlarged Socialist bloc facing an emerging (and dominant) 'free market' alliance between the EPP, the ELDR and the non-attached Conservatives.

From 'Transnational Party Cooperation' to 'Nascent Euro-Parties'

There was thus a considerable change in the nature of party organisation beyond the Parliament from its beginnings in the mid–1970s to the new situation in the mid–1990s. The combination of internal (party decision-making structures) and external (linkages to the political system) developments constituted a transformation from one 'type' of party organisation to another. This is illustrated in Figure 7.2. When the party federations were established, their internal organisations were weak and they were only linked to one European institution (through the groups in the EP). The main aims of these new European-level party organisations were the coordination of the European election campaigns and the adoption of common election manifestos. This was the classic conception of 'transnational party cooperation' described by Geoffrey and Pippa Pridham in the early 1980s (as shown in the top-left box in Figure 7.2) (Pridham and Pridham, 1981).

After the direct election of the EP, however, the EP groups developed large supporting bureaucracies, stable recruitment and decision-making structures, and substantial financial resources derived directly from the EC budget. As a result, the internal

FIGURE 7.2   Types of parties in the EU system

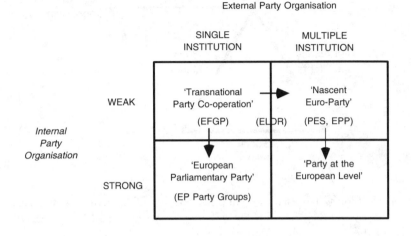

External Party Organisation

organisation of the EP groups was significantly stronger than the flimsy structures of the extra-parliamentary federations. This thus constituted the emergence of a different type of party organisation at the European level: the 'European parliamentary party' (in the bottom-left box in the figure) (see Bardi, 1994; Attinà, 1990). The aims of this organisation are to secure and maintain a particular set of political offices (the seats in the EP), and to coordinate the policy behaviour of the holders of this office. The office goal is secured through the domestic party machineries (because of the structure of MEP selection), and the policy goal is secured through the internal organisation of the groups in the EP. The MEPs hence have little incentive to contribute to the development of the extra-parliamentary organisations.

However, independent of the EP party groups, the extra-parliamentary party organisations have developed their connections with the other institutional sites in the EU system. Links began to be established with the party actors in the Council of Ministers and the Commission. However, the most significant change was the specific organisation around the European Council. The Party Leaders' Meetings (attended by the actors in the European Council) were institutionalised as the central decision-making organs of the EPP, ELDR and PES. Furthermore, the party federations increasingly sought to influence the behaviour of the European Council: through the organisation of Party Leaders' Meetings in the weeks immediately before or after (and often in the same venue as) a European Council, and through the adoption of common positions on the specific subjects of the European Council.

This development from single to multiple institutional sites was thus a movement to a third type of European party organisation: a 'nascent Euro-party' (in the top-right box in the figure) (Hix, 1995a). This type of party organisation is suitable for parties which seek some office rewards from the political system, such as seats in the EP and the post of the Commission President, and which seek policy outputs from the system. From the original shape of party federation organisation to this new type of organisation, the central goal of the parties thus shifted from loose cooperation in the European election campaigns to the pursuit of common policy goals in the EU system at the highest political level: by the domestic party leaders, and through the European Council. The success of this strategy is reflected in the growing rate of party leaders' participation in the leaders' meetings.

Nevertheless, if the main aim of parties is to pursue policy outputs from the EU system, it also would be in their interests to develop stronger internal organisational structures. Only with a stable decision-making pattern, and measures to secure binding decisions, can party policy be enforced on party actors in the European institutions. This would thus imply the emergence of a new type of European party organisation: a true 'party at the European level', as envisaged in the Maastricht Treaty Party Article (in the bottom-left box in the figure). By the middle of the 1990s, however, the transition from 'nascent Euro-parties' to real 'parties at the European level' has not yet taken place. The EPP and the PES, with the most sophisticated internal organisational structures, have made some moves in this direction. Nevertheless, the internal organisations of the EPP and the PES are still very weak in comparison to parties at the domestic level, and the ability of the party federations to enforce their positions across the whole EU system remains low. As a result, real parties at the European level are still some way off.

8

Conclusion: Towards a Europe of Parties

A turning point: *Europe des patries* or *Europe des partis*?

The Community's chances of moving beyond the narrow limits of the present 'Europe des patries' depend crucially on the emergence of a 'Europe des partis', in which the political forces that matter at the national level are bound together by the need to fight for power at the Community level.

David Marquand (1978)

David Marquand's distinction between a 'Europe of nations' and a 'Europe of parties' is even more salient for the development of the European Union in the 1990s than it was for the future of the European Community at the end of the 1970s. Marquand was writing in the build-up to the first direct elections to the EP, when he was not alone in hoping that this experiment in European-wide democracy would produce a fundamental transformation in the politics of European integration. Behind the decision to hold European elections, and behind Marquand's assessment, was the belief that the only way out of the period of 'Euro-sclerosis' – the stagnation of European integration in the early and mid-1970s – was to inject an element of classic representative democracy into the system.

Nearly twenty years on, however, the election of the EP has done little to prevent the development of a new and much deeper wave of scepticism towards European integration. At the beginning of the negotiation of the Maastricht Treaty, between 1989 and 1990, there was little reason to suggest that a bargain struck behind closed doors by senior national government ministers would not be legitimate in

198

the eyes of Europe's citizens. Yet, the process of ratifying the Maastricht Treaty between 1991 and 1993 demonstrated a deep public ambivalence about the way the negotiation of the treaty had been conducted and about the general future of political and economic integration in Europe. It seemed that the so-called 'permissive consensus' (Lindberg and Scheingold, 1970), that had guaranteed public acceptance of bargains between Europe's governmental elites since the Treaties of Rome and Paris in the 1950s, had come to an abrupt end.

Under this permissive consensus system, the basis of public support for elite agreements was a specific conception of politics at the European level. First, the vast majority of citizens perceive that for whatever political, economic, cultural, territorial or historical reason, they have more in common with people from their own 'nation' than with anyone from another nation. In other words, all the citizens of the same nation state share a common and indivisible 'national interest'. Second, this 'national interest' is articulated by national governments, who derive their (*a priori*) legitimacy from democratic elections. Third, agreement is reached through unanimously adopted package deals between these governments, that protect the vital interests of all the member states. As a result, a national government can veto a package deal with the full support of its citizens if the deal threatens the national interest. In this conception of European-level politics there is thus a coherent link between individual identity (based on an indivisible 'national interest'), articulation and representation of this interest (through national governments), and policy-making to protect this interest (through intergovernmental bargaining). This conception was classically stated by Charles de Gaulle when he described a '*Europe des patries*' (a 'Europe of nations') as the only acceptable form of authority at the European level. He consequently argued that if any of the elements of a 'Europe of nations' are undermined, legitimacy will break down. He hence blocked plans to increase majority voting in the Council of Ministers. A similar argument was made by Margaret Thatcher in her 1988 speech at the College of Europe in Bruges, when she stated that, 'willing and active cooperation between independent sovereign states is the best way to build a successful European Community'.

Problems arise, however, when some of the elements of this conception start to erode. If individuals no longer identify with the national interest, they will not feel that their government will be representing their private concerns. If decisions are taken by majority rules, or tasks are delegated to supranational institutions (such as the European Commission), individual governments are less able to protect their own national interests. Such supranational or majority decisions inevitably lead to a distribution of resources or values between one group of interests and another. If this distribution is between groups which are not defined along nation-state lines (such as farmers, employers, workers, consumers, or environmentalists), it will increase the salience of non-national identities and interests. In turn, this will mean that national interests are less clearly defined, and governments are less capable of articulating the views of their citizens. The result is that Europe's citizens are less willing to passively accept bargains struck between governments, because they do not necessarily reflect a coalition of wider societal interests.

Nonetheless, this 'legitimacy deficit' is not an inevitable consequence of European integration. With a different conception of the link between interests/identities and decision-making, the legitimacy of European-level politics may be reestablished. A possible alternative conception is a '*Europe des partis*'. As with the term '*patries*' in the classic conception of EU politics, the term '*partis*' in this alternative conception refers to party-political identities, interests, ideologies, organisations and behaviour. First, citizens identify with other people who have similar social or economic positions or values, regardless of their territorial or national location in the EU. Second, these interests or values are articulated by political parties, who advocate coherent socioeconomic '*Weltanschauungen*' (world-views) – such as Liberalism, Conservatism, Christian Democracy or Socialism – and compete with each other for the support of the socioeconomic groups. Third, political decision-making is based on majority coalitions between these partisan organisations. In Marquand's argument, therefore, if the EU is to reestablish a legitimacy, European-level politics should be very similar to politics in most (domestic) political systems in the democratic world.

A transformation from a 'Europe of nations' to a 'Europe of parties' consequently has fundamental empirical, theoretical (or methodological) and normative implications. These are summarised in Table 8.1. On the *empirical level*, the main issue is whether nation states or political parties align Europe's citizens, articulating their views at the EU level, and organise the way actors behave in the decision-making process. However, the study of these different empirical realities is best conducted using completely different *theoretical and methodological* perspectives: by analysing the EU as an international organisation

TABLE 8.1

From a 'Europe of nations' to a 'Europe of parties'

	'Europe des patries'	'Europe des partis'
Empirical:		
Individual identity	Nation	Social group
Interest articulation	National governments	EP groups/party federations
Decision-making	Intergovernmental bargaining	Executive–legislative process
Style of decision-making	Unanimity of governments	Majority based on party strengths
Underlying policy aim	Preserve 'national sovereignty'	Reallocate resources or values
Theoretical:		
Sub-field of politics	International Relations	Comparative politics
Description of EU	International organisation	Political system
Dominant theory	Neo realism	Pluralism
Main agents	Cabinet ministers	Party leadership cadre
Institutional constraints	Nation states/international institutions	Multi-level consensus and rules
Normative:		
Executive authority	European Council	European Commission
Legislative authority	Council of Ministers	European Parliament
Role of elections	No election of EU-level officials	Direct election of EP/ Commission President
Selection of Commission	European Council	Majority in the EP or direct election
Treaty changes	Intergovernmental Conference	'Constitutional Convention'

with the main actors the national ministers; or seeing the EU as a political system with an internal political arena. Finally, on a *normative* (prescriptive) level, if a 'Europe of parties' would reduce the legitimacy deficit in the EU, how should the EU institutions be designed? In the next section we will tackle the theoretical/methodological issues, before turning to the empirical issues in the subsequent section, and the normative questions in the final section.

A clash of paradigms: international versus internal politics

A paradigm is a set of assumptions, arguments and propositions about a particular subject that is accepted by the majority of theorists of that subject at a particular point in time. If one set of assumptions and propositions no longer explains the subject in a straightforward and convincing way, however, theorists begin to search for alternative explanations. When a completely new and coherent set of assumptions and arguments has been developed, and a majority of theorists are convinced that this new framework is better than the old one, the previous 'paradigm' is abandoned and the new one is adopted (Kuhn, 1962). Sometimes the old paradigm is completely replaced. More often than not, however, either two rival interpretations exist side by side for some time before the new paradigm emerges as dominant, or the old paradigm is reformed to incorporate some of the new assumptions and propositions (Lakatos, 1970).

Since the 1950s, the dominant paradigm in the study of European integration is the International Relations (IR) approach. The core assumption of this approach is that the EC, and now the EU, is a hybrid form of international organisation, where the central actors are the European nation states. The two main variants of the IR programme recognise different constraints on the behaviour of the nation states. Neo-Realists (or Intergovernmentalists) accept that non-state groups compete in the domestic arena over the definition of and right to represent the 'national interest' in the European arena (Hoffman, 1996; Moravcsik, 1993). Similarly Neo-Functionalists argue that transnational non-state groups and the supranational institutions of the EU compete with the nation states in the European decision-making process (Haas, 1958; Sandholtz and Zysman, 1989). However, these two variants of the IR paradigm share a central proposition about how EU politics works. They both maintain that all interests – whether nation states, non-state groups, or the EU institutions – are aligned along a single dimension of politics: where one end of the dimension is 'supranational integration' and the other end is 'national independence'. If the pro-integration interests win, EU integration proceeds. If the anti-integration interests win, EU integration stands still (or is partially reversed). This IR paradigm, with its central assumption of nation-state interests and its central proposition of unidimensional politics, is consequently the theoretical underpinning of the 'Europe of nations' conception of the EU. However, as the EU develops beyond a pure *Europe des patries*, the ability of the IR paradigm to explain how EU politics works is reduced.

In contrast, a fundamentally different paradigm underpins the conception of a *Europe des partis*. The behaviour and organisation of, and competition between, political parties has been a central subject of the study of domestic political systems for over one hundred years. Consequently, there already exists a deep and complex set of theories, methods and arguments (from the field of Comparative Politics) that can be used to study how parties are developing in the European Union. To have access to this body of knowledge, however, we need to abandon the assumption that the EU is an international organisation, where the nation states are the central aggregate actors, and accept that the EU is a nascent political system, where political parties are the central aggregate actors (see Hix, 1994). In this rival paradigm, politics in the EU is inherently similar to politics in any 'polity' or 'system of governance'. Against the IR proposition that EU politics is inherently unidimensional, moreover, political conflict in the EU between rival socioeconomic and territorial interests is manifest as competing ideologies (or 'world-views'), and is articulated by partisan actors in the legislative and executive arenas of government. The centrality of political parties in this comparative-political approach leads to the presumption that 'democracy is unthinkable save in terms of parties' (Schattschneider, 1942, p. 1).

However, this difference between the International and the Internal (or comparative) paradigms of the study of EU politics is less (meta)theoretical than it is methodological. The main theoretical dispute in political science, between agency-biased approaches (like rational choice) and structure-biased approaches (like new institutionalism), is the same in both IR and Comparative Politics. The fundamental difference between the two paradigms pertains more to 'what aspects of the EU should we study?' and 'how should we study them?'. In studying a 'Europe of nations', the core subjects for theoretical explanation are such things as national interest and sovereignty, interstate power relations, economic interdependence, international institution-building, and transnational policy regimes. Moreover, in the IR approach these variables are analysed by comparing their current manifestation to other examples of international cooperation in the international system, or (and more often) to a previous period of European integration. In studying a 'Europe of parties', in contrast, the theoretical focus shifts to such variables as the structure of society, the dimensions of ideological and party conflict, the institutional framework of the political system, the behaviour of political actors within this system, and the making of public policy. Moreover, in the Comparative Politics approach these subjects are analysed by comparing their structure in the EU to their structure in other political systems, or to 'ideal types' (such as pluralism, federalism, or consociationalism) that summarise a wide-range of experiences (for example, Streek and Schmitter, 1991; Sbragia, 1992; Shapiro, 1992; Majone, 1993; Lange, 1993; Bulmer, 1994; Scharpf, 1994; and Taylor, 1994).

There is thus a fundamental difference in the way politics in a 'Europe of nations' as opposed to a 'Europe of parties' should be analysed. In a system where nation states are the primary agents (an international system) it is best to use theories and methods from the field of International Relations. In a system where political parties are the primary agents (an internal political system), however, it is more appropriate to use theories and methods from the field of Comparative Politics. In the evolution from a 'Europe of nations' to a 'Europe of parties' there would hence be a transformation in the way we build-theory to explain EU politics: a shift between different paradigms.

Is the EU a 'party democracy'?

But how far has the EU already developed towards a *Europe des partis*? To answer this question one could simply look at the retrospective development of the EP party groups and the party federations. However, this would be seeing how far the EU has moved away from a 'Europe of nations' rather than how far it has moved towards a 'Europe of parties'. A better method would be to compare the present structure of parties in the EU to how we would expect them to look in a 'Europe of parties'; but we do not yet know how a Europe of parties would look. Alternatively, using a Comparative Politics approach, we can compare the present structure of parties in the EU to a generalisable model of parties in all democratic systems.

Hence, 'party democracy' is an ideal type that describes a system of democratic government where political parties are the key actors, and against which the role of parties in all systems can be measured. There are five basic criteria of 'party democracy':

- *organisational cohesion* – leaders and/or supporters with similar interests establish common, cohesive and hierarchical decision-making structures (political parties);
- *office-seeking* – the basic aim of these political parties is to secure political power through placing their representatives in positions of public office;

- *policy/ideological competition* – political parties develop rival political agendas and policy platforms and compete over how and when they should be enacted;
- *electoral legitimacy* – the primary means of choosing office-holders and between political agendas is through party competition in democratic elections; and
- *recruitment/accountability* – office-holders are recruited within political parties and are held accountable to their parties' electoral platforms and policy positions.

These criteria are an amalgamation of the work of many scholars of political parties; but see, in particular, Schattschneider (1942), Schumpeter (1943), Epstein (1967), Sartori (1976), Katz (1986), Budge and Keman (1990) and Katz and Mair (1995).

These interrelated criteria describe a system of government that exists to a greater or lesser extent in all democratic polities. The closest approximations to this ideal type are the West European democracies (at the domestic level). The United States, on the other hand, meets the criteria for office-seeking, electoral legitimacy and policy competition, but falls short on the questions of organisational cohesion and recruitment/accountability. This does not mean that European systems are more democratic than in the USA. It simply reveals that in the democratic process in the USA, political parties are constrained by the institutional structures of government (the separation of powers and the federal system) and are rivalled by other political organisations (such as powerful interest groups). Consequently, when comparing the role of parties in EU politics to the 'party democracy' model we are not judging whether the EU is democratic, but simply how far the democratic process in the EU is channelled and articulated through political parties.

Organisational cohesion

As we have shown in the previous chapters, European-level political parties were formed in the earliest years of the EP between politicians from the same historical 'party families' but from different member states. Similarly, in the build-up to the first direct elections to the EP in 1979, the domestic party organisations and the EP groups of the main European party families established the 'transnational party federations', to draft European electoral programmes and cooperate in the development of common positions on European-level issues. By the early 1990s, there were thus four parties at the European level: the European People's Party (of Christian Democrats and some Conservatives); the Party of European Socialists; the European Liberal Democratic and Reform Party; and the European Federation of Green Parties/Green group in the EP.

Moreover, these 'European parties' have established hierarchical and decision-making structures comparable to political parties in the domestic arena. The EU parties have party constitutions and rules of procedure (with provisions for majority voting), annual or biannual party congresses, executive committees, party and parliamentary leaders, and common manifestos and programmes. Moreover, the EP group presidents play a similar role to leaders of parliamentary factions in domestic parliaments: they are the key spokespersons in debates, and the chairs of the group leadership committees; they can threaten to discipline members who deviate from the group line in key votes; and they are increasingly the 'face' of the EU-level parties in the domestic and European media (particularly Pauline Green of the PES Group and Wilfried Martens of the EPP Group). The party groups in the EP also have a relatively high level of cohesion in their legislative behaviour. Similarly, within the party federations, the six-monthly 'Party Leaders' Meetings' (of the leaders of the domestic parties, the EP groups, and the European Commissioners from the same party family) constitute a collective leadership structure, where policies towards major issues on the EU agenda are coordinated (such as towards the IGC or economic and monetary union) and the electoral and legislative strategies of the domestic parties and the EP groups are scrutinised. In addition, the party federations adopt some policy platforms by a majority of party leaders, of executive committee members, or of votes in the party congresses.

However, these emerging European-level parties still fall far short of the level of organisational cohesion of most political parties in democratic systems. The EP party groups and the party federations are fundamentally corporate rather than unitary organisations: where the basic party organisational units at the European level are the national party delegations (in the EP groups) and the domestic political parties (in the party federations). As a result of this corporate structure, centralised party decision-making is extremely weak. If a national delegation or a domestic political party disagrees with a collective decision, there is very little the EP group leader or the party leaders' meeting can do to prevent dissension. Also

because of this corporate structure, there is almost no direct accountability between individual party members and the European-level
party organisations; few members of the domestic parties are even
aware that they are also indirect members of European-wide parties,
or could indicate in which group their party sits in the EP. In general,
therefore, the level of organisational cohesion of the EU political
parties is closer to the Democrats and Republicans in the United
States than it is to the integrated and permanent party organisations
in the domestic arena in Europe.

Office-seeking

Despite this weak organisational cohesion, parties at the European
level increasingly *behave* like political parties in other democratic
systems. The central aim of parties in democracies is to gain control
of the instruments of power by placing their representatives in the key
political offices, or at least supporting the nominations of parties with
similar objectives. In terms of influence over the agenda of the EU,
the hierarchy of political offices in the EU is as follows: national prime
ministers (in the European Council); Commission President; Commissioners; ministers in the Council of Ministers; President of the EP;
and Members of the EP.

   As we have shown, the EP party groups and the party federations
actively seek to place their members in at least four of these offices.
First, and above all, the President of the EP is selected through a pact
between the PES and EPP groups in the EP; where for the first half of
the parliament's term, one group supports the other's candidate, and
the situation is reversed in the second half of the term. Second, but to
a lesser extent, in the selection of the Commission President (under
the procedure used since June 1994), the party federations adopt
common positions in the Party Leaders' Meetings on who should be
nominated in the European Council, and the EP groups vote *en bloc* in
the ratification of the European Council nominee. Third, in the
choice of the individual Commissioners, under the procedure first
used for the selection of the Santer Commission (1994–9), the EP
groups vote *en bloc* after the Commissioners that do not support their
partisan agendas have been severely criticised in the EP Committee
hearings. Fourth, in the selection of the MEPs, through the direct
elections to the EP, the European-level parties (the EP groups
through the party federations) adopt and fight the campaigns on
the basis of common electoral manifestos.

However, the actual ability of the EU parties to secure any of these political offices is restricted. The Commission President is really chosen by a bargain between the leaders of the national governments (i.e., the parties in power in the domestic arena), and the individual Commissioners are nominated by the national governments and presented to the EP as almost a *fait accompli*. The Party Leaders' Meetings may discuss who are being put forward by their member parties in government, but can do little to effect their choices. Moreover, in the EP votes on the Commission President and the whole Commission, the national delegations almost universally vote against the EP group positions where their domestic party interests are opposed to the group positions (Hix and Lord, 1996). In addition the decision about who stands as an MEP rests fundamentally with the domestic party organisations, and there is very little even the national party delegations in the EP can do against the power of the domestic party central offices. Finally, in two of the most important offices in the EU system, the European parties have hardly any say: the choice of the candidate for Prime Minister is made exclusively within the domestic party organisations (with perhaps a small input from the parties' MEPs); and the selection of the other government ministers is made by the Prime Minister, in cooperation with the other senior domestic party officials. In sum, therefore, parties at the European level may seek to place their representatives in the key political offices in the EU, and prevent other parties from obtaining these positions. However, they can do little to secure these ambitions. The power to obtain political office in the EU ultimately rests with the sub-units of the EU parties: the domestic party organisations.

Policy/ideological competition

In addition to public office, political parties in democratic systems pursue public policy: by developing coherent policy positions, and competing over the implementation of these positions, through alliances with parties with similar agendas. It is in this aspect of party behaviour that the parties at the European level are most similar to domestic European parties. As the previous chapters have shown, the EP groups and the party federations both have relatively sophisticated systems for developing policy positions: with special working groups, draft reports and final policy declarations. In the EP groups, this policy network is used to maximise cohesion among the members when a specific policy issue is debated on the floor of the EP. In the party federations, the policy network is designed to coordinate the positions of the national parties on the main issues on the EU agenda.

Moreover, there is a growing coherence in the policy platforms pursued by each Euro-party. The positions are ever more detailed and directly related to policy action at the European level, and clear distinctions are growing between the platforms of each party. The five key issues of the four main EU parties are shown in Figure 8.1. These rival platforms consequently constitute rival 'world-views' of EU politics: the EPP is the most radical supporter of European integration and advocates a 'social market economy' and traditional social values (such as preservation of the family); the PES pursues EU policies like EMU and the Social Chapter as a means of securing high employment and social and environmental protection; the ELDR supports individual economic and social freedom and hence advocates a 'democratisation' of the EU institutions; and the Greens support EU policies for environmental protection and development

FIGURE 8.1   Competition between Euro-party platforms in the EU policy space

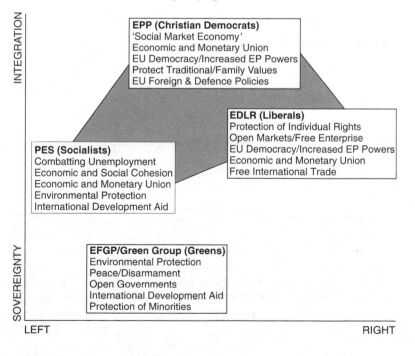

aid but reject the replication of a capitalist/industrialist state at the European level.

In addition, in an attempt to implement these platforms, the Euro-parties compete with each other and form rival alliances. The main coalition driving the EP agenda is between the PES and the EPP. However, when this coalition breaks down, the ELDR is a key player in determining whether the PES or the EPP controls the EP agenda. Similarly, through the organisation of the Party Leaders' Meetings, the PES and EPP attempt to secure their policy platforms in the European Council. When the Christian Democrats and Socialists are in a large majority in the European Council, the PES–EPP alliance has a significant impact on the policy outputs of this institution. As Figure 8.1 illustrates, therefore, the core of the EU party system is the triangular set of alliances between the policy platforms of the PES, the EPP and the ELDR. This 'grand coalition' between the three main ideological viewpoints in European politics is the driving-force behind EU policy-making.

Electoral legitimacy

European political parties have also competed in democratic elections ever since the first direct elections to the EP, in 1979. Indeed, the main impetus behind the formation of the party federations was the need to coordinate transnational election strategies in the build-up to the first European elections. As a result, in all four European elections between 1979 and 1994 (and in the last two in the case of the Greens), the EP groups in cooperation with their party federations have spent at least a year drafting and adopting European election manifestos. The European parties have also made an effort to manage the European election campaigns of their member parties: by printing posters and pamphlets, arranging European rallies, and exchanging speakers and electoral information. Finally, after the 1994 elections, the PES and ELDR groups and party federations for the first time attempted to connect the outcome of the elections to the choice of the Commission President.

However, despite these efforts, the EP elections have contributed little to the legitimacy of the EU parties. There is little knowledge of the EP groups and party federations among the European electorates, and even among the rank-and-file members of the national parties (who are the doorstep campaigners during any election). Moreover, voters and party members tend to be more concerned with specific local or national issues than the distant and abstract issues in European-level politics. As a result, voter turn-out in the European elections is much lower than in national elections, and in fact fell between 1989 and 1994. Some 'European' issues (such as economic and monetary union and common European environmental concerns) are present in the European elections in some member states (Smith in Gaffney, 1996). However, the main issues for voters and politicians in the European elections are the same as those in national, regional or local elections: the economy, health care, unemployment, education and so on. It is thus almost impossible for the EP groups or the party federations to attract attention for their rival agendas for EU policy-making.

The main reason why EU-level parties cannot claim legitimacy as a result of the European election is the institutionalised interests and behaviour of the national political parties. For the national parties, the sub-units of the European parties, European elections are 'second-order national contests'. The central aim of domestic political parties in any electoral contest is gaining control of national government office. European elections are thus fought on the performances of the parties holding national government offices. In this respect, they are little different to regional or local elections, or even certain national referendums. As long as the national parties decide who are the candidates in the elections and control the attention of the media during the campaigns, there is little the EP groups or the party federations can do to break their hold over the process. As a result, European elections are not contested on the political agenda of the EU, let alone on the performance of the EP groups or the party federations.

Recruitment/accountability

Nevertheless, European-level office-holders are to a certain extent recruited through the European-level parties. As Table 8.2 shows, seven of the current members of the European Commission were MEPs, and eight have been presidents, vice-presidents or active participants (i.e., have regularly been present) in the Party Leaders' Meetings of the party federations. Moreover, because Santer was a long-standing president of the EPP party federation (from 1987 to 1990), he was an acceptable compromise for the Christian Democrat prime ministers (and the EPP group in the EP) following the rejection of Dehaene by the British Conservatives and Lubbers by Chancellor Kohl. Also, the three Commissioners from the new EU member states (underlined in the table) cannot really be included in an analysis of recruitment patterns, as they could not have been MEPs or senior figures in the party federations prior to taking up their posts. Consequently, 11 out of a possible 17 (65 per cent) of the main executive office-holders at the European level were 'recruited' from the European parties.

The European parties have also attempted to hold EU legislative and executive office-holders accountable to European-level party programmes and policy statements. The EP group leaders and executive bureaux use the European election manifestos to justify group positions and votes, and the party federation leaders' meetings occasionally refer the EP group leaders to manifesto statements if they disagree with a position taken by their Groups. These links are most developed in the EPP, with the adoption of Action Programmes at the beginning of each EP session, but are also present in the PES and the ELDR. The party federations have also begun to scrutinise the behaviour of the Commissioners from their member parties. This is most developed in the PES, where there is an informal caucus of Socialist Commissioners, and all nine Socialist Commissioners regularly attend the PES leaders' meetings. The EPP and PES also try to hold their actors in the European Council accountable to party positions, by organising leaders' meetings immediately before each European Council and adopting Leaders' Declarations on the specific agenda of the European Council. This strategy was particularly effective during the IGCs leading to the Maastricht Treaty.

However, the role of European-level parties in the recruitment of office-holders in the EU system remains weak. Commissioners, MEPs, ministers in the Council of Ministers, and prime ministers in the European Council are primarily chosen by, and recruited from within, the domestic political party organisations. The European parties provide important European-level experience (as MEPs or party federation vice-presidents) for members of national parties who subsequently hope to be chosen by their domestic parties to be European Commissioners. Similarly, the accountability of EU office-holders to the European parties is low. The EP groups or the party federations do not possess the necessary powers or incentives to impose their wishes on Commissioners or ministers in the Council.

TABLE 8.2

Members of the Santer Commission recruited from the Euro-parties

		Previously involved in the party federations:	
		YES (Pres./V-Pres./ Leaders' Meets)	NO
Previously involved in the EP groups	YES (MEP)	Santer (EPP–Pres) Bangemann (ELDR–VP) Van Miert (PES–VP) Papoutsis (PES–VP)	Oreja (EPP) Cressen (PES) Bonino (ELDR)
	NO	Marin (PES–VP) Van Den Broek (EPP–LM) Pinheiro (ELDR–LM) Kinnock (PES–LM)	Brittan Flynn Monti De Silguy Bjerregaard (PES–LM) Wulf-Mathies (PES–LM) *Gradin* (PES–LM) *Fischler* (PES–LM) *Liikanen* (PES–LM)

Implementation of party positions consequently relies more on the voluntary acts of the actors in the EU institutions than on the enforcement by European parties.

The empirical reality, therefore, is that the EU has made some progress towards a 'Europe of parties'. However, the position of European-level parties is still extremely weak in comparison to parties in most democratic systems. Parties at the European level certainly advocate competing ideological visions of the direction of EU policy-making, and form alliances on the basis of these positions. They also possess a level of organisational cohesion, seek to place their supporters in positions of power in the EU system, and attempt to hold these actors accountable to European party policy positions. However, on each of these three later criteria, European-level parties fall far short of the role of parties in a 'party democracy'. Moreover, European-level parties are weakest of all in comparison to classic political parties on the most vital criteria of all: the question of electoral legitimacy. Without electoral legitimacy, there is little possibility for European parties to control the individuals holding positions of authority in the EU system and for policy competition between the parties to be translated subsequently into EU action.

Implications for the design of EU institutions

Finally, turning to the normative implications of the change from a 'Europe of nations' to a 'Europe of parties', we need to ask the question: how should EU institutional reform facilitate this transformation? As we have found, a fundamental constraint on parties at the European level is that the shape of the EU system is not conducive to 'party democracy'. First, executive authority at the European level is divided between two institutions (the Commission and the Council), and in both institutions the actors are primarily aligned (or nominated in the case of the Commission) on national rather than partisan grounds. Moreover, in the legislative process at the European level, the directly elected chamber (the EP) – the natural arena for political parties in any system – is weak in comparison to a chamber of the national executives (the Council). Second, the division of executive and legislative powers between two levels of government, the maintenance of a majority of policy-making levers at the national level, and the power of national office-holders within the European-level institutions, creates strong incentives for sub-units of the EU parties (the national parties) to pursue political strategies that are contradictory with European-level party positions. Third, in many issues in EU politics, political interests are divided on national/territorial lines (i.e., British versus French, or north versus south) rather than on socioeconomic lines (i.e., consumers versus producers, or environmentalists versus industrialists). These issues inherently undermine any parties at the European level that are based on the historical *familles spirituelles* and are aligned along a single left–right dimension. In sum, there is an extremely 'low partyness' of the EU system (Katz, 1986).

However, before reforming the EU institutions to facilitate strong European-level parties, we should question Marquand's assumption that a 'Europe of parties' is an answer to the legitimacy question. Since Schattschneider's assertion in the early 1940s that 'democracy is unthinkable save in terms of parties', the relationship of political parties to the democratic process has changed in two important respects. First, in the ideal cases of 'party democracy', there is a growing disillusionment with the role of political parties. Rather than compete with each other, rival party elites have formed 'cartels' and used the powers and resources of the state to strengthen the collective dominance of parties in the political system. Instead of party democracy, the result is *partitocrazia* ('partiocracy') or the *Parteienstaat* ('party state') (Katz and Mair, 1994, 1995). Consequently, is there not really a danger that strong European-level parties would undermine EU democracy rather than strengthen it? Second, the traditional ideological divisions between political parties have effectively disappeared. Almost all parties on the left, and certainly all the members of the PES, now fully accept the rigours of the free market, and hence advocate the privatisation of state monopolies. Moreover, the vast majority of parties on the right now accept the social reforms of the 1960s, like equal rights for women, abortion rights, the liberalisation of divorce laws, and rights for homosexuals. Consequently, if there is very little difference between Socialists, Christian Democrats, Liberals and Conservatives, how can they present real choices for Europe's citizens?

A 'Europe of parties' is thus not a panacea. Nonetheless, democratic government cannot function without organisations to structure electoral choices and legislative and executive behaviour, and hence link popular opinion to public policy-making. And, whether we like them or not, political parties are the only organisations that can really fulfil these roles. The challenge, therefore, is to design EU institutions that strengthen party organisations where they are needed and in ways that increase EU legitimacy, while preventing them where they could do more damage than good. We will hence focus on three areas of institutional reform that could contribute to the emergence of a 'Europe of parties' in a positive rather than a negative way (the specific proposals are in bold): institutions to promote parties in European elections; institutions to facilitate party competition; and institutions to prevent party domination.

Institutions to promote parties in European elections

For 'party democracy' to work in the EU, parties must be able to establish legitimacy from European elections (as we pointed out in the previous section). For this to happen, however, elections to the EP must become 'European' contests rather than purely national ones. An essential condition for this development would be a **uniform electoral procedure**, rather than fifteen individual sets of rules. However, this would not by itself be sufficient, since national parties would still want to fight the elections on the performance of the national governments. EP elections will only be 'European' elections if the role of the national parties in the campaigns is almost completely replaced by European parties. This would mean allowing

European parties to control the selection of candidates, the adoption of manifestos, and the attention of the national and European media. This could be facilitated through **a body of EU 'party law'**, based on Article 138A of the EC Treaty, giving European parties special rights and responsibilities in the European elections. For example, these rules would allow national parties to get subsidies from the EU budget for their European election campaigns if they agreed to cooperate with their European parties in the selection of candidates and to use only the European party manifestos in their election campaigns. Similarly, the activities of the European parties would receive funds if they have member parties in most member states, adopt common manifestos for the EP elections, and have internally democratic decision-making rules.

Alternatively, if we acknowledge that EP elections will be fought primarily by national and not European parties for some time to come, a possible other way of legitimising EU action is through the **direct election of the Commission President**. In a presidential system, as opposed to a parliamentary system, the head of the executive is elected independently of the legislature. The EP has consequently opposed this strategy since it would mean disconnecting the choice of the Commission President from the EP. However, in terms of electoral legitimacy for European-level parties, a separate election for the Commission President would have a number of advantages over the present EP elections: it would be difficult for national parties to fight the election on the performance of national governments; each European party could support a separate candidate; and once the President is elected they could be made accountable to the manifesto of the parties that backed them. For example, if an election had taken place for the person to succeed Delors, the PES would probably have supported Felipé González, the EPP would most likely have backed Jean-Luc Dehaene, the British Conservatives (and some of the other Conservatives that are not in the EPP) would have backed Leon Brittan, and the ELDR, the Greens, and the Anti-Europeans would probably have proposed their own candidates. Moreover, to prevent purely 'national' candidates, and to promote the role of parties in the election, candidates could be required to secure the support of national parties from a specific number of member states and who won a certain percentage in the last national elections. This would truly allow Europe's voters to choose between rival agendas for EU-level action.

Institutions to facilitate party competition

In addition, after a decline of ideological divisions between the European party families, parties also need to be encouraged to compete with each other in the electoral and legislative processes, rather than to establish cartels. The ideal institution for promoting party competition is a clear division between 'government' (winners) and 'opposition' (losers). However, because of the deep national/ territorial divisions in the EU, allowing a simple majority to dominate decision-making would be dangerous. Nevertheless, certain elements of the government–opposition framework could be introduced into the areas of the EU system where political parties are involved. As we have discovered, parties at the European level already propose relatively different agendas for EU policy-making, but in their behaviour in the EP the main political groups (PES, EPP and ELDR) tend to form a cartel instead of competing to form rival majorities. However, this would change if **all EP votes are by a simple majority of those in attendance**, instead of a majority of the total number of MEPs (which invariably requires the PES and EPP to work together). This would allow certain stable patterns of competition to emerge in the EP, such as a centre-right majority (based around a core of the EPP and ELDR) on economic issues and a centre-left majority (based around a core of the PES and ELDR) on social issues. Moreover, if this is applied to the annual vote on the Commission's legislative programme, the Commission would be forced to build a coalition of partisan support rather than simply assume that an EPP–PES alliance would guarantee its approval.

Furthermore, certain measures could be taken to ensure that parties at the European level continue to develop rival proposals for EU action. The parties will only be able to do this if they have ongoing access to knowledge and expertise about EU politics and policy options from other democratic systems. A provision could be included in a body of EU party law (based on Article 138A) requiring political parties to play a role in public education and policy analysis through the establishment of **European party research foundations**. These would be similar to the German parties' *Stiftungen*, but with less ambitious aims (and hence less costly!). The operating costs of the foundations could be funded from the EU budget, and the EP groups and the member parties of the party federations could be obliged to make financial contributions or to second staff. The foundations could then be commissioned to write reports by the EP groups, the EP Secretariat, national parties, the Council, the Commission, or private interest groups or businesses. These would be similar to reports written by private think-tanks or political consultants for the EU institutions, but would most likely be on more general questions of EU integration (such as institutional reforms or EMU). The EPP and the PES have tried to establish similar institutions in the past, but have failed because of a lack of finances and/or political commitment.

Institutions to prevent party domination

Nevertheless, parties at the European level must not be allowed to take control of the political process, as they have done in some domestic political systems. Moreover, strong parties could be particularly dangerous in the EU because of the underlying non-partisan divisions between the nation states. Some of the EU structures that prevent the emergence of strong parties at the European level by allowing for the articulation and representation of national and territorial interests are hence blessings in disguise. For example, because the Commission is a collegiate and predominantly technocratic body it can construct alliances across partisan and national–territorial lines. Consequently, in addition to the rules on the national make-up of the Commission, **the Commissioners should come from at least four European parties**. This would be very similar to the rules used in the formation of the Swiss executive, which ensure a balance of partisan, cantonal and linguistic interests. Until now, the Commissioners have always come from at least four European party traditions. However, if the Commission becomes dependent on an ongoing majority in the EP, or if the Commission President is directly elected, there will be pressure for the Commission to be composed of individuals from a single partisan point of view.

Similarly, there is an inherent balance between the representation of national interests in the Council and the European Council on the one hand, and the representation on the other hand, of socioeconomic and partisan interests in the EP. This is a classic solution to overcoming territorial divisions in many political systems: as in the system of representation in the German Bundesrat and Bundestag. Consequently, although parties may begin to establish connections between ministers or prime ministers from the same member parties, these **partisan links in the Council and the European Council**

should not be allowed to undermine the current structure of voting on national lines. Furthermore, in many systems of 'party democracy', interest group pluralism is undermined because parties dominate the legislative process. This inevitably prevents policy-makers from benefiting from the opinions of a wider public, and allows special groups close to the parties to monopolise policy initiatives. Consequently, **the EU institutions should actively seek to involve private interest groups in the policy-making process**.

Finally, there are advantages to the maintenance of a 'two-level' party system in the EU: where there are independent party organisations at national and European levels, and the structure of party competition in national elections is different to that in European elections. By allowing national member parties to preserve their independent identities, they always have the possibility of breaking away from a European party if a certain party position is severely detrimental to the interests of a particular national party. Again, this preserves the balance between national and transnational interests. Consequently, in any body of EU party law, **the internal decision-making structures of European parties should be based on the principle of subsidiarity**, where European-level party action can only be taken if the objective cannot be achieved by national parties acting independently.

As Lipset pointed out, 'legitimacy is the capacity of the system to reflect the values of society' (Lipset, 1959, p. 77). If a 'Europe of parties' is to increase the legitimacy of the EU system, the European institutions hence need to be designed to enable parties to strengthen the link between EU policy-making and citizens' opinions on vital socioeconomic issues (the defining issues of the party families), without allowing parties to dominate the political process or undermine national, cultural and territorial interests. A strength of the American system is that political parties play an important role in the electoral and legislative processes, but are limited by the separation of powers and the institutions of federalism, and are forced to construct wide coalitions of socioeconomic and territorial interests. This is perhaps a good model for parties in the EU to follow.

In sum, a central dilemma in the European integration project is how to make effective and efficient political and economic decisions that are at the same time accountable to Europe's citizens. This is an age-old issue of democratic politics. In the 1990s, the system of

European-level governance based on the articulation of interests primarily through the nation states, and decision-making primarily by national governments, is not by itself sufficient to resolve this dilemma. It is thus the contention of this book that political parties are an essential complement to the present structure of national and territorial decision-making: on the one hand, enabling policy pro-grammes to be enacted through cohesive legislative and executive action; and, on the other hand, enabling political elites to be 'thrown out' or the policy direction to be altered by a majority in democratic elections. As a result, if European political and economic integration is to succeed, the central role of political parties in securing the democratic bases of this process needs to be better understood, explained, theorised and prescribed. We hope this book has gone at least some way towards achieving this goal.

Guide to Further Reading

Chapter 1

The idea that parties could have an important role as carriers of European integration is to be found in Haas (1958). Marquand (1978) and Pridham and Pridham (1981) consider the possibility that party politics at the European level would be stimulated by the institutional development of the Union. Pridham and Pridham (1981) also analyse the constraints on pan-European party political activities. However, these works all predate the EU's contemporary political system, as defined by Treaty changes since 1986. More recent reflections on incentives and constraints for parties to develop at the European level are to be found in the works of Attinà (1990 and 1992) and Bardi (1992, 1994 and 1996) and Gaffney (1996).

Chapter 2

Lipset and Rokkan (1967) is the seminal work on the social and issue cleavages that have dominated the formation of party politics in Western Europe. Subsequent attempts to estimate the dimensions of party competition and the positions of individual parties on those dimensions are to be found in Castles and Mair (1984), Budge, Robertson and Hearl (1987), Laver and Hunt (1992), and Huber and Inglehart (1995).

Chapter 3

Little has been written on how the party federations, EP party groups and national parties interact. However, Gaffney (1996) includes invaluable case studies of the party politics of European integration at both the Union and national levels. Hanley (1994) contains a useful chapter on the EPP. The methodology of using organigrams to analyse the structure of political parties is to be found in Katz and Mair (1992); and the publications of the PES, EPP, ELDR and Greens that are listed in the bibliography provide some further guidance on the internal structures of particular Euro-parties.

Chapter 4

For the argument that European elections are 'second-order' in character see Reif and Schmitt (1980), and for accounts of the European elections held in 1994 see Guyomarch (1995), Lodge (1996) and Smith in Gaffney (1996). Lécureuil in Lodge (1996) considers the most recent evidence on the link between European elections and the development of European political parties. There is little written on the second theme of this chapter – the politics of party group formation in the European Parliament. However, Corbett, Jacobs and Shackleton (1995) provide some useful insights in their pen portraits of the party groups at the beginning of the 1994–9 Parliament. The work of Attinà (1990 and 1992) and Bardi (1992, 1994 and 1996) underscores the extent to which the shape of the party system in the EP has tended to adapt itself to institutional rules that govern the exercise of parliamentary powers and the formation of groups, subject to interruptions by the electoral cycle (1996).

Chapter 5

The powers of the European Parliament are now well documented. Corbett, Jacobs and Shackleton (1995) and Westlake (1994) are based on the first-hand observations of those who work in the EU institutions. Nugent (1994) and Middlemas (1995) analyse the position of the EP in the EU's overall political system and thus capture inter-institutional relationships with the Commission and Council. An understanding of the role of the party groups in the parliamentary work cycle of committees, group weeks and plenaries is also provided by Corbett, Jacobs and Shackleton 91995). Abelès (1992) is an engaging evocation of the atmosphere of the EP and its party groups.

Chapter 6

Work on measuring the cohesion of the party groups of the EP through roll-call analysis was pioneered by Attinà (1990). Factors that govern the political behaviour of the groups and their capacity to reach agreements across national delegations are considered in Attinà (1990), Abelés (1992), Westlake (1994a) and Corbett, Jacobs and Shackleton (1995). The extent to which the groups are genuinely transnational and fit together to form a stable party system is discussed by Bardi 91996).

Chapter 7

The earlier history and performance of the party federations is discussed in Pridham and Pridham (1981). Low public awareness of the federations and their relative failure to develop their expected role as coordinators of electoral programmes are covered in Niedermayer 91984 and 1989). Analysis of the development of the federations as sites for political co-ordination between EU party leaders prior to meetings of the European Council has been pioneered by Hix (1993 and 1995b) and Hix in Gaffney 91996).

Chapter 8

The international relations or intergovenmentalist approach to the study of European integration is best represented by Hoffman (1966) and Moravcsik (1993a). The contrasting comparative politics approach – that the EU is a political system with its own internal political arena – is to be found in contributions to Sbragia (1992) and in Hix (1994).

Bibliography

Abelès, M. (1992) *La vie quotidienne au Parlement Européen*. Paris, Hachette.

Andolfato, D. (1994) 'Les Euro-députés en Question', *Revue Politique et Parlementaire*, Mars–Avril, no. 970.

Attina, F. (1990) 'The Voting Behaviour of European Parliament Members and the Problem of the Europarties', *European Journal of Political Research*, vol. 18, pp. 557–79.

Attinà, F. (1992) 'Parties, Party System and Democracy in the European Union', *International Spectator*, vol. 27, no. 3, pp. 67–86.

Bardi, L. (1992) 'Transnational Party Federations in the European Community', in Richard Katz and Peter Mair (eds), *Party Organisations: A data Handbook on Party Organisations in Western Democracies 1960–90*. London, Macmillan, pp. 931–73.

Bardi, L. (1994) 'Transnational Party Federations, European Parliamentary Party Groups, and the Building of Europarties', in R. S. Katz and P. Mair (eds), *How Parties Organize: Adaptation and Change in Party Organizations in Western Democracies*. London, Sage, pp. 357–72.

Bardi, L. (1995), 'Transnational Trends in European Parties and the 1994 Election of the European Parliament', Party Politics, vol. 2, no. 1, pp. 99–114.

Baumgarten, J. (ed.) (1982 *Linkssozialisten in Europe: Alternativen zu Sozialdemokratie und Kummunistischen Parteien*. Hamburg, Junius.

Blondel, J. (1993) *Comparative Politics*. London, Harvester.

Bogdanor, V. (1986) 'The Future of the European Community, Two Models of Democracy', *Government and Opposition*, no. 2, pp. 161–73.

Bowler, S. and Farrell, D. M. (1993) 'Legislator Shirking and Voter Monitoring: Impacts of European Parliament Electoral Systems Upon Legislator–Voter Relationships', *Journal of Common Market Studies*, vol. 31, no. 1, pp. 45–61.

Bowler, S. and Farrell, D. (1995) The Organising of the European Parliament: Committees, Specialisation and Co-ordination, *British Journal of Political Science*, no. 25, pp. 219–45.

Budge, I., Crewe, I. and Farlie, D. (eds) (1976) *Party Identification and Beyond: Representations of Voting and Party Competition*. London, Wiley.

Budge, I. and Keman, H. (1990) *Parties and Democracy: Coalition Formation and Government Functioning in Twenty States*. Oxford, Oxford University Press.

Budge, I., Robertson, D. and Hearl, D. (eds) (1987) *Ideology, Strategy and Party Change: Spatial Analysis of Post-War Election Programmes in 19 Democracies*. Cambridge, Cambridge University Press.

Bulmer, S. (1984) 'Domestic Politics and European Community Policy-Making', *Journal of Common Market Studies*, vol. 24, no. 1, pp. 349–63.

Bulmer, S. (1994) 'Institutions and Policy Change in the European Communities: The Case of Merger Control', *Public Administration*, vol. LXXII, pp. 425–46.

Castles, F. and Mair, P. (1984) 'Left–Right Scales: Some Expert Judgements', *European Journal of Political Research*, vol. 52, pp. 73–89.

Castles, F. and Wildenmann, R. (eds).(1986) *Visions and Realities of Party Government*. Berlin, de Gruyter.

Christian Democrats. (1976) *CD–Europe Bulletin*. Brussels: Christian Democratic Group in the European Parliament.

Corbett, R. (1993) *The Treaty of Maastricht – From Conception to Ratification: A Comprehensive Reference Guide*. Harlow, Longman.

Corbett, R., Jacobs, F. and Shackleton, M. (1995) *The European Parliament*. London, Longman.

Cotta, M. (1980) 'Classe Politica e Integrazione Europea. Gli Effecti delle Elezione Dirette del Parlemento Communitario', *Revisita Italiana di Scienza Politica*, vol. 10.

Cox, G. W. and McCubbins, M. D. (1993) *Legislative Leviathan: Party Government in the House*. Berkeley, University of California Press.

CSP (Confederation of the Socialist Parties of the EC) (1974) *Rules of Procedure of the Confederation of the Socialist Parties of the European Community*, adopted by the Bureau of the CSP, Brussels, 27 September 1974. Brussels, CSP.

CSP (Confederation of the Socialist Parties of the EC) (1990) *Party Leaders' Declaration on the Intergovernmental Conferences*, leaders' meeting of the CSP, Madrid, 10 December 1990. Brussels, CSP.

CSP (Confederation of the Socialist Parties of the EC) (1991a) *Luxembourg Declaration: The Intergovernmental Conferences*, leaders' meeting of the CSP, Luxembourg, 3 June 1991. Brussels, CSP.

CSP (Confederation of the Socialist Parties of the EC) (1991b) *Party Leaders' Summit Declaration*, leaders' meeting of the CSP, Brussels, 3–4 December 1991. Brussels, CSP.

Daalder, H. and Mair, P. (eds) (1983) *West European Party Systems: Continuity and Change*. London, Sage.

Dehousse, R. (1995) 'Institutional Reform in the European Community: Are there Alternatives to the Majoritarian Avenue?', EUI Working Paper RSC No. 95/4.

Delwit, P. and De Waele, M. (1993) *La gauche face aux mutations en Europe*. Bruxelles, Université Libre de Bruxelles.

Dinan, Desmond (1994) *Ever Closer Union: An Introduction to the European Community*. London, Macmillan.

Downs, A. (1957) *An Economic Theory of Democracy*. New York, Harper & Row.

Dunleavy, P. (1990) *Democracy, Bureaucracy and Public Choice: Economic Explanations in Political Science*. Hemel Hempstead, Harvester Wheatsheaf.

Duverger, M. (1954) *Political Parties: Their Organization and Activity in the Modern State*. London, Methuen.

Dyson, K. (1994) *Elusive Union: The Process of Economic and Monetary Union in Europe*, London, Longman.

226 *Bibliography*

ECGP (European Co-ordination of Green Parties) (1984) *Statutes of the European Co-ordination of Green Parties*, adopted by the First Congress of the ECGP, Liège, 1 April 1984. Brussels, ECGP.

EFGP (European Federation of Green Parties) (1993) *Statutes of the European Federation of Green Parties*, adopted by the last meeting of the EFGP, Helsinki, 20 June 1993. Brussels, EFGP.

EFGP (European Federation of Green Parties) (1994) *Demokratie ist Europas Kern-Gesamteuropa ist unser Haus*, Committee of the EFGP, Essen, 5–8 December 1994. Brussels, EFGP.

ELD (Federation of Liberal and Democratic Parties in the EC) (1976) *Constitution of the Federation of Liberal and Democratic Parties in the European Community*, adopted by the Executive Committee of the ELD, Stuttgart, 26–7 March 1976. Brussels, ELD.

ELDR (Federation of Liberal, Democratic and Reform Parties in the EC) (1991) *Final Adopted Text*, leaders' meeting of the ELDR, Brussels, 3 December 1991. Brussels, ELDR.

ELDR (Federation of Liberal, Democratic and Reform Parties in the EC) (1992) *Leaders' Resolution: The European Community Before the European Council in Edinburgh*, leaders' meeting of the ELDR, Brussels, 7 December 1992. Brussels, ELDR.

ELDR (European Liberal, Democratic and Reform Party) (1993a) *Statutes of the European Liberal, Democratic and Reform Party*, adopted by the Congress of the ELDR, Torquay, 9–10 December 1993. Brussels, ELDR.

ELDR (European Liberal, Democratic and Reform Party) (1993b) *Building a Citizens' Europe*: ELDR Election Manifesto 1994, 16th Congress of the ELDR, Torquay, 9–10 December 1993. Brussels, ELDR.

ELDR (European Liberal, Democratic and Reform Party) (1994) *European Council Meeting in Essen: The ELDR Position*, Council of the ELDR, Paris, 6 December 1994. Brussels, ELDR.

EPP (European People's Party) (1976) *Statutes of the European People's Party*, adopted by the Political Bureau of the EPP, Luxembourg, 8 July 1976. Brussels, EPP.

EPP (European People's Party) (1990) *Statutes of the European People's Party*, adopted by the Congress of the EPP, Dublin, 15–16 November 1990. Brussels, EPP.

EPP (European People's Party) (1991) *Communiqué: Conférence des Chefs de Gouvernement et du Parti du PPE*, leaders' meeting of the EPP, The Hague, 6 December 1991. Brussels, EPP.

EPP (European People's Party) (1992) *Déclaration du Président du Parti Populaire Européen*, leaders' meeting of the EPP, Brussels, 4 December 1992. Brussels, EPP.

EPP (European People's Party) (1993a) *Statutes of the European People's Party*, adopted by the Congress of the EPP, Brussels, 8–10 December 1993. Brussels, EPP.

EPP (European People's Party) (1993b) *European People's Party: Manifesto for the European Elections 1994*, leaders' meeting of the EPP, Brussels, 9 December 1993. Brussels, EPP.

EPP (European People's Party) (1994) *Compte rendu de la Conférence des Chefs de Gouvernement et de Partis du PPE*, leaders' meeting of the EPP, Brussels, 8 December 1994. Brussels, EPP.

Epstein, L. D. (1967) *Political Parties in Western Democracies*. New Brunswick, NJ. Rutgers University Press.

European Parliament (1988) *Political Parties in the EC and European Unification*. Research and Documentation Papers, Political Series, No. 14, 10/1988. Luxembourg, European Parliament Directorate General for Research.

European Parliament (1994a) *Bibliographical Notes on the 567 Members*. Luxembourg, European Parliament Directorate General for Research.

European Parliament (1994b) *Legislation Governing Elections to the European Parliament*, Working Paper, Political Series, No. 13. Luxembourg, European Parliament Directorate General for Research.

Featherstone, K (1987) *Socialist Parties and European Integration: A Comparative History*. Manchester, Manchester University Press.

Franklin, M. N., Mackie. T., and Valen. H. (eds) (1992) *Electoral Change: Responses to Evolving Social and Attitudinal Structures in Western Countries*. Cambridge, Cambridge University Press.

Gaffney, J. (ed.) (1996) *Political Parties and the European Community*. London, Routledge.

Georg-Betz, H.. (1994) *Radical Right-Wing Populism in Western Europe*. New York, St Martin's Press.

Girvin, B. (ed.). (1988) *The Transformation of Contemporary Conservatism*. London, Sage.

Guyomarch, A. (1995) 'The European Elections of 1994', *West European Politics*, vol. 18, no. 1, pp. 173–87.

Haahr, H. H. (1993) *Looking to Europe: The EC Policies of the British Labour Party and the Danish Social Democrats*. Aarhus, Aarhus University Press.

Haas, E. (1958) *The Uniting of Europe*. Stanford, Stanford University Press.

Haas, E. (1990) *When Knowledge is Power*. Berkeley, University of California Press.

Habermas, J. (1992) 'Citizenship and National Identity: Some Reflections on the Future of Europe', *Praxis International*, vol. 12 (April 1992), pp. 1–19.

Hanley, D. (ed.). (1994) *Christian Democracy in Europe: A Comparative Perspective*. London, Pinter.

Held, D. (1987) *Models of Democracy*. Cambridge, Polity.

Higley, J., Hoffmann-Lange, U., Kadushin, C. and Moore, G. (1993) in 'Elite Integration in Stable Democracies', in Marvin Olsen and Martin Marger (eds) *Power in Modern Societies*. Boulder, Colorado, Westview.

Hix, S. (1993) 'The Emerging EC Party System? The European Party Federations in the Intergovernmental Conferences', *Politics*, vol. XIII, no. 2, pp. 38–46.

Hix, S. (1994) 'The Study of the European Community: The Challenge to Comparative Politics', *West European Politics*, vol. XVII, pp. 1–30.

Hix, S. (1995a) 'Political Parties in the European Union System: A 'Comparative Politics Approach' to the Development of the Party Federations', unpublished doctoral thesis, Florence: European University Institute.

228   *Bibliography*

Hix, S. (1995b) 'Parties at the European Level and the Legitimacy of EU
Socio-Economic Policy', *Journal of Common Market Studies*, vol. XXXIII,
pp. 527–54.

Hix, S. and Lord, C. (1996) 'The Making of a President: The European
Parliament and the Confirmation of Jacques Santer as President of the
Commission', *Government and Opposition*, vol. XXXI, pp. 62–76.

HM Treasury (1993) 'Growth Competitiveness and Employment in the
European Community', paper by the United Kingdom on the Commission
White Paper, 30 July 1993. London, HMSO.

Hoffmann, S. (1966) 'Obstinate or Obsolete? The Fate of the Nation-State
and the Case of Western Europe', *Daedalus*, vol. XLV, pp. 872–7.

Holland, S. (1980) *The Uncommon Market*. London, Macmillan.

Huber, J. and Inglehart, R. (1995) 'Expert Interpretations of Party
Space and Party Locations in 42 Societies', *Party Politics*, vol. 1, no. 1,
pp. 73–111.

Irving, R. E. M. (1979) *The Christian Democratic Parties of Western Europe*.
London, Allen & Unwin.

Jacobs, F. (ed.). (1989) *Western European Political Parties: A Comprehensive Guide*.
Harlow, Longman.

Jansen, T. (1995) 'Die Einbeziehung der Konservativen in die EVP', paper
presented to Leeds University seminar on Transnational Parties and the
EU, Brussels, 18–19 May 1995.

Judge, D., Earnshaw, D. and Cowan, N. (1994) 'Ripples or Waves: The
European Parliament in the European Community policy process', *Journal
of European Public Administration*, vol. 1, no. 1, pp. 27–51.

Katz, R. S. (1986) 'Party Government: A Rationalistic Conception', in F. G.
Castles and R. Wildenmann (eds), *Visions and Realities of Party Government*.
Berlin, de Gruyter.

Katz, R. S. and Mair, P. (eds). (1992) *Party Organizations: A Data Handbook on
Party Organizations in Western Democracies, 1960–90*. London, Sage.

Katz, R. S. and Mair, P. (1994) 'The Evolution of Party Organizations in
Europe: Three Faces of Party Organization', in W. Crotty (ed.), Political
Parties in a Changing Age, special issue of the *American Review of Politics*,
vol. XIV, pp. 593–617.

Katz, R. S. and Mair, P. (1995) 'Changing Models of Party Organization
and Party Democracy: The Emergence of the Cartel Party', *Party Politics*,
vol. I, pp. 5–28.

Kaupi, N. (1996) 'European Union Institutions and French Political Careers', *Scandinavian Political Studies*, vol. 19, no. 1, pp. 1–24.

Kinnock, N. (1991) *Statement at the meeting of the leaders of the Socialist Parties of
the EC*, 3 June 1991. London, Labour Party.

Kirchner, E. (ed.) (1988) *Liberal Parties in Western Europe*. Cambridge, Cambridge University Press.

Kuhn, T. S. (1962) *The Structure of Scientific Revolutions*. Chicago, University of
Chicago Press.

Labour Party (1990a) *Meet the Challenge, Make the Change: A New Agenda for
Britain. Final Report of Labour's Policy Review for the 1990s*. London, Labour
Party.

Labour Party (1990b) *Economic and Monetary Union*, 6 November 1990. London, Labour Party.
Labour Party (1991a) *Economic and Monetary Union*, 8 July 1991. London, Labour Party.
Labour Party (1991b) *Labour and Europe*, 30 October 1991. London, Labour Party.
Laffan, B. (1996) 'The Politics of Identity and Political Order in Europe', *Journal of Common Market Studies*, vol. 34, no. 1, pp. 81–103.
Lakatos, I. (1970) 'Falsification and the Methodology of Scientific Research Programmes', in I. Lakatos and A. Musgrave (eds), *Criticism and the Growth of Knowledge*. Cambridge: Cambridge University Press.
Lange, P. (1993) 'Maastricht and the Social Protocol: Why Did They Do It?', *Politics and Society*, vol. XXI, pp. 5–36.
Laver, M. J. and Hunt, W. B. (1992) *Policy and Party Competition*. London, Routledge.
Layton-Henry, Z. (ed.) (1982) *Conservative Parties in Western Europe*. London, Macmillan.
Lenaerts, K. (1991) 'Some Reflections on the Separation of Powers in the European Community', *Common Market Law Review*, vol. 28, no. 1, pp. 11–35.
Lindberg, L. N. and Scheingold, S. A. (1970) *Europe's Would-Be Polity: Patterns of Change in the European Community*. Englewood Cliffs, Prentice-Hall.
Lindberg, L. and Scheingold, S. (eds) (1971) *Regional Integration: Theory and Research*. Cambridge, Mass., Harvard University Press.
Lipset, S. M. (1959) *Political Man: The Social Bases of Politics*. Garden City, NJ, Doubleday.
Lipset, S. M. and Rokkan, S. (1967) 'Cleavage Structures, Party Systems and Voter Alignments: An Introduction', in S. M. Lipset and S. Rokkan (eds), *Party Systems and Voter Alignments: Cross-national Perspectives*. New York, Free Press.
Lodge, J. (ed.) (1993) *The European Community and the Challenge of the Future*. London, Pinter.
Lodge, J. (ed.) (1996) *The 1994 Elections to the European Parliament*. London, Pinter.
Lord, C. (1991) 'From Intergovernmenal to Interparliamentary Union', *Contemporary European Affairs*, vol. 4, no. 2/3.
Lord, C. (1994) 'Party Groups in the European Parliament: Rethinking the Role of Transnational Parties in the Democratisation of the European Union', paper presented to 22nd ECPR sessions, Madrid, April 1994.
Mair, P. and Smith, G. (1990) *Understanding Party System Change in Western Europe*. London, Frank Cass.
Majone, G. (1993) 'The European Community: An 'Independent Fourth Branch of Government?', Working Paper SPS No. 93/9. Florence, European University Institute.
March, J. and Olsen, J. (1984) 'The New Institutionalism: Organizational Factors in Political Life' *American Political Science Review*, vol. 78, pp. 734–49.

Marcus, J. (1995) *The National Front and French Politics: The Resistible Rise of Jean-Marie Le Pen*. London, Macmillan.

Marquand, D. (1978) 'Towards a Europe of the Parties', *Political Quarterly*, vol. IL, pp. 425–45.

Mavgordatos, G. (1984) 'The Greek Party System: A Case of Limited but Polarised Pluralism', *West European Politics*, vol. VII, pp. 156–69.

Mazey, S. and Richardson, J. (1993) *Lobbying in the European Community*. London, OUP.

Menke, K. and Gordon, I. (1980) 'Differential Mobilisation and Europe: A Comparative Note on Some Aspects of the Campaign', *European Journal of Political Research*, vol. VIII, pp. 63–89.

Michels, R. (1949) *Political Parties*. New York, Free Press.

Middlemas, K. (1995) *Orchestrating Europe: The Informal Politics of the European Union*. London, Fontana.

Moravcsik, A. (1993a) 'Preferences and Power in the European Community: A Liberal Intergovernmentalist Approach', *Journal of Common Market Studies*, vol. XXXI, pp. 473–524.

Moravcsik, A. (1993b) 'Idealism and Interest in the European Community: The Case of the French Referendum', *French Politics and Society*, vol. 11, no. 1, pp. 57–69.

Morgan, R. and Silvestri, S. (eds) (1982) *Moderates and Conservatives in Western Europe: Political Parties, the European Community and the Atlantic Alliance*. London, Heinemann.

Muller-Rommel, F. (ed.) (1989) *New Politics in Western Europe*. Boulder, Colorado, Westview.

Niedermeyer, O. (1984) 'The Transnational Dimension of the Elections', *Electoral Studies*, vol. III, pp. 235–43.

Niedermeyer, O. (1989) 'The 1989 European Elections: Campaign and Results', *European Journal of Political Research*, vol. XIX, pp. 3–15.

Nugent, N. (1994) *The Government and Politics of the European Union*. London, Macmillan.

Offe, C. (1985) 'New Social Movements: Challenging the Boundaries of Institutional Politics', *Social Research*, vol. 52, pp. 817–69.

Ordeshook, P. (1986) *Game Theory and Political Theory*. Cambridge, Cambridge University Press.

Padgett, S. and Paterson, W. E. (1991) *The History of Social Democracy in Postwar Europe*. London, Longman.

Panebianco, A. (1988) *Political Parties: Organization and Power*. Cambridge, Cambridge University Press.

Paterson, W. E. and Thomas, A. H. (eds) (1986) *The Future of Social Democracy: Problems and Perspectives of Social Democrat Parties in Western Europe*. Oxford, Clarendon Press.

PES (Party of European Socialists) (1992a) *Statutes of the Party of European Socialists*, adopted by the Congress of the PES, The Hague, 9–10 November 1992. Brussels, PES.

PES (Party of European Socialists) (1992b) *Leaders' Conference: Declaration, leaders' meeting of the PES, Edinburgh*, 9–10 December 1992. Brussels, PES.

PES (Party of European Socialists) (1993a) 'Extraordinary Summit in Arrábida', *PES-FAX- INFO*, No. 07/1993. Brussels, PES.

PES (Party of European Socialists) (1993b) *Declaration of the Leaders of the Party of European Socialists*: 'The European Employment Initiative' – Put Europe Back to Work, leaders' meeting of the PES, Brussels, 9 December 1993. Brussels, PES.

PES (Party of European Socialists) (1994) Party Leaders' Summit Meeting: Final Declaration, leaders' meeting of the PES, Essen, 7–8 December 1994. Brussels, PES.

PES (Party of European Socialists) (1995) Statutes of the Party of European Socialists, adopted by the Congress of the PES, Barcelona, 6–8 March 1995. Brussels, PES.

PES (Party of European Socialists) (1996) *Minutes of the PES Leaders' Conclave*, Sintra, 9–10 March 1996. Brussels, PES.

Peters, B. G. (1994) 'Agenda-Setting in the European Community', *Journal of European Public Administration*, vol. 1, no. 1, pp. 9–26.

Peterson, J. (1996) 'Co-decision: An Early Assessment and Future Prospects', presentation to *Colloque Jean Monnet sur la CIG*, Bruxelles, 6–7 May 1996.

Pridham, G. and Pridham, P. (1981) *Transnational Party Cooperation and European Integration: The Process Towards Direct Elections*. London, Allen & Unwin.

Reif, Karlheinz and Schmitt, Hermann (1980) 'Nine Second Order National Elections. A Conceptual Framework for the Analysis of European Election Results', *European Journal of Political Research*, vol. 8, pp. 3–44.

Riker, W. H. (1962) *The Theory of Political Coalitions*. New Haven, Conn., Yale University Press.

Riker, W.H. (1986) *The Art of Political Manipulation*. New Haven, Conn., Yale University Press.

Rokkan, S. and Urwin, D. (eds).(1982) *The Politics of Territorial Identity: Studies in European Regionalism*. London, Sage.

Rudolph, J. R. and Thompson, R. J (eds) (1989) *Ethnoterritorial Politics, Policy and the Western World*. Boulder, Colorado, Lynne Reiner.

Sandholtz, W. and Zysman, J. (1989) '1992: Recasting the European Bargain', *World Politics*, vol. XLII, pp. 100–2.

Sartori, G. (1968) 'The Sociology of Parties: A Critical Review', in O. Stammer (ed.) *Party Systems, Organisations, and the Politics of New Masses*. Berlin, Free University.

Sartori, G. (1976) *Parties and Party Systems: A Framework for Analysis*, Vol. 1. Cambridge, Cambridge University Press.

Sartori, G. (1987) *The Theory of Democracy Revisited*. NJ, Chatham House.

Sbragia, A. M. (1992) 'Thinking About the European Future: The Uses of Comparisons', in A. M. Sbragia (ed.) *Euro-Politics: Institutions and Policy-making in the New European Community*. Washington, DC, The Brookings Institution.

Scharpf, F. W. (1988) 'The Joint-Decision Trap: Lessons from German Federalism and European Integration', *Public Administration*, no. 66, pp. 239–78.

Scharpf, F. W. (1994) 'Community and Autonomy: Multi-Level Policy-Making in the European Union', *Journal of European Public Administration*, vol. I, pp. 219–42.

Schattschneider, E. E. (1942) *Party Government*. New York, Rinehart.

Schmitter, P. (1966) 'Is It Really Possible to Democratise the Euro-Polity?', paper given to 24th ECPR joint sessions, Oslo.

Schumpeter, J. (1943) *Capitalism, Socialism and Democracy*. London, Allen & Unwin.

Shapiro, M. (1992) 'The European Court of Justice', in A. M. Sbragia (ed.) *Euro-Politics: Institutions and Policymaking in the New European Community*. Washington, DC, The Brookings Institution.

Streek, W. and Schmitter, P. C. (1991) 'From National Corporatism to Transnational Pluralism: Organized Interests in the Single European Market', *Politics and Society*, vol. XIX, pp. 133–64.

Strom, K. (1990) 'A Behavioural Theory of Competitive Political Parties', *American Journal of Political Science*, vol. 34, no. 2, pp. 565–98.

Thatcher, M. (1993) *The Downing Street years*. London, HarperCollins.

Tsebelis, G. (1994) 'The Power of the European Parliament as a Conditional Agenda-Setter', *American Political Science Review*, vol. 88, no. 1, pp. 128–42.

Von Beyme, K. (1990) *Political Parties in Western Democracies*. Aldershot, Gower.

Werts, J. (1992) *The European Council*. Amsterdam, North-Holland.

Wessels, W. (1996) 'The Evolution of the European Parliament: A New Kind of Parliament for a New Kind of Political System', presentation to *Colloque Jean Monnet sur la CIG*, 6–7 May 1996.

Westlake, M. (1994a) *Britain's Emerging Euro-Elite? The British in the European Parliament, 1979–1992*, Aldershot, Dartmouth.

Westlake, M. (1994b) *A Modern Guide to the European Parliament*. London, Pinter.

Index